PRINCIPAL HIGHWAYS
OF
MEXICO

———— Paved road
••••••••• All weather road
———— Dry weather road
•••••••••••• Projected road

100   0   200 MILES

TRAVEL DIVISION OF THE PAN AMERICAN UNION
1953

FRANCES TOOR'S
NEW GUIDE TO MEXICO

LIST OF MAPS

FRANCES TOOR'S NEW GUIDE TO MEXICO

Including Lower California

SEVENTH EDITION AUGMENTED AND COMPLETELY
REVISED BY FREDERICKA MARTIN

CROWN PUBLISHERS, INC.

NEW YORK

ACKNOWLEDGMENTS

My gratitude to the many friends and acquaintances who have helped me with information for this book — too many to mention their names.

The organizations which cooperated generously are: Asociación Mexicana de Turismo, Asociación Mexicana Automovilistica, Instituto de Antropologia e Historia, Compania Mexicana Aerofoto, the Dirección General de Turismo, and the Mexican Government Tourist Bureau. Special thanks are due to Senor Marcelo Rodríguez, chief of the Av. Juárez office of the Dirección General de Turismo.

Thanks are also due to the Mexican National Tourist Council, the Mexican Consulate General, Aeronaves de México, and particularly to the Mexican Government Tourism Department for permission to reproduce pictures used in the book; to the Travel Division, Pan American Union, for permission to reproduce most of the maps; and to the American Automobile Association for permission to reproduce the Mexican street and road signs.

CONTENTS

INTRODUCTION

Mexico, our nearest neighbor to the South, is from the point of view of scenery, peoples, history, social progress, and artistic achievement the most interesting Latin country of the Americas.

GEOGRAPHY: Outstanding topographical features are a high central plateau, dominated by huge mountains, many of volcanic origin. The two principal ranges are the majestic Sierre Madre Oriental (East) and Occidental (West). The total area of the country is approximately 760,000 square miles.

CLIMATE: The mountain ranges and their extensions form many valleys, resulting in a great variety of scenery and climates. Along the sea coasts and in the lowlands, called Tierra Caliente, it is always hot and it rains almost constantly; in altitudes from 3,000 to 6,000 feet, it is fairly hot during the day but cool in the evening. On elevations above 6,000 feet, the days are seldom hot and the nights always cool or cold. The rainy season on the Central Plateau lasts from May into October, but it does not spoil sightseeing as it generally rains late in the afternoon. Mexico is an all-year vacation land! It is especially beautiful in the fall, when the countryside is green and alive with wild flowers.

HISTORY: Mexican history may be divided into four well-defined periods—1) the pre-Conquest, which began thirty thousand years B.C., according to some experts, when some nomad tribes began invading and settling the country: 2) the Colonial, beginning with the Conquest in 1521, after which the country became a Spanish colony and was called Nueva España: 3) the Independence, after the revolution of 1810, when Mexico freed itself from Spain; 4) the Revolutionary-Reconstruction period, following the Social Revolution of 1910-1920, since which all the advanced social and cultural movements have been initiated. Each of these epochs has left its mark in the cultural and social traits of Mexico, as well as in the architecture.

OUTSTANDING EVENTS since 1821, when Mexican Independence was finally established: the loss of Texas in 1836; the U. S.-Mexican war in 1846-47; the Reform Laws instituted by Benito Juárez, the Oaxaca Zapotec President, in 1859; the victory of the French and reign of Maximilian of Hapsburg as Emperor from 1863 to 1867, when he was executed and the French driven out of Mexico; the Social Revolution, 1910-20; the expropriation of the foreign oil companies by the government of General Lázaro Cárdenas in 1938.

GOVERNMENT: Mexico's government is a Republic of Federated States with executive, legislative, and judiciary branches. The constitution permits the executive branch extraordinary powers. The Senate is called Cámara de Senadores and the House of Representatives, Cámara de Diputados; their members—*senadores* and *diputados* respectively. In 1934, the presidential term was extended to six years; there is no Vice-President. Adolfo Lopez Mateos, elected July 6, 1958, is now President of Mexico.

POPULATION: Mexico is a country of diverse cultures. Descendants of many pre-Conquest people still live in the regions inhabited by their forefathers. Almost half of the population, which, according to a 1957 U.N. estimate is 31,426,000, is native; about 40 per cent or more, *mestizo* (Indian and white, mixed), and the rest, non-Indian. The tribes that achieved the highest degree of civilization, leaving the most magnificent monuments, are the Teotihuacans, Toltecs, and Aztecs of the Central Plateau; the Zapotecs and Mixtecs of Oaxaca; the Totonacs of Veracruz; and the Mayas of the South. The present-day natives have kept alive the plastic ability which they inherited from their ancestors; they can make beautiful things with their hands and love color, music, and the dance.

A VACATION IN MEXICO

A trip to Mexico from the U.S. is now as easy and comfortable as going from one state into another. Yet the moment you cross the border you are in a foreign country —new language, customs, and rhythm.

A vacation in Mexico is a unique experience. It is an adventure into a country of great contrasts, where one may see all the various degrees of civilizations from the most primitive to the most modern within a short period of time.

If you have only two weeks at your disposal, you can quickly reach Mexico City—the capital and center of the Republic. Then, while living in perfect comfort, see the remains of magnificent pyramids; splendid Colonial and contemporary architecture; fine ancient and modern frescoes; visit native markets and villages. There are also great contrasts in the scenery of this small area—from magnificent mountains to lush tropics. If you have more time and can take extended trips, your experiences will be so much the richer. But even during a short stay, you can see the entire gamut of the social, economic, and cultural life of Mexico, as well as its scenic beauties.

If you prefer to concentrate on a good time, Mexico City has horse races, bullfights, golf, good cabarets, fine restaurants, and plenty of sunshine the year round.

Mexico has interests for every taste. For many it is a land of magical enchantment.

LANGUAGE: Spanish is the official language, but there are still villages in which the native tongues are used almost exclusively. Much English is spoken in tourist centers. One can get along quite well without knowing any Spanish, but the traveler who will devote a little time to acquiring even a meager Spanish vocabulary will be amply rewarded. There are a number of helpful phrase books on the market, one of them by the author—*Easy Spanish for Mexico, Cuba and All Latin-American Countries*. Look under "Miscellaneous Information," for a list of useful phrases.

PRODUCTS AND INDUSTRIES: Too industrialized now to be labeled a purely agrarian country, Mexico is tackling urgent problems due to changing from its former largely self-sufficient rural village economy to widespread dependence on the output from manufacturing, and the population shift from villages to urban centers. Encouraging industry and seeking new markets run parallel with modernizing farming methods, renewing worn-out soils, reforesting large regions, building gigantic irrigation systems and power plants for new factories and to electrify remote hamlets, and constructing new roads for the flow of goods and the increase of tourist attractions.

Major crops for home use and/or export include maize, beans, chick-peas, wheat and other cereals, coffee, cotton, fruit and vegetables, henequen and other plant fibers, and oil-producing seeds—sesame, castor, etc. Mining, the oldest pre-Conquest industry, has recovered impetus. Oil production prospers. The booming building industry cannot keep pace with urban needs. Only villages tucked away among the mountains or lost in arid semi-wastes like Hidalgo's *mezquital,* remain primitively self-sufficient, but their inhabitants are gnawed by hunger for modern goods.

As machine production satisfies growing demands for useful appliances and gadgets, handmade articles lose status as objects of personal or local use and become cash-earning merchandise, often vulgarized and debased in quality or design to satisfy misconceptions of tourist taste or to meet the competition of cheaper counterparts made in mechanized workshops. True regional handicrafts, many encouraged, even subsidized by the federal government, do exist. Government schools for craft artisans are training a new generation of handworkers. Tourists are still tempted by far too many attractive wares for their budgets and baggage allowances.

OPPORTUNITIES FOR STUDY AND RESEARCH: Because every social, artistic, historic, and economic facet of life is essentially and uniquely its own, Mexico is a rich field for writers, scientists, artists, folklorists, and students. Foreign students attend Mexican schools in ever-increasing numbers, either the summer courses offered by the national and many state universities or the regular academic year courses. Details of Mexico City courses appear on pages 154 and 156. Consult the Mexican Consulate, Tourist Bureau, or your local university about others.

TRAVEL FACILITIES AND ACCOMMODATIONS have increased enormously during recent years. Excellent graded, paved highways run the length and breadth of Mexico and new paved links are constantly added to this network. Conspicuously colored new road signs aid motorists. Clean modern hotels and motels provide comfortable stopovers. Sanitary restaurants eliminate food and water health hazards. There are frequent gas stations and auto service and repair shops. Main highways are serviced by the green cars of the Radio Patrulla de Auxilio Turistico, the Tourist Aid Radio Patrol (see p. 161), extending free help to all travelers as a courtesy of the federal government's tourist department. Air lines reach the remotest, still roadless, parts of the Republic, but one should not miss the joyous informality and holiday spirit of a train trip in Mexico.

There are first-class, comfortable hotels and tourist courts in all large towns, cities, and frequented resorts. The elegant luxury hotels of the Capital and many resorts match their peers elsewhere. Intimate, friendly, inexpensive hotels and *posadas* (inns) are common. Hotel rates will be indi-

Typical Market Scene—Toluca

cated where needed, according to a general scale: "modest" will designate a single room without meals (European Plan —Eur. Pl.) costing up to 35 *pesos* a day ($2.80 U.S. currency); "moderate" up to 75 *pesos* ($6.00 U.S.); "expensive" above 75 *pesos*. A meal, without tips or drinks included, priced under 15 *pesos* ($1.20 U.S.) will be classified "modest"; from 15 to 30 *pesos* ($2.40 U.S.) as "moderate"; over 30 *pesos* as "expensive." If traveling out of season, ask for discounts. Always ask at motels to see "economy" rooms —there are usually three or four.

THE FOOD QUESTION: Eating is part of vacation fun. U.S. menus and food tastes are known and catered to in Mexico, but visitors should sample Mexican dishes—if well prepared, they are delicious. Hygienic conditions have improved greatly, but milk products and salads should be ordered only in first-class restaurants. Eat cooked fruits or raw fruits which can be peeled, such as mangoes, pineapples, bananas. Even the smallest village hotels serve "safe" cooked foods. Be careful of your diet, but not overanxious. Excessive worry is responsible for more upset digestions than Mexican microbes.

In Mexico City and elsewhere in high altitudes, digestion is slower. It is important not to yield to the temptation of overeating, especially in the evening. The same is true of immoderate drinking. So eat lightly, drink sparingly, and sample new foods, fruit, and drinks gradually. (And do not overexert yourself in high altitudes!)

MEXICAN DISHES: The most festive of all is *mole de guajolote* (Aztec for turkey, pronounced gwa-ho-*lo*-teh). The *mole* is a rich, piquant sauce, dating from pre-Conquest times—Moctezuma served it to Cortés. *Tacos* and *enchiladas* are meat or chicken rolled in *tortillas*—the maize pancakes, made as before the Conquest, of corn previously soaked and boiled in lime water, ground, patted, and baked. *Quesadillas* (pro. ke-sah-*dee*-yas) are turnovers of corn dough, filled with cheese, beans, savory meat mixtures, potatoes, or exotic "greens" such as squash blossoms, and fried in lard. *Tamales* are corn dough dumplings, filled with many kinds of sweet or savory fillings, and steamed in corn husks or banana leaves. Every region has its own kind. *Frijoles* or Mexican beans, fried and refried, are a daily dish. There are also many egg and rice dishes fixed in special ways.

DULCES, OR SWEETS: Quince and other fruits are made into pastes or candied in their original forms. *Chongos* are made of curdled cheese with a sweet sauce. *Cajetas de Celaya* are caramel goat milk candies sold in boxes or glass jars. *Morelianas, ates,* and *cueros* (fruit candies of Morelos) are delicious.

FRUIT: In addition to all the common fruit available in the U.S., Mexico offers a variety of delicious tropical and semi-tropical seasonal ones. Summer is the time for the delicately flavored *mango* and *tuna;* winter for the *zapotes*: *chicos, negros,* and *borrachos.* The pasty black pulp of the *zapote negro,* when beaten up with orange juice or wine, makes a unique and delicious dessert. Among the other exotic fruits are the *mamey, chirimoya,* and *guanabana,* the latter two of especially pleasing flavor.

WATER: Some of the larger cities have good water systems, but elsewhere water from faucets is not safe to drink. Many of the first-class hotels have artesian wells; others serve purified bottled water. When in doubt, drink bottled mineral water or beer, of which there are several excellent varieties. A cheaper, but less agreeable, alternative is to use chlorine tablets.

SOFT DRINKS: Most bottled soft drinks, *refrescos,* bear familiar U.S. names. Popular Mexican drinks of fruit and flower-flavored water, *aguas frescas* (cooling waters) are sold from big glass jars on almost every street corner. Avoid these, but ask your hotel to serve you the most exotic ones (commonplace to Mexicans)—*tamarindo, jamaica, guanabana, mamey,* and other seasonal fruit ones.

ALCOHOLIC DRINKS: *Pulque,* a thick, slightly sweetish drink, made by fermenting juice taken from the heart of the *maguey* plant, is consumed in enormous quantities by the natives, but it does not appeal to the foreign palate. *Tequila,* one of the most popular as the smoothest of the *mescales,* (liquors distilled from crushed hearts of several small *maguey* species), is named for the Jalisco town where it is made. Oaxaca calls her brand *mescal;* Guerrero, *chichi-hualco*—the fieriest of *mescales,* extinguished by sucking orange slices. *Aguardiente* (fire water), sugar-cane brandy of varying taste and potency, is made in every sugar-growing district. Mexico's red and white wines are good and less expensive than imported ones and her beers are superb. Sweet fruit liqueurs are numberless, many produced only in a single region. City and resort bars and stores stock U.S. and European wines and liquors.

MEXICAN MEALS: A formal dinner or *comida* is a long, leisurely affair, generally served from 2 to 4 P.M. It begins with cocktails, *antipasto* or *hors d'oeuvres,* followed by consommé or soup, rice with fried eggs or shrimps, a fish or meat dish, the main meat course, *frijoles fritos,* or fried beans, fruit, dessert, cheese, coffee and a liqueur, with wines throughout the meal. Breakfast, or *desayuno,* generally consists of fruit, bread, and coffee; the brunch, or *almuerzo,* is heavier. At night one may have *merienda*—chocolate with *pan dulce,* followed by a glass of cold milk; or *cena,* with meat, beans, and coffee with milk.

Festival in Tehuantepec, Oaxaca

14

PREPARATIONS FOR YOUR TRIP

PLAN YOUR OWN TOURS! Even if you are traveling with a tourist agency, you should make your own general plans with respect to what you are going to do and see. Otherwise you will find yourself in the position of so many who included in their itineraries a tiring and expensive trip which they later regretted having taken. Had they read about it in advance, they could have spared themselves time and trouble and gained greater pleasure.

BOOKING WITH A TOURIST AGENCY—although not necessary—has many advantages. If your time is limited and you come during the heavy tourist seasons, it is very convenient to have a reliable tourist agency make your hotel reservations; furnish you with cars and guides, and special information. Above all, during the heavy tourist seasons, don't fail to make hotel reservations in advance, either personally or preferably through a tourist agency. See list of tourist agencies in DIRECTORY OF MEXICO CITY, p. 160.

CLOTHING: Although Mexico lies in southerly latitudes, one's wardrobe should always be planned for both warm and cool weather. For Mexico City and other places at high altitudes, spring or fall clothing is suitable for all times, with a heavier topcoat or an extra sweater for winter and a raincoat for the summer rainy season. A warm bathrobe and slippers are useful, as there is practically no central heating and the night air in high altitudes is chilly even in the summer months. Summer sport clothes are comfortable almost everywhere in the day time, especially in altitudes such as Cuernavaca, Taxco, and Guadalajara. Typical seaside resort clothes are suitable but not necessary for Acapulco, Veracruz, Mazatlan, Guaymas, and other seashore places. They are *not* suitable for Mexico City. Evening clothes are not necessary even for the opera or theater, unless your Mexican friends invite you to attend social affairs or diplomatic functions. Other useful articles are stout walking shoes and stockings for hilly and cobbled streets, dark glasses for the tropical sun, sun hats, which may be obtained locally, and hiking or riding outfits, depending upon one's plans. In matters of dress there is a lack of formality, but Mexicans object strongly to women wearing slacks, shorts, or bare-shouldered dresses in public places.

Trip Expenses: The cost of living in Mexico is increasing. One should allow at least ten American dollars per day, aside from fares between towns, with a reserve fund to meet emergencies, but hardy adventurers or experienced persons can get by on a minimum of about five dollars and still enjoy themselves. Living in smaller cities, towns, and villages costs less than in Mexico City. For an extended stay it is possible to reduce expenses by boarding, or renting an apartment. Fares on trains and buses are still so low that traveling inside Mexico is cheap. In general, even the most expensive hotels and night clubs can be enjoyed for less than in the U.S.

Mexican Money: The Mexican unit of money corresponding to the American dollar is the *peso*. Mexico is on a silver standard and the U.S. dollar is worth $12.50 (*pesos*) at the present time. Fractional coins, all based on the decimal system, are *centavos* issued in denominations of 5, 10, 20, and 50. There are silver one-*peso* pieces, and bills of 1, 5, 10, 20, 50, 100 *pesos* and higher.

The dollar sign is standard in Mexico, always signifying *pesos,* and as such it is used in this book. To determine the cost in dollars of an item or a service in Mexico, simply divide the cost in *pesos* by 12½. For example, a meal costing $25.00 (*pesos*) is $2.00 (U.S.). See conversion tables, page 301.

Travelers' checks in dollars are most easily cashed at tourists' hotels, fairly easily in tourist-goods shops, but regular stores as well as banks usually demand more absolute proof of identity than the counter-signature or tourist card. Expect variable small service charge discounts everywhere. An old-fashioned money belt is useful on long trips through small towns.

Entering Mexico: Starting on January 1, 1964, free courtesy cards will be issued to visitors entering Mexico. They will be good for 30 days and can be used in place of the former $3.00 cards that were valid for 180 days. Tourists who plan to remain in Mexico for longer than 30 days will continue to need the $3.00 card for a single entry or the $5.00 card which permits multiple entries during a 180-day period. Citizens of other countries must travel on passports.

It is always advisable to carry evidence of citizenship in the form of birth certificates, passports, or permits in order to avoid difficulties with immigration authorities. Never go out-of-doors without your tourist card, as the law demands. *Do not lose it!* If you do, seek help at the National Tourist Office, Av. Reforma 35, Mexico City. Replacement may use up your vacation time. If prone to losing belongings, arm yourself with a photostatic copy, certified by a Mexican notary, and leave the original in your hotel safe. Engaging in remunerative activities of any kind without the authorization of the Secretaría de Gobernación in Mexico City (authorization can be arranged through a Mexican Consul in the U.S.) is penalized by arrest, heavy fines, expulsion, sometimes preceded by a stay in jail. Tourists may study legally at any school during the permitted 180-day stay. For prolonged studies, a special student visa must be obtained from a Mexican Consul *before* entering Mexico. Students may study—not work. Special information for the motorist will be given under TRAVELING BY CAR, page 22. Regulations change. Check with your nearest Consul just before take-off time.

HEALTH REGULATIONS: A smallpox vaccination certificate is required for entry into Mexico and re-entry into the U.S. Typhoid shots are a sensible precaution, other immunizations to suit your phobias.

HUNTING AND FISHING: Preliminary arrangements to obtain temporary hunting licenses must be made in the U.S. with one's Mexican Consul. Upon compliance with current regulations, the Consul will issue an identification certificate and firearm description to be presented at the point of entry —first to the Delegado Forestal de Caza (Game Warden) who issues licenses, then to the office of the Military Garrison to get the firearm entry permit, and, lastly, to the Customs Office. Obtain fishing licenses from the warden at the entry point or later from local wardens. Licenses of authorized fishing boats cover passenger fishing. The Mexican government encourages fishing as a good-will sport, and annual fishing tournaments are held, on movable dates, with valuable prizes, at the principal resorts—Acapulco, Guaymas, La Paz, Tampico. For information on fishing tournament dates, write to the Pemex Travel Club, Av. Juarez 89, or Dirección General de Turismo, Reforma 35, Mexico, D.F.

MEXICAN CUSTOMS: Only personal baggage entering Mexico with the tourist is allowed in duty-free. *Never ship your belongings separately!* Different regulations govern the kind and quantity of personal articles a tourist may bring in duty-free, depending upon his mode and place of entrance, a contradiction due for quick readjustment. Air passengers fill out a declaration during their flight which meticulously enumerates the number of articles of any one kind they may bring in. Only air passengers can bring in gifts, up to $80.00 (U.S.) worth. Unless volume of baggage suggests discrepancy with declaration, there will be no inspection. Land border-crossing regulations permit no gifts, and unless a tip is forthcoming, agents may mess up your baggage. Get the latest lists of the personal belongings you may bring in from your travel agent or Consul and carry them with you. Successive inspection points between border and capital, three or more to each highway, are irritants the Government plans to eradicate soon. Report any abuses or attempts to extract tips (forced tip is a *mordida,* a bite) to the Tourist Bureau in Mexico City or the Servicio de Aduana. For permission to take archeological and colonial objects out of the country, apply to the Instituto Nacional de Antropología e Historía, Córdoba, No. 73, Mexico City.

U.S. CUSTOMS REGULATIONS: Tourists may take home one hundred dollars' worth of Mexican popular art and other objects not for resale. Modern paintings are not dutiable but proof of their authenticity must be presented. This can be arranged through the artist or his gallery. You may mail or express any part of your allotted duty-free objects by sending a statement to the U.S. Customs at their port of entry. On your declaration slip make one heading "Miscellaneous," in order to be able to add anything you may have forgotten and thus avoid trouble. Also to avoid trouble—if you are taking to Mexico any valuable articles of foreign make, register them with the U.S. Customs before leaving the country.

Inform yourself of the latest custom regulations before leaving either country. Ask at your Consulate or the Mexican Tourist Bureau offices in U.S. cities, or write Dirección General de Turismo, Reforma 35, Mexico, D.F.

MENTAL AND EMOTIONAL PREPARATION: Remember that Mexico offers a more leisurely tempo and rhythm than the U.S., so cast aside your nervous tension and ideas of speed before crossing the border. Never forget that you are a guest in a foreign country, where customs are different from those in your own. When something displeases you, a display of temper will not accomplish nearly as much as a smile and a courteous request. Try to understand Mexico and the Mexicans. Be leisurely! Relax! Linger, loiter, and loaf in the beauty of Mexican landscapes, clear skies, and warm sunshine. You will be amply rewarded.

Cuernavaca—Mexico City Highway

TRAVELING FROM THE U.S.
TO MEXICO CITY

Air, train, and bus services to Mexico City are excellent.

By Air: Mexico is connected with the whole world by its own national, U.S., and international airlines offering every modern service and facility: first class, tourist, even "go slow" fares; stop-over and direct flights; etc. Companies which offer daily direct flights to Mexico City, the Republic's hub of flights to points within its own borders as well as beyond, from key U.S. cities are: *Air France, Aeronaves de Mexico,* and *Eastern Airlines* from New York; *American Airlines* and *Mexicana de Aviación* (*C.M.A.,* affiliate of Pan American Airlines) from Chicago; *Aeronaves de Mexico* (Guest Airlines has been incorporated with this company), *Mexicana de Aviación,* and *Western Airlines* from Los Angeles. Except for *Air France,* these companies schedule many stop-over flights, and *American Airlines* maintains excellent connections between about a score of U.S. cities from coast to coast.

Both *Mexicana de Aviación* and *Aeronaves de Mexico* schedule many flights between Los Angeles and/or Tijuana which serve Mexico's West Coast resorts and larger cities throughout the country, with many stop-over privileges enroute to the Capital. Don't plan an air-hopping trip inside the Republic without consulting both companies' current schedules. *Aeronaves* has a popular new flight from Los Angeles to La Paz, Baja California, to Acapulco.

Jet flights between Mexico City and U.S. cities include the following: *Aeronaves de Mexico* and its subsidiary, *Guest Aerovias Mexico,* to New York. *American Airlines* Astrojets to San Antonio, Dallas, Chicago, or Washington. *Braniff* super-jets, Boeing El Dorado, to San Antonio, Dallas,

Kansas City, Minneapolis–St. Paul. *Eastern Air Lines* Golden Falcons to New York, daily jets to New Orleans. *Mexicana de Aviación* to Chicago and Los Angeles. (The latter company also provides jet flights inside Mexico between Mexico City and Mérida, and Mexico City and Monterrey, and is preparing other jet routes.) *Pan Am* has jets to Houston as well as South American countries. *Western Airlines* has evening jet flights to Los Angeles.

Canadian Pacifico has new super DC-8 Jet Empresses to the Orient.

BY TRAIN: The nation-wide system of government owned and operated railroads, denoted by the initials *F.F.N.N. de M.* (*Ferrocarriles Nacionales de México*), has direct or branch connections with seven border towns and two U.S. railroads. The still independent Mexican line, *Ferrocarril del Pacifico, S. A.* (*F. A. de Pacifico,* Pacific Railroad), runs from Guadalajara to Mexicali and Nogales, connecting at the latter with the U.S. *Southern Pacific Railway*. At Guadalajara southbound passengers transfer to a *F.F.N.N. de M.* train crossing the states of Guanajuato, Queretaro, Hidalgo, and Mexico to Mexico City. *F.F.N.N. de M.* trains between Ciudad Juárez and the Capital connect with the U.S. *Southern Pacific* across the border in El Paso, Texas. Chief Mexican stops on this line are Queretaro, Aguascalientes, Zacatecas, Torreon, and Chihuahua. The fast luxury *Aguila Azteca* (Aztec Eagle), the *National Railroads'* pride, between the Capital and Laredo, meets the U.S. *Missouri Pacific* there, and has through cars to San Antonio and St. Louis.

A branch of *F.F.N.N. de M.* runs from Monterrey to Reynosa, opposite McAllen, Texas, and another to Matamoros, opposite Brownsville, Texas; another line runs from Saltillo to Piedras Negras. The new *F. C. Chihuahua al Pacifico, S. A.* has lines from the Mexican border towns of Ojínaga and Ciudad Juárez which join at Chihuahua and cut across the spectacular mountains of the Sierra Madre Occidental to San Blas, Los Mochis, and the Gulf of California port, Topolobampo, one of the most scenic rides in the Hemisphere.

Train trips not only are a pleasant way to see scenic regions, but open sesame to making friends with Mexican fellow passengers. Fares are so low as to seem a courtesy to tourists. Main line trains have Pullman and diner service; short routes serve drinks and villagers offer local-recipe snacks, fruits, and their crafts at many stops. (See DIRECTORY OF MEXICO CITY for list of railroad offices.)

BY BUS: U.S. *Greyhound* buses connect with first-class Mexican bus lines from Mexico City at six border towns, *Continental Trailways, U.S.A.,* at three. From the Capital, two runs daily on *Transportes del Norte* connect with *Greyhound* at Brownsville (24-hour trip costs $7.00 U.S.!); two to Laredo on the same bus line (29 hours, $7.60 U.S.); two to Ciudad Juárez–El Paso on *Transportes Chihuahuaense* (30 hours, $13.30 U.S.); two to Nogales on *Tres Estrellas de Oro* or *Transportes Norte de Sonora* (48 hours, $17.35 U.S.) Using the last-named bus line, the 50-hour trip to Mexicali costs $20.85 U.S. and, with another 4 hours on the same run to reach Tijuana, the whole fare is $22.85 U.S.

Continental Trailways, U.S.A. connects with *Omnibus de Mexico* from the Capital at El Paso, Texas; with *Autobuses Blancos* at Laredo (the Mexican bus crosses the border). Buses of the latter line from Mexico City to Matamoros and Reynoso do not cross the border—passengers must change to a local bus or taxi to get to bus terminals on the U.S. side.

Buy tickets to a destination in the U.S. at offices of the U.S. companies in Mexican cities to insure connections (cheaper, too)—not at Mexican bus offices. In Mexico City *Greyhound Agentes Generales* have their offices at La Fragua 4, and *Continental Trailways* at Reforma 34-3.

BY CAR: Excellent major highways from the border, interconnected by an evergrowing number of new or newly paved roads, afford motorists from anywhere in the U.S. an opportunity to really see the country on the way to the Capital. From east to west the border crossing points, the route numbers, and approximate mileages are: (*1*) Brownsville, Texas–Matamoros (C.N. [Carretera Nacional, Na-

tional Highway] 101 and 85), 638 miles; (2) McAllen, Texas
–Reynosa (C.N. 40 and 85), 762 miles; (3) Laredo, Texas–
Nuevo Laredo (Pan American Highway and first of these
highways, opened July 1, 1935; C.N. 85), 765 miles; (4)
Eagle Pass, Texas–Piedras Negras (least varied and easiest to
drive, C.N. 57), 822 miles; (5) El Paso, Texas–Ciudad Juárez
(Central Highway; C.N. 45 and 57), 1,265 miles; (6) Nogales,
Arizona–Nogales (Pacific, International, or West Coast
Route; C.N. 15), 1,500 miles.

Preparations are not much more exacting than for a
long trip in the U.S., the trip the most intimate and rewarding way of seeing Mexico.

MOTORIST NOTE: The spectacular new Mexican Gulf
Coast or Circuit Route from the U.S. border along the Gulf
of Mexico to Puerto Juárez in Quintana Roo at the tip of
the Yucatán Peninsula (a link of the projected Caribbean
circuit by automobile ferries to Cuba and Florida and back
to the starting point along the U.S. Gulf Coast), a labor of
connecting existing roads by new ones cut through jungle
terrain, offers exciting trips in the tropically cooler, dryer
months of December to February.

A cross-country route from Tampico to Barra Navidad
lacks only a few links and already connects major U.S. highways, affording autoists many engaging side trips.

Inquire at your home or border AAA or at the organizations listed below, or, for the freshest report, at *SOP (Secretariat de Obras Publicas)*, Av. Cuauhtemoc and Xola,
Mexico City, at its *Oficina de Informes,* Tel. 19-74-63, of
the *Dirección General de Planeación de Carreteras Feder-
ales,* Building *Cuerpo H,* fourth floor, for information regarding progress of the steadily extending Pacific Coastal
Route, designed to complete a circuit tour of the Republic.

LEADING ORGANIZATIONS which supply information and
service to motorists are the *AAA (American Automobile
Association)*; other automobile associations and oil companies; the *AMA (Asociación Mexicana Automovilística)*,
Club Consejo Nacional, Chapultepec 276, Mexico, D.F.,
Tel. 14-93-57. For a longish stay, it is advisable to join. Dues
for three months are $3.00, for six months $6.00, for one

year, $12.00. *AMA* agents all over the country will help solve difficulties and give emergency and road service and information, as well as their illustrated monthly travel magazine and maps. *Asociación Nacional Automovilística,* Miguel Shultz, 136-140, Mexico City; Tel. 46-99-65; information 46-02-67, emergency service 35-03-43; annual dues only $16.00. *The Pemex Travel Club,* Av. Juárez 89, Mexico, D.F., is a courtesy organization. Anyone may receive the club's illustrated monthly bulletin, booklets, folders, and road maps gratis. Material is not always up-to-date or accurate.

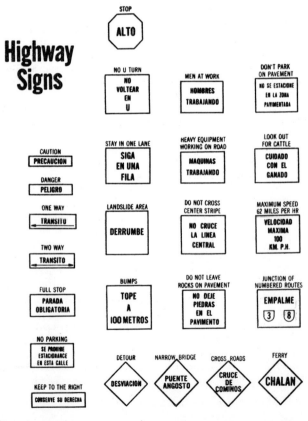

Highway Signs

STOP
ALTO

NO U TURN
NO VOLTEAR EN U

MEN AT WORK
HOMBRES TRABAJANDO

DON'T PARK ON PAVEMENT
NO SE ESTACIONE EN LA ZONA PAVIMENTADA

CAUTION
PRECAUCION

DANGER
PELIGRO

STAY IN ONE LANE
SIGA EN UNA FILA

HEAVY EQUIPMENT WORKING ON ROAD
MAQUINAS TRABAJANDO

LOOK OUT FOR CATTLE
CUIDADO CON EL GANADO

ONE WAY
TRANSITO

TWO WAY
TRANSITO

LANDSLIDE AREA
DERRUMBE

DO NOT CROSS CENTER STRIPE
NO CRUCE LA LINEA CENTRAL

MAXIMUM SPEED 62 MILES PER HR
VELOCIDAD MAXIMA 100 KM. P.H.

FULL STOP
PARADA OBLIGATORIA

BUMPS
TOPE A 100 METROS

DO NOT LEAVE ROCKS ON PAVEMENT
NO DEJE PIEDRAS EN EL PAVIMENTO

JUNCTION OF NUMBERED ROUTES
EMPALME 3 8

NO PARKING
SE PROHIBE ESTACIONARCE EN ESTA CALLE

KEEP TO THE RIGHT
CONSERVE SU DERECHA

DETOUR
DESVIACION

NARROW BRIDGE
PUENTE ANGOSTO

CROSS ROADS
CRUCE DE COMINOS

FERRY
CHALAN

24

DOCUMENTS AND INSURANCE: For crossing the border you need your own tourist card and a Mexican government permit for your car, good for 180 days only and obtainable at point of entry, plus your car registration certificate and driver's license, which is good in Mexico. Your car equipment may be listed, in which case you must account for it when leaving the country. If your car insurance is void in Mexico, be sure to get a short-term policy with a Mexican company at the border at a reasonable rate.

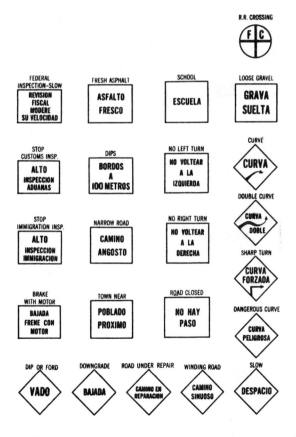

FROM LAREDO TO MEXICO CITY

VIA THE PAN AMERICAN HIGHWAY (C.N. 85)

LAREDO, Texas, is the principal entry port to the Pan American Highway, C.N. 85, which meets branch roads from Brownsville and McAllen at Monterrey. Get pre-border crossing advice at local Pemex Travel Club office, 3104 San Bernardo Street, or at the AAA office in the Plaza Hotel, 904 Hidalgo Street at Laredo. (In Brownsville the AAA is at 1307 Central Blvd.—junction of U.S. 77 and 281.)

NUEVO LAREDO, Tamaulipas, across the bridge from Laredo, is a dignified city, with all the usual border attractions—bars, cabarets, restaurants, handicraft shops—and fishing 80 miles away at Don Martin and Del Azucar Dams.

The Pan American Highway is a scenically varied and thrilling narrow road that makes a prosaic start through arid cactus, mesquite, *anacahuite,* and sagebrush country, climbing easily after SABINAS HIDALGO across tropical canyons, valleys, rivers, and desert mountains, 2,300 feet high, to Mamulique Pass and down to the last baggage inspection beyond CIENAGA DE FLORES (Flower Swamp), from which Monterrey is visible. Entering the city, you can refresh yourself with free beer in the garden of the Cervecería de Moctezuma, if you are in time for one of the weekday hourly brewery tours.

MONTERREY (Pro. Mon-teh-*rray;* "King's Mountain"), capital of Nuevo León (Alt. 1,762 ft., Pop. 615,009), was settled 1596 by Spaniard Diego Montemayor by order of the Viceroy, Conde de Monterrey, and named by the latter for the Spanish Virgin of Monterrey. This great industrial city, Mexico's steel center, with Latin tempo and customs, lies in a lovely mountain valley, cut by the Santa Catarina River. To the East is the famous Cerro de la Silla (Saddle Rock).

26

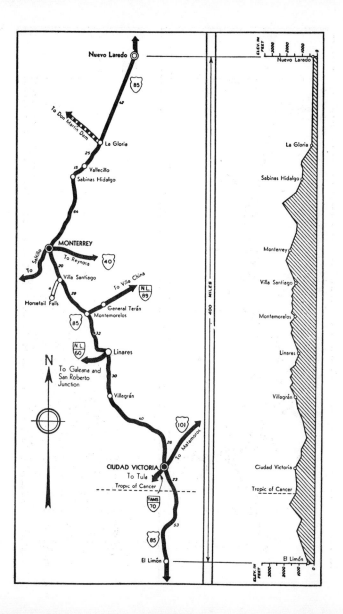

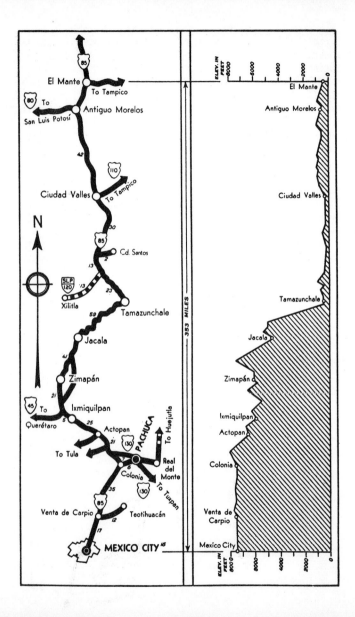

Hotels: Among the best known are the Rio, Ambassador, Ancira, Colonial, Monterrey, Yamallel, Favorita, San Francisco, Amega, and Posada Carápan (small but most de luxe). The Ancira is the most Mexican and a favorite. California Courts, El Bosque, Motel Alamo, El Paso Autel, and Roma are good motels; moderate. Motel Monterrey is de luxe, with gardens and swimming pool. Dancing: Ambassador Hotel, Rio Hotel, and El Patio. The Anfa Super Motel is air-conditioned, has a playground, swimming pool, restaurant, and pleasant rooms.

Restaurants: The large hotels and motels have restaurants and bars. Sanborn's has a new modern home. The Louisiana is a long-time favorite, offering international cuisine. Rosita Restaurant and Patio, in a genuine *hacienda* featuring a Mexican menu. One can dance there.

Amusements: Movies, band concerts, bullfights, night clubs. Night clubs include El Toro, the Barrio Bar at Hotel

Flower Sellers

Rio; Calabria; Chipps Restaurant and Piano Bar; Cita Alacranz with composer Alacranz and his band; and many more. Guest cards for tennis and golf may be secured. Swimming in pools and outdoor dancing in parks. Tourist bureaus and hotels make arrangements for hunting and sightseeing trips, also for drivers and guides.

Outstanding Buildings: The Cathedral, on the Zaragoza Plaza, completed in 1851, has a good Baroque façade. Above the main altar is a copy of Murillo's "Assumption of the Virgin."

There are three government buildings: the nineteenth-century Colonial-style Palacio Municipal contains city offices and the Municipal Library; the modern Palacio Federal on Zaragoza Ave. houses all federal offices, telephone and telegraph offices (Government booklets and souvenir cards on sale); and Palacio del Gobierno, the state capitol, modern with Spanish patio and tiled decorations, guards historical trophies. Six stained glass windows, portraits of military heroes, are near the main entry. Fortress-like El Obispado (Bishopric), a dominating landmark, built 1787-1790 on Chepe Vera Hill, was a fort in 1817, 1847, and 1864; an isolation hospital during yellow fever epidemics, 1898 and 1903; and Pancho Villa's fort in 1913. From 1927 to 1937 its terrace was an open-air night club, Cafe Obispado. The part still standing is a historical museum.

Churches and Neighborhoods of the People: Church of La Purísima, bold, ultramodern, on the corners of Serafino Pena and Hidalgo across from La Llave (Key) Plaza, houses the city's patron saint, famed for saving the city from destruction by flood. The Church of El Roble (The Oak), Juárez and Cinco de Mayo Streets, is a massive eighteenth-century structure. The legend is that a native woman who possessed the image of this virgin claimed that one night it disappeared, that the following morning she found it at the hollow oak in a nearby pond, wet and covered with burrs— proof that it had walked. The tree soon became a sacred spot and the clergy decided to build a church there. Around these churches and in other sections of the city are many typically Mexican streets, with gaily-painted houses, grilled windows, and lovely patios with flowers, plants, and birds. On holidays, *fiestas* are celebrated in these neighborhoods.

Shopping: Monterrey has no important local handicrafts, but such shops as Helena's and the museum-shop Carápan carry excellent popular art goods from all Mexico; the modern Public Colón Market has pottery and craft stalls.

Shopping advice: There are handicraft shops all along the highways and in many hotels. When you see something you like exceptionally well, buy it. Handmade objects are never repeated exactly. Do not haggle over prices unless bargaining is customary.

Excursions via Saltillo Highway (C.N. 40): CHIPINQUE MESA, 3 miles, then 10 more on paved toll road (2½ *pesos* per person) winding up through woodland over 4,000 feet to the mesa. Panoramic view, sports. Food and lodging at Chipinque Inn. At Santa Catarina, 9 miles from Monterrey, turn left to HUASTECA CANYON entrance, 2 miles away, through which Santa Catarina River runs, its cliffs weatherworn to dramatic shapes. The most notable resembles the Holy Virgin. In the villages of the canyon you will find folk customs and dances, the typical one being the *huapango*.

About 4 miles beyond Santa Catarina, turn right on paved road, 15 miles to Villa de Garcia, Nuevo León. Take paved road to spectacular GARCIA CAVES. Hourly funicular service to their mouth and guided excursions from 8 A.M. to 5 P.M. There are restaurant and horseback-riding facilities.

MOTORIST NOTE: C.N. 40, cross-country route from the Gulf to the Pacific, 53 miles west of Monterrey at Saltillo, joins C.N. 57, newest, quickest border-to-Capital route. Cross the Eagle Pass, Tex., toll bridge to Piedras Negras; then via Monclova to SALTILLO, 260-mile trip with two customs stops, one 15 miles below border, the next 60 miles beyond. After Saltillo, C.N. 57 runs via Durango, San Luis Potosí, and Queretaro to Capital.

SALTILLO (Little Falls) (Alt. 5,145 ft., Pop. 99,101), capital of Coahuila, is the oldest, most Mexican, northern city; pre-Conquest Indian town occupied by Spaniards in 1568 and repopulated with Tlaxcalans. This industrial weaving center is clean and picturesque with narrow, hilly streets and pleasant parks. Dry, even, salubrious climate at its mile-high elevation makes it North Mexico's natural health and summer resort. Long established schools for foreigners: Universidad Interamericana, at State University, offers accredited summer and regular courses while International Academy at Normal School offers intensive credit-earning Spanish studies. Visitors enjoy all sports. Locally made: tin masks, pottery, woolen blankets, famous light-weight, multi-colored striped *serapes.*

Churrigueresque-faced Santiago Cathedral (1735) has superbly carved doors, and San Esteban de la Nueva Tlaxcala, begun in Indian district 1592, is much remodeled. Ruins of Landin Chapel, pre-dating Saltillo, near Rancho Morillo, still display exquisite Plateresque carvings. San Francisco, behind the Cathedral, has notable bas-reliefs. Regional dance of Matachines highlights church *fiestas*; chief ones are May 3, and August 1 and 30. Visit Buena Vista Battlefield, where U.S. troops defeated Mexicans, 1847. New Tourist Department office is on Bulevar Constitución.

Hotel Arizpe Saenz, popular, central, moderate, has a restaurant; new Hotel de Anda is good, modest. Comforta-

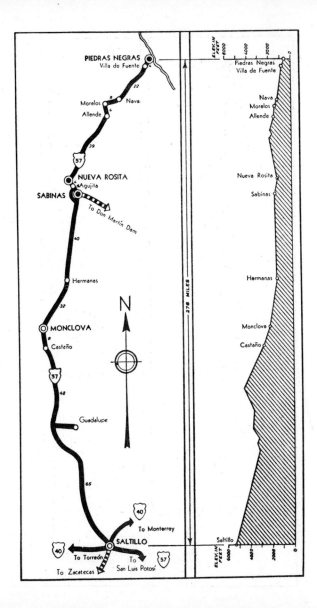

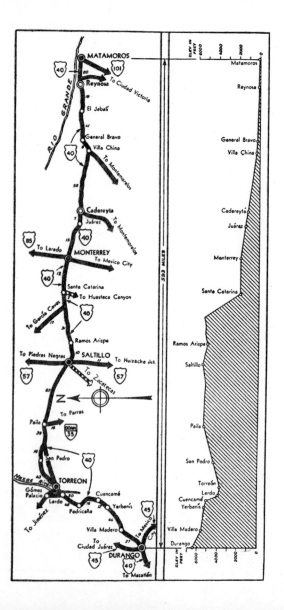

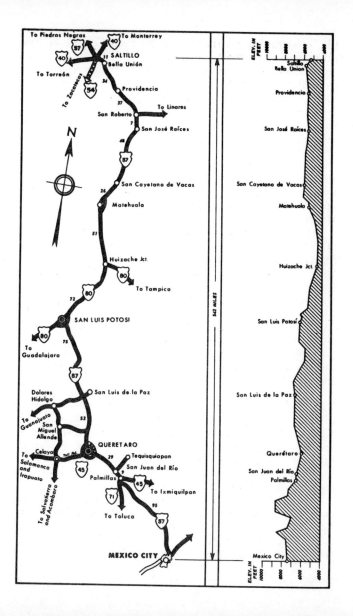

ble, moderate outskirts motels: El Paso Courts, no restaurant; new Estrella, bar, restaurant.

PARRAS DE LA FUENTE, en route to Torreón (C.N. 40) from PAILA, 84 miles from Saltillo, 16 miles left on paved road. A placid Colonial town in grape-growing wine center, it has an Art Institute. See the mansion, birthplace of the leader of the 1910 Revolution, Francisco I. Madero. There are a host of impressive mansions and *haciendas* in and around town.

TORREON, Coahuila, 180 miles west of Saltillo on C.N. 40, forms with nearby GOMEZ PALACIO and LERDO in Durango, the tri-city center of cotton and wheat-growing cooperatives of the immense Laguna area of reclaimed land. Hotels: Nazas, Elvira, Naves. Restaurant: El Apolo Palacio.

FROM MONTERREY TO CIUDAD VALLES: If you plan to take two days to reach Mexico City (over 600 miles), the logical overnight stop is CIUDAD VALLES; but take longer, if your time permits. Leaving Monterrey, C.N. 85 soon enters the beautiful aisle of HUAJUCO CANYON, then becomes the charming single riverside street of SANTIAGO, with its quaint plaza and church. For an interesting side jaunt at EL CERCADO, two miles beyond, turn right on the paved road to Cola de Caballo (Horsetail Falls), a mile's stroll from the parking area on the privately owned Hacienda Vista Hermosa. Small admission fee, lodgings. Swimming, other sports.

MONTEMORELOS: This town of grill-windowed homes with unique roof-high chimneys in back walls is in a citrus orchard area. Take State road C.E. 89 (by which McAllen-Reynosa traffic by-passes Monterrey) left at gas station, to visit GENERAL TERÁN, sixteen miles off C.N. 85, and the great orange groves of nearby *hacienda* Soledad de la Mota.

BACK ON THE HIGHWAY, C.N. 85, the road leads past a *maguey* plantation and many farms.

LINARES, next large town on C.N. 85, in a farming, ranching region, has pleasing plazas, an old casino and delightful Iglesia del Senor Misericordia. Don't miss Sr. Pablo Salce Arredondo's petroglyph collection! Exciting fair, February 23-25. (New paved connection with C.N. 57 is the

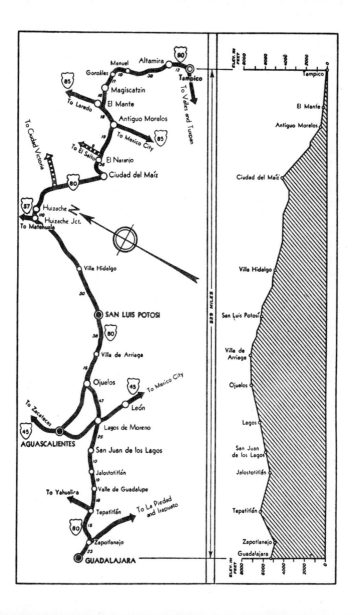

easiest route to oddly named Indian mountain towns Iturbide and Galeana.) Hotel Ramal, the town's best. Motel: Escondido Court, north of town. Others beyond in Villagran, where *henequén* plantations begin. At Km. 805 the scenic climb of Cuesta de Salero begins. Beyond Hidalgo, flat country bristles with *huisache*, mesquite, and the flowering *anacahuite*.

Hacienda Santa Engracia guest ranch, Tamaulipas, eleven miles off highway. Modern accommodations in a century-old ranch house, near mountains and a river, and cottages surrounded by lovely gardens and orchards. Fishing, swimming, horses, and polo; hunting and mountain lodges.

CIUDAD VICTORIA, capital of Tamaulipas (Alt. 1,473 ft., Pop. 50,727), is a *henequén* center and convenient overnight tourist stop. City institutions include State Capitol, Agricultural College, vocational school. Swimming, good fishing and hunting nearby. Hotel Sierra Gorda (Fat Hill) in town and San Antonio Motel on highway have some air-conditioned rooms. Turner's Restaurant at junction of C.N. 85 and C.N. 101 (Brownsville-Matamoros road) is popular. Good food, quicker service at nearby Café Florida.

TROPIC OF CANCER crosses road 5 miles south of Victoria between Km. 688 and 687 and you are now in the Torrid Zone. Beyond, climbing to Mesa de Llera, the road offers panoramic views, and later you enter the Canyon of Galeana, a paradise of tropical birds, trees, and flowers, and orchids within reach. (Try to catch a hummingbird here—they bring good luck in love.) Road drops gradually to

CIUDAD MANTE, tropical heart of the sugar-cane belt. The large refinery serves surrounding cane co-operatives (*ejidos*). See the federal tropical tree nursery, south edge of town. Swimming, fishing, hunting. Hotels: Naola, Mante, in town. Motel Los Arcos has a good restaurant.

MOTORIST NOTE: Just south of town, State Road 80 (C.N. 100) branches east to TAMPICO, 2 hours or 95 miles away. Better than State 110 route from Ciudad Valles.

TAMPICO, largest city of Tamaulipas (Pop. 122,197), is an oil center, vital Gulf port; 7 miles inland on Panuco

River. Site of Huastecan town razed by Cortés' forces, 1523. Sole Huastecan relic crumbles in Colonia de las Flores, a small rounded structure with stairway, probably a temple base. Pirate raids succeeded Indian mutinies; then, after 1810, battles between Insurgent patriots and Spaniards. U.S. troops landed in 1914. Cutthroat economic strife flared later when oil was discovered. The city has recovered from boom-day violence and is conventionally modernized; the landscape bristles with oil wells and refineries, monuments of prosperity.

Diversions: Excellent fishing, hunting; swimming at Miramar Beach. By horseback, bus, boat to many interesting spots.

Accommodations: Hotels: Inglaterra and Imperial, with good night club. El Flamingo, another good night spot. Motel: Colorado Courts, good. Many others. Unsurpassed seafood cuisine in all restaurants from lowliest to most elegant.

MOTORIST NOTE: At Antigua Morelos, 18 miles south of Mante, State Road 80 (link in C.N. 100, Tampico-to-Mazatlan Coast-to-Coast Route) crosses C.N. 85 and runs west via San Luis Potosí 443 miles to Guadalajara.

SAN LUIS POTOSÍ, capital of San Luis Potosí (Alt. 6,290 ft., Pop. 159,640), in rich farming, mining region (logical overnight stop before Guadalajara), was settled as Misión San Luís, in nearby San Pedro Hills, in 1589, the year before gold was found there, and was shifted to its present site to have water. Tractable Tlaxcalans settled here as examples to sullen pacified Chichimecas and Huachichiles. Wealth and progress did not destroy the city's Colonial air. There are cobbled streets to roam. A modern steel mill is neighbor to ancient potteries. The Cathedral and Church of Nuestra Señora del Carmen are ornate Baroque, the latter's façade one of Mexico's finest. San Francisco has a Mudejar tiled dome. The Teatro de la Luz and the Caja de Agua by Tresguerras are noteworthy.

Tourists' happy hunting grounds are the shops and Public Market on tile-decorated Calle de Hidalgo. Try the local cactus candy, *queso de tuna*. Murals of Fernando Leal depict the "Triumph of the Locomotive" in the railroad station, the machine age in San Juan de Dios Church. There is a State University and museum.

Hotels: Colonial, Progreso, Gante and Tuna Courts are moderate. Café La Lonja, good restaurant.

CIUDAD VALLES, San Luis Potosí, next big modern town on C.N. 85, is a citrus center. Thermal baths, swimming, hiking, riding, fishing, hunting. Hotels: Casa Granda, Valles, de luxe Taninul Spa on C.E. 110, alternate road to Tampico. Mexico City less than a day's trip, but the unhurried can repose at such oases as Banito Courts, 7 miles away, bathing in sulphur springs or swimming pool. Or enjoy a side trip such as:

TAMUIN: About 20 miles east on C.E. 110. Its predecessor was a holy city built by the Huastecas, offshoots of the Maya race, during their second cultural epoch in this area, about 950 A.D. The partially excavated ruins on the anciently terraced banks of the Tamuín River may be reached on foot—a rugged hike. Fading frescoes on a carved altar are the major sight. Of the statuary found here, the masterpiece is a Huastec youth, tattooed with intricate symbols. The figure clinging to the boy's back is a symbol of the sun's birth. On the Tamuín River a French archeological mission is exploring Tantóque.

CIUDAD SANTOS: 38 miles south of Valles on C.N. 85. Turn east at Xolol on paved road to this Huastecan village; its inhabitants still call it *Tancanhuitz* (Huastecan, "Canoe of Flowers"). Pre-Hispanic ruin in the churchyard. Huastecan mountain villagers attend the busy Sunday market. Holy Week festivities are still markedly pagan. True adventurers may follow C.E. 55, gravel road branching off C.N. 85 about 25 miles further south, to peek at secluded Indian hamlets, XILITLA and XILITIA.

TAMAZUNCHALE (Tam-as-un-*cha*-leh, Huastecan, "Governor's Residence"), former Huastec capital, is a tropical village in Moctezuma River valley on C.N. 85; its sixteenth-century church has been disfigured by recent renovation. A naturalists' and sportsmen's Eden—river fishing from dugouts, mountain game. Moderate hotels are Texas, San Antonio, Quinta Chilla, Mirador.

MOTORIST NOTE: Drive on to Zimapan only during the day to avoid fog when crossing the steep mountain barrier —there is one 5,000-foot winding scenic climb. Stretches of the road are cut from the solid rock flank of mountains.

CHAPULHUACAN, at onset of climb, near old village of that name, is Government road camp with restaurant, post office, telephone, telegraph—splendid vista!

JACALA (Ha-*ka*-la; Azt., "Town of Huts"), Hidalgo. Its white houses on a fertile valley slope are a welcome sight from high above. Restful to eat here. Simpson Courts and restaurant.

ZIMAPAN (See-ma-pan; Azt., "Place of Arid Mountains"), Hidalgo, 3 miles west of highway. Mining town, settled in 1522 in beautiful country, has a tree-bowered plaza, aging Colonial buildings and churches—an almost Oriental-styled parish church. Otomí Indians sell their handicrafts at Sunday market. Colonial-style Posada del Rey has pool, good food. Hotel Fundición, near the Plaza, is a former mining *hacienda*, guarding Colonial relics. Modest, excellent service.

TASQUILLO, a pre-Conquest Otomí capitol, 15 miles farther south and half a mile east of highway. This tree-shaded village uses the massive Colonial bridge over the Tula River. Motel and Balneario Tzindejéh on outskirts is a delightful, moderately priced retreat. About 5 miles beyond, junction with Queretaro road, C.N. 45; another 5 miles to Federal Car Inspection point.

IXMIQUILPAN (Eesh-me-*keel*-pan; Azt., "Place Where Edible Wild Greens Abound"), just east of C.N. 85, flourishing pre-Conquest Otomí city, still center of Otomí industry and culture. As Otomí women sit in market or walk about, their deft hands spin *maguey* fiber thread with their forefathers' simple stick and whorl technique. To Monday market they bring hand-woven articles: geometrically designed, colored bags; *quexquematls* (pre-Conquest woman's triangular shoulder shawls); sashes and the indigenous netlike, square carrying cloths, *ayates*. Two Colonial bridges span the Tula River. A glorious legacy is the massive Augustinian church-monastery, founded about 1550, occupied by busy teaching monks before 1571. Legends cluster about its re-

Market Scene

nowned Cristo de Santa Teresa, once a refugee in the Carmelite convent of this lady saint. Recently discovered on
church walls under layers of paint, still being restored, are
the first-known frescoes with predominately Indian figures
and designs in a religious edifice. Full panoplied Indian
warriors wield native weapon against mythic creatures—
figures, perhaps symbols of sins, and monsters blended of
European and Indian fantasy. A centaur, shod with Indian
sandals, wears a plumed Indian headdress and brandishes
an obsidian knife-edged club. Vivid colored figures swirl

within network of creepers and tendrils. Although Indians battle personified evil, no Christian symbol appears. Only place to stay, Dobb, Km. 159. Good food, service.

ACTOPAN (Azt., "Fertile Land"), pre-Conquest sister city of the above, is still Otomí but more modern. Here is a majestic Augustinian church-monastery, also founded about 1550—a forceful counterpoint to pagan temple grandeur. The black and white frescoes are well-preserved. Houses religious museum and fine exhibits of Otomí life and craft—many old articles identical to those on sale at Wednesday market.

MOTORIST NOTE: One road to Tula (see p. 28) runs west from here. C.N. 85 climbs to its highest point at HACIENDA DE LA CONCEPCIÓN, 8,206 feet. At COLONIA is junction with road to PACHUCA (see p. 28). On through VENTA DE CARPIO (road to Teotihuacan), across Spanish stone causeway into San Cristobal Ecatepec. At right is the foursquare House of the Viceroys, now a historical museum, but once the prison of Independence leader Father Morelos, executed where his statue stands beside the road.

At SANTA CLARA, C.N. 85 forks left to Capital past Basílica de Guadalupe with police inspection at ATZACOALCO; and ahead to Av. Insurgentes Norte. The inspection station is near the Indios Verdes statues. The pyramid monument beyond is dedicated to the founding of Mexico City's predecessor, Tenochtitlan. The tourist service booth at entrance gives free information; guide service must be paid for.

FROM EL PASO TO MEXICO CITY
VIA THE CENTRAL HIGHWAY (C.N. 45)

This highway runs mostly through flat semi-desert, agricultural, cattle-raising, and mining country, with views of mountains, some climbing, but no spectacular scenery.

The entry port is Ciudad Juárez (Hoo-áh-res). Cross from EL PASO on one of two cheap toll bridges or on free, less-traveled Cordova Island Bridge. Get information and travel literature in El Paso at the Pemex Travel Club office, Chamber of Commerce Building; the AAA office, 506 E. Paisano Drive on U.S. 80A; or at one of many travel agencies on either side of the border. Don't break the baggage custom seals stuck on at the bridge until past the inspection points, first 19 miles below Juárez, and last 156 miles below, outside Chihuahua.

CIUDAD JUÁREZ, Chihuahua (Alt. 3,700 ft., Pop. 261,683), largest border city, was founded in 1662 as Paso del Norte and renamed in 1888 for President Juárez, whose capital it was in the 1860's. There are many tourist shops, amusements, local industries, a lively market, good public buildings, and modern residences. The handsome carved wooden beams and stairway in the Mission of Nuestra Señora de Guadalupe have been preserved. The Mission was founded in 1659—before the town.

CASAS GRANDES (Large Houses): Turn right on C.E. 10 at Gallego, 137 miles south of the border for a 123-mile run to modern NUEVO CASAS GRANDES. (Can also be reached by National Railroad and is an Aeronaves plane stop.) The town is a farming, dairy center and sportsmen's base. Tourist accommodations. 4 miles to OLD TOWN OF CASAS GRANDES. Turn south in the second plaza as sign *"A las Moctezumas"* directs, for ½ mile on a dirt road, to the ruins of the ancient "border town," a trade crossroads and melting pot, a

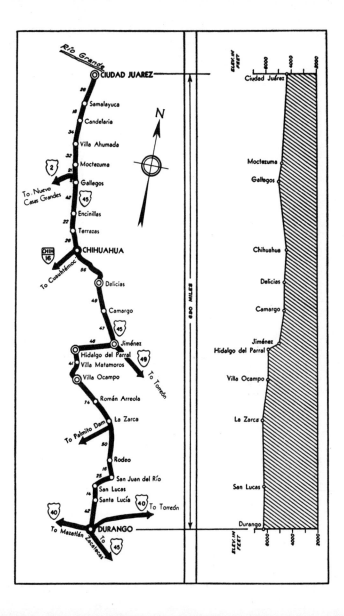

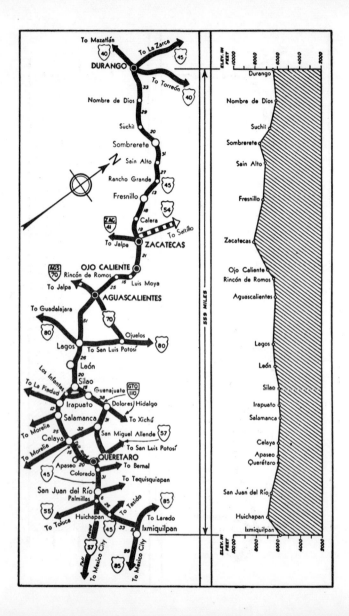

conspicuous fusion of many cultures. There are southwest Indian adobe apartment houses and irrigation-drainage systems; pyramids and ball courts of Toltec and other Meso-American cultures; shells from Gulf of Mexico trade.

CHIHUAHUA (Chee-*wah*-wah) (Alt. 4,593 ft., Pop. 149,-437), capital of Chihuahua, is ringed by mountains rich in minerals and game and has spacious streets, stone mansions, gardens, parks, and public buildings hallowed as sites of imprisonment, execution, and temporary burial place of the Father of Mexican Independence, Cura Miguel Hidalgo y Costilla, in 1811. The modern Palacio de Gobierno, rebuilt on the ruins of its burned predecessor, has a carved cedar Hall of Sessions and an elegant marble stairway. Outstanding are the Baroque cathedral, Santa Rita Church, and San Francisco Church, where Hidalgo's headless body was buried until 1827. Quinta Luz, former home of General Francisco Villa, is a museum of his possessions. The bustling Sunday market displays local leather goods, tiles, wrought-iron objects (also sold in shops), national handicraft articles, and hairless Chihuahua dogs—check their pedigrees! Barefoot Tarahumaras in regional dress—men of this hardy mountain race are famous endurance runners—may play their homemade violins in the streets for coins. Chihuahua, Tarahumara for "Place of Work," became, because of its satisfying explosive sound, an exclamation of surprise, admiration, and consternation throughout Mexico.

Pleasant drives out from the city are to the Colonial aqueduct with huge arches, still in use; to the old Quintas Carolinas, paved with cobblestones in geometric patterns; to the old regional mining town of Santa Eulalia; and the attractive Jesuit village of Aldama. Longer excursions for the adventurous to Basaseáchi Falls and Barranca de la Tarahumara. There is a train trip on the new Chihuahua Railway through spectacular canyon country to Topolobampo.

Accommodations: Palacio Hilton Hotel, moderate to expensive, popular restaurant and bar; Hotel Del Real, new and air-conditioned, moderate; Colonia Victoria Hotel, gardens and swimming pool. On the highway, El Capitan Motel and Santa Rita Courts, both moderate, good.

47

CIUDAD CAMARGO, a small industrial city in green Conchos River Valley, was founded about 1740 as Mission of Santa Rosalia. Her festival begins September 4. The hot sulphur springs on the outskirts were a pre-Conquest spa. Good fishing at Toronto Lake (Boquillo Dam).

Accommodations: Hotels—Baca, in town. Motels—Santa Rosalia Courts and Baca on highway.

HIDALGO DE PARRAL. Former State capital, rich mining center, picturesquely unmodernized, just off highway. Relics of past opulence are the gilded Churrigueresque altars of the parish church and the graceful, warm church the Indians love best, dedicated to the Virgin del Rayo (Virgin of Thunder). Local ores lavishly adorn the newer church of Our Lady of Fatima. The fantastically decorated private residence of the La Palmilla Silver Mine's owner is called Palacio de Pedro Alvarez. Shop fronts diminish the dignity of the last home of Pancho Villa, assassinated here.

Accommodations: Hotel Burciaga, Motel Camino Real, moderate.

DURANGO (Alt. 6,263 ft., Pop. 97,520), capital of Durango, is situated in a fine agricultural valley, surrounded by mountains rich in iron, silver, and gold. Its dry sunny climate attracted both Indians and Spaniards, the latter having established the city in 1563 and given it its Basque name. Among the Colonial edifices the massive, ornate cathedral (1695) is outstanding. Now the city has many modern buildings and homes, pleasant parks, and an attractive promenade along the river. To the north stands the huge, 700-foot-high Cerro del Mercado (Iron Mountain), said to be the largest in existence, and nearby are thermal baths and hunting in the mountains, as well as old mines.

Accommodations: Hotel Casablanca, Mexico Courts, and the Colonial-style Posada Duran, all moderate, are pleasant hostelries.

MOTORIST NOTE: The first connection between the Central and West Coast Highways is between Durango and Villa Union, 12 miles south of Mazatlán. Gorgeous mountain scenery, but dangerous driving. Minor improvements going on. Inquire as to conditions.

From Durango the highway enters the State of Zacatecas, offering a change of scene to rolling, cactus-dotted countryside through mellowing mining towns—NOMBRE DE DIOS, Durango, and SOMBERETE, Zacatecas, the latter noted for its thermal springs; the highway crosses the TROPIC OF CANCER shortly before FRESNILLO, a mine center.

ZACATECAS (Alt. 7,377 ft., Pop. 31,851), capital of Zacatecas (Azt., "Place of Grass"), was founded in 1548 under the high-sounding title of "The Very Noble and Loyal City of Our Lady of Zacatecas." It is an opulent Colonial city stagnating of late due to silver market problems. Custodian of a Colonial architectural legacy, this comely city still uses its ancient aqueduct. Clustered houses overhang cobbled stairs up abrupt Cerro de la Bufa (*bufa*—Spanish wine sack). As for centuries, leather-suited *aguadores* (water vendors) trudge between homes and public fountains. From the cerro, crowned by Los Remedios Chapel (its Virgin revered by local Indians for frequent miraculous cures), the view embraces the city and surrounding mountains. Stately unspoiled is the exterior of the cathedral (1617-1752), its façade a carven expression of intense faith. The exterior of the former Jesuit Baroque church, La Companía, now called Santo Domingo, has been slightly spoiled by renovations. Fine old secular buildings: Palacio Municipal, Teatro de Calderón. The museum-monastery of Guadalupe, founded 1707, 6 miles from the city, has one of the finest collections of Colonial painting in the country; the adjoining Capilla de Napoles is a neoclassic gem. Guadalupe villagers make *serapes*.

Accommodations: Hotel Ruis, Posada del Parque, Condesa; Zacatecas Courts. Restaurant—Los Petates.

LA QUEMADA (Burned Place). Take the road to VILLANUEVA, then the paved road to these archeological ruins (a full day's trip), which are a group of buildings, courts and pyramids, built up steeply on a hill with terraced walls, summits artificially leveled and terraces broadened; an imposing construction—the transition type between the Southwest and Mexico. The area's culture was most potent between 900 and 1200 A.D. Water still runs from fountains abandoned before the Conquest.

CHALCHIHUITES (Azt., "Precious Stones"), archeological zone. The ruins are of the same era as La Quemada, but better preserved.

AGUASCALIENTES (Hot Waters) is the capital of Aguascalientes (Alt. 6,222 ft., Pop. 126,222). The city has a good temperate climate, many parks and orchards, and thermal bathing. The underground is perforated by a network of tunnels, their origin and purpose unknown, but they have given rise to the name of La Cuidad Perforada. The State Palace is in the feudal Castle of the Marques of Guadalupe and the churches of interest are San Marcos and San Antonio, the architecture of the latter reminiscent of that of St. Basil in Moscow.

Attractive pottery and hand-drawn work are the local crafts. Together with others, these appear for sale in shops and at the market. A very popular *fiesta* and fair, with dances, fireworks, cockfights, and bullfights in honor of the patron saint San Marcos, begins April 25 and continues for two weeks.

Accommodations: Hotels—Paris, Francia, Imperial. Motels—San Marcos Courts, Campo Medrano. Restaurant—Fausto. All moderate.

LAGOS DE MORENO, a nice drowsy town, at junction with San Luis Potosí–Guadalajara Highway, C.N. 80.

STATE OF GUANAJUATO, despite increasing industrialization, encloses and cherishes so many cities of Colonial atmosphere or towns hallowed as Independence War shrines that it merits a long stay or a return visit from Mexico City.

LEON, Gto. (Alt. 6,183 ft., Pop. 209,469), the largest city in the state, is a vital agricultural, industrial center—the shoe capital of Mexico. Among its specialties are *rebozos,* and craftsmen still produce inlaid leather articles—belts, bags, horse trappings.

Accommodations: Hotels—Leon, Capri, Mexico. Motel—Yolanda Courts on highway. All moderate. Balneario de Comanjilla, near Leon, is a pleasant semi-resort hotel with thermal bathing. Inexpensive.

SILAO produces *serapes*, toys, inlaid boxes. Junction

outside city with C.E. 110, 15 miles to Guanajuato, state capital, via Marfil Canyon. The hillside above the road is sprinkled with the shacks of jobless miners; in the canyon below a dirt road wanders between the melancholy semi-ruined country mansions of mine-enriched, later impoverished, families of Guanajuato City. Mexicans and foreigners are beginning to restore some of them. Motel Marfil is a strategic station for exploring this romantic spot.

GUANAJUATO ("Hill of the Frogs" in Tarascan) is the state capital (Alt. 6,681 ft., Pop. 28,135). Founded in 1534, it was for centuries an immensely rich mining center and is still one of the loveliest and most unspoiled of Mexico's

Street in Guanajuato

Colonial cities. Narrow, cobblestoned streets and houses with Moorish balconies climb up the hillsides with many examples of good architecture. Lively social activities are available evenings, as well as many band concerts and serenades by the students of the State College, who also give street performances of Spanish medieval plays.

Hotels: Castillo de Santa Cecilia, impressive, dour keep on Valencia Hill some patrons love—others loathe. The Orozco, Paseo de la Presa, roomy, pleasant. Posada de la Presa, across street, small, modest, homey, Am. Pl., as is nearby Villa Goerne. Las Ambajadoras, same street, friendly, good service. Posada Santa Fé, Plaza Jardín Unión, is central, convenient.

Occupied in ancient times by Otomí, then by Tarascans (their name, Cuanaxhuata, Hispanicized to Guanajuato), then by Aztecs. Descendents of one or all of these peoples make *rebozos*, homespuns, toys, and pottery—sold in the city market or their workshops.

Some of Mexico's most magnificent old churches are here. San Diego on Jardín Unión Plaza has a remarkable Churrigueresque façade. Nearby is the parish church, Basílica de Nuestra Señora de Guanajuato (formerly San Francisco), which cherishes the miracle-performing image of its patroness in a side chapel. The Jesuit church of La Compañía, a short distance from the center, is a splendid edifice constructed of Guanajuato marble. The *retablos* are in many instances works of art.

La Valenciana, famous church of San Cayetano, and La Valenciana Mine, both 3 miles out, should not be missed. The church is one of the finest examples of Churrigueresque art inside and out (façade carvings are Mudejar design) in Mexico. It was built in 1788 by Conde de Rul, owner of the mine. The miners contributed generously and it is said that the foundation contains much silver ore.

Secular Buildings: The historic shrine, Alhóndiga de Granaditas, is a dignified edifice, built as a grain storehouse and market. During the Revolution for Independence it served as a fort and prison—later the state prison. Now the state historical museum, its main stairway has an appropriate mural by Chavez Morado. Simple, even charmingly childlike exhibits in the upper rooms depict the harsh Colonial restrictions which inspired the 1810 revolt. The rebuilt State University (its excellent summer school attracts many U.S. students) is a stately green and white edifice. The regal home of Conde de Rul, built by Celaya genius Eduardo Tresguerras, is on the same plaza as the Basílica, near the plainer birthplace of great historian Lucas Aleman, and the State Legislature. The birthplace of Diego Rivera will soon open as a museum.

A landmark is the huge statue on Valenciana Hill of José Barajas Martinez, the miner-hero affectionately remembered as Pipila (Little Turkey), holding a flaming torch. Balancing a heavy stone slab on his shoulders, Pipila reached and fired the doors of the Alhóndiga unscathed. Through this blazing breach the Insurgentes charged to victory.

Guanajuato

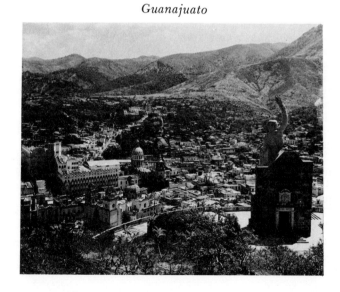

The non-squeamish find cemetery catacombs, lined with well-preserved mummies, interesting.

Excursions: The country is inviting for hikes and horseback trips. It is a unique experience to visit the mines with their ancient shafts and the villages around them with their churches rich in votive paintings.

IRAPUATO, Gto., back on highway C.N. 45, a pleasant town and industrial farm center, is famous for its strawberries and hand-drawn work. See San Francisco Church.

CELAYA, Gto. (Alt. 5,766 ft., Pop. 58,762). Both the El Paso and Guadalajara trains stop here. The specialties here are *cajetas de Celaya,* caramelized milk sweets, sold everywhere in Mexico; also toys and masks. The city market and surrounding country are very attractive.

Celaya is the birthplace and home of Francisco Eduardo Tresguerras (1765-1833), Mexico's most celebrated academic architect, poet, and painter, disciple of Herrera, who built the Escorial. Nuestra Señora del Carmen, completed in 1807 and deemed his masterpiece, is crowned by a noble green and gold tile dome, the finest of this type in the Republic. All the sculptures and paintings were done by him. La Capilla del Juicio (the Chapel of the Last Judgment) contains some of his best frescoes and two of his self-portraits. His works include the Monument to Independence on the main plaza and El Puente de la Laja (the Flagstone Bridge). He is buried in the old parish church of San Francisco, to which he added the chapel, altars, and murals, including his self-portrait.

Accommodations: Motels—Campestre, Royal Courts. Hotel—Isobel. Restaurant—El Gaucho.

MOTORIST NOTE: Junction with paved road via COMONFORT to SAN MIGUEL ALLENDE, Gto. (Alt. 6,068 ft., Pop. 14,-853), was founded in 1542 by the Franciscan Juan de San Miguel, with Allende added to its name in honor of the native revolutionary hero of 1810. It is a delightful city, on hilly terrain, with cobbled streets and adobe huts as well as modern and Colonial houses. There are many notable churches and chapels, but the most exquisite is the chapel of San Miguel Viejo, defenseless against time's abuse, in the fields beyond the railroad station, an unpardonable aesthetic negligence. Nearly 40 buildings built before 1810 are honored as birthplaces of national heroes, vanished institutions (House of the Inquisition), mansions of Colonial nobles, or for preserved Colonial features—for example, the House of the Dogs for its carved balcony posts.

There is a permanent colony of foreign writers and artists, temporarily increased and enlivened by newcomers attending Instituto del Arte de Allende, an accredited school of fine arts that gives excellent instruction in many crafts at summer sessions. Intensive Spanish and related studies (with credit) are offered at Academia Hispana, a vital new influence stimulating cultural activities in the city. A branch of the National Instituto de Bellas Artes occupies the hallowed precincts of the San Francisco monastery. A part is reserved as a museum—admission 2 *pesos*.

Festivals, taken over by city officials, lack their former spontaneous vitality. *Conchero* dancers from some neighboring towns attend the September 29 San Miguel *fiesta*. Shops and workshops sell local craft goods—tin and copper wares, carvings, handsome leather bags and belts. A tasteful selection of national arts and crafts is displayed at Casa Maxwell's new headquarters, Calle de Canal 14; contemporary art is also exhibited in its gallery. A branch of Artes

Art School in San Miguel Allende

Populares de Tequis (see Tequisquiapan) in a Posada de San Francisco shop, offers superlative woolens, wire jewelry, stone carvings.

Hotels: Posada de San Francisco is a Colonial mansion on Zócalo; friendly Vista Hermosa, Casa Sautto; Rancho Atascadero on height above city. *Motel*: Siesta.

Excursions: On the paved state road via Dolores to Guanajuato city, to the popular thermal pools of Taboada —thermal bathing at nearby (7½ miles from San Miguel) Atotonilco (Azt., "Where There is Hot Water"), a pathetic village in the shadow of a huge, dilapidated Jesuit sanctuary (1740-1748), a potent pilgrim's magnet. The tarnished interior and chapel wall decorations are unusual. The vestibule paintings by Miguel Antonio de Pocosangre are medieval fantasies of sin and punishment and scrolled verses on the same themes. The first stop on Hidalgo's march to battle, he borrowed the church's Guadalupe portrait to be the Insurgents' standard.

Dolores Hidalgo, 25 miles from San Miguel, is a simple pottery town. Patriot priest, Miguel Hidalgo y Costillo, was curate here from 1803 to 1810. Casa de Diezma, 1779, was his home from 1804 to 1810 and is now Casa de Hidalgo, a national shrine and a poignant museum of his effects. Here Mexico's Paul Revere, horseman Ignacio Pérez, brought word at dawn on September 16, 1810, that, the rebels' plans betrayed, Spanish troops were riding to arrest leaders. While its bell (now hung in National Palace in Mexico City) clanged a call to arms, from the parish church steps Cura Hidalgo proclaimed Mexico's Independence in saltier words than the "Viva Mexico" of "El Grito de Hidalgo" cried from official posts in every hamlet each September 15 at 11 p.m. Local potters, abandoning earlier charming, simple designs, produce high-colored, glazed wares—some very handsome.

Queretaro (Azt., "Ball Court") (Alt. 6,160 ft., Pop. 67,277), capital of Queretaro, grew on the site of an Otomí town conquered first by Aztecs and occupied not long after (1531) by Spaniards. Still picturesquely Colonial center inside ring of modern factories; water still supplied by lofty arched aqueduct (1726-1738).

Accommodations: Hotels—Grand Hotel and Hotel del Marquis on Zócalo, moderate, near best lunchroom (Café Flor de Queretaro). Modern highway motels—Flamingo, Casa Blanca, Barón, Jacal, etc., too expensive for variable, chilly, perfunctory services.

The natives of the region are Otomís, who do good weaving. Markets and shops sell local textiles and handicrafts. Opals (*only* semi-precious stones mined in area!) sold in matrix or cut and polished, as are imported gem stones, by local experts. Be wary of street vendors. Buy only in reliable stores like El Rubí or cutters' home workshops.

Fiestas: Christmas Eve, February 2, May 5, August 15 and 19, September 13-16. All entertaining.

Public Buildings: Secular ones of note include Palacio Municipal, former Casa Real (1770) and governor's residence, former home of the Corregidor Dominguez and his heroic wife, Josafina Ortiz, who warned Hidalgo Spanish troops were en route to seize rebel ringleaders. Her face is on the five-*centavo* coin, a "Josefina." Herself betrayed, she was the Royalists' prisoner in the same building, a national monument containing a historical museum. Palacio Federal, former great Augustinian monastery (1731-1745) on main plaza, has wondrous carved patio and gallery decorations.

El Convento Colegiata de Santa Rosa de Vitervo, on Calle Santa Rosa, a seventeenth-century edifice, with a fine simple façade; remodeled by Tresguerras (see CELAYA) in the eighteenth century. In the sacristy hangs one of his finest murals, showing Santa Rosa at work in the garden with her pupils. The little chapel is filled with elaborate gilded altars.

Church of Santa Clara, on the Plaza de Santa Rosa, founded in 1706; also remodeled by Tresguerras, who designed the glazed dome and tower. The interior is richly ornamented.

The cathedral and all the other churches and convents, of which there are many, have interesting architectural details. The Church of Santa Cruz (Holy Cross) stands on the site where the Otomí Indians fought the invading Spaniards; Fra Junipero Serra officiated there before going to

57

California, and Iturbide and later Maximilian used it as barracks.

Nearby Places: Cerro de las Campanas, or Hill of the Bells, where the Emperor Maximilian and his two faithful generals, Miramón and Mejía, were executed; the place is marked by a little chapel. At a short distance by car is the picturesque old village of San Pedro de la Cañada, where there are natural hot springs; also El Pueblito, where there are interesting archeological ruins and a Christian sanctuary. The remains of a fine sturdy Colonial aqueduct stand at the edge of the city.

SAN JUAN DEL RIO produces strong willow and reed baskets and furniture. Nearby is the palatial old Hacienda de la Llave, converted into a government agricultural school.

TEQUISQUIAPAN, on a paved road 12 miles north, a serene Otomí village and spa, is Mexico's kindest retreat from modern tensions. Thermal pools at every inn. A favorite haven is charming, inexpensive Posada del Virrey, its quiet pool in a garden close. Posada del Camino has more sophisticated ambiance. Tequisquiapan, El Reloj, and San Francisco, larger, less quiet but delightful. Artes Populares de Tequis makes and sells, at Centenario 44, exceptionally beautiful wool rugs and *serapes,* original, handsome wire jewelry, carved stone figures. Other shops handle local willow and reed woven articles and baskets. Opal miners and dealers meet and bargain at Sunday market in the plaza. Nice buys in uncut stones. Excursions include a trip to one of two opal mines; to the bull ranch on Don Fernando de la Mora's *hacienda* (ask to see the garden); to the great cactus nursery in Cadereyta; to the weavers' village, Bernal, at the foot of a fantastic isolated rock peak.

MOTORIST NOTE: From San Juan del Rio choice of quick trip to Capital by toll road, C.N. 55, or by more interesting, older, longer C.N. 57 via State of Mexico's capital, Toluca, to Pan-American Highway.

TOLUCA (Azt., "Place of Reeds"), capital of the State of Mexico, lies in farming, cattle-raising valley, higher than Mexico City (Alt. 8,793 ft., Pop. 76,871), and is market center for the network of mining and handicraft towns of Aztec, Otomí, and Matlatzinca Indians, whose presence and products account for the size and fame of the city's Friday market. Beware of pickpockets and tire slashers. Don't waste breath bargaining. *Hotels*: San Carlos, Rex, Colonial.

Toluca is a windy, chilly (icily cold in winter), clean, prosaic city of severe architecture decorated with wrought-iron grillwork. The *portales* in section El Mercado Riva Palacio shelters booths of handicrafts and delicious candies. Next door is an old Franciscan church with a handsome façade. In the atrium of El Carmen church, near the Public Market, is one of the last of the weird Little Hand trees—its hand-shaped flowers are red. The tourist Department is in Colonial-style Palacio del Gobierno on the main plaza. Nearby, the Biblioteca Publica guards valuable old books. For a view and folkloric interest visit El Calvario on the hill beyond El Paseo de Colon to see an image like the Señor de Chalma (see p. 61).

The State Museo de Arqueología on Calle Cura Merlin has a collection of superb statuary and objects from the state's pre-Hispanic ruins. Across the street the Fine Arts Museum displays Colonial paintings and an exciting exhibit of equestrian objects. The Museo del Arte Popular, open daily (except Monday) from 9 A.M. to 1 P.M. only, has a charming display of the region's arts and crafts. Artes Regionales, Juárez 34, has excellent local handicrafts.

The State University has summer session for foreigners. Southeast of the city is an important agricultural institute.

Excursions: A fair road leads to the Nevado de Toluca, a thrilling ride, with splendid views. At the top are the extinct craters with their deep blue lakes. The ride to San Bartolo Otzelotepec (Azt., "Hill of the Tiger"), with *haciendas* on the way and villages nearby, is interesting. The festival there is on New Year's Day. Valle de Bravo, a picturesque town, where the government has constructed a big dam, has a pleasant hotel near a waterfall. Nice pottery is made here.

CALIXTLAHUACA (Azt., "Houses on the Plain") is a ½-square-mile archeological zone 5 miles from Toluca. There are several interesting restored temples to see. Occupied in archaic times, the first serious builders were Matlatzinca (an Otomí tribe), influenced first by their Teotihuacan contemporaries, later strongly influenced by Tolteca-Chichimeca, lastly and briefly by the Aztecs who conquered the city in 1510. Refugees returned from the Tarascan country after Spaniards arrived. Some of the greatest pre-Hispanic sculpture is found here—pieces of it are exhibited in the archeological museums of Toluca and Mexico City. The most remarkable restored edifices include the semi-rounded Temple of the Wind God, Pyramid of the Rain God, and a building containing a cruciform altar with a skull frieze. The site was pillaged by nearby builders, and valuable carved stones appear in the parish church walls. Small museum at the ruins.

ARTS AND CRAFTS VILLAGES SCATTERED AROUND TOLUCA: One can visit all of them in one day with a car. Check the state of the few dirt stretches. Seek general advice from the director of Museo del Arte Popular. All are farming towns supplementing their income by continuing to make for sale one or more kinds of articles for home or personal use. Local fruit liqueurs, *moscas,* seem sweet but have a tangy bite.

OCOYOACAC (Azt., "Entrance to Pine Grove"), 14 miles from Toluca, makes homespuns, blankets, sashes, has many feast days, from January 10 to Ash Wednesday. On the first date, the gaieties include an elaborate muleteer dance, "Danza de los Arrieros," stepped to music part of the time, then to a chant of old prayers about protection from robbers, the trade's chief hazard. The inhabitants of the nearby village of LERMA, feared a century ago because the farmers were highwaymen between harvest and sowing, now are law-abiding reed mat weavers and toy and chair makers.

TIANGUISTENCO (Azt., "In a Market"), a *serape* town, lives up to its name with its big Tuesday market. Ten minutes away is a weaving hamlet, GUADALUPITA (Little Guadalupe), where cloth, *serapes,* bags, and sashes are made. At the headwaters of Lerma River, a few miles away, is AMOLAYA DEL RIO (Azt.-Span., "Where Water Springs from

River"). Specialties: embroidered tablecloths and napkins, unbleached cotton bags, wool sashes woven on a pre-Conquest kind of loom, and handmade caned chairs. VILLA VICTORIA is another embroidery town. Between here and Metepec is basket-making SANTA ANA. Another road from Tianguistenco to Metepec through quaint MEXICALTZINGO permits a stop at famed bull-breeding Hacienda de Atenco.

MOTORIST NOTE: One of the most varied lovely drives in Mexico is from Toluca to Taxco, C.N. 55, which meets the Grutas–Cuernavaca–Mexico City route above Las Grutas; there is a junction with the Mexico City–Taxco–Acapulco road, C.N. 95, at Km. 138 before Taxco. Bus service for all C.N. 55; *turismo* limousines as far as Ixtapán de la Sal from Mexico City via Toluca. The Toluca-Taxco trip is a short cut in miles, but the need to at least peek at each interesting town will make the trip a full day or longer.

METEPEC (Azt., "Maguey Hill") is off C.N. 55, only 5 miles from Toluca; frequent bus service. Potters turn out gorgeous, polychromed, imaginative bric-a-brac, figurines, toys—rarely seen in the local Monday market but sold in potters' home workshops and their co-operative store in Toluca at Guillermo Prieto 301, along with their charming everyday pots and pitchers. Prices moderate, fixed.

TENANGO (Azt., "Walled Place"), terminal of a railroad branch from Toluca, has several crumbling forts of many epochs, from pre-Conquest times to 1910.

TENANCINGO (Azt., "Near the Walled Place") is a large old town (Alt. 5,710 ft.), beyond a beautiful canyon after Tenango, where *rebozos* and woven palm furniture are made. Delightful Sunday market in a shady plaza blazing with racks of *rebozos* and serapes. Local goods are always on sale in roadside shops and craftsmen's homes. It is possible, but not easy, to visit nearby EL DESIERTO by car; it is easier by horseback. This village of huts in the shadow of the noble, semi-ruined Carmelite Convent in a beautiful hilly woodland, holds gay fiestas January 3, July 16, and October 15. More exciting, and easier, side trip from here takes in two famous sanctuaries—pre-Columbian MALINALCO and post-Conquest CHALMA—by car over all-weather road to first; by bus to both from Tenancingo.

MALINALCO (Azt., "A Turn in the Road"), secluded in an exuberant tropical valley, has an impressive sixteenth-century Augustinian church and monastery with a novel cloister; roomy old residences; and adobe village homes smothered in flowering gardens and orchards. It is a 20-minute hike up Cerro de los Idolos to the extraordinary never-to-be-finished cluster of sacred edifices cut from the hill's living rock. Begun 1487 by order of Emperor Ahuitzotl (The Scourge), after the Aztecs subjugated the resident Malinalca, work slackened in 1490. So, in 1501, the Emperor sent skilled stonecutters from Tenochtitlan. He died in 1503. Annually whiplashed by Moctezuma's sharp orders, the workers still had not finished it when Spaniards burned the town and sacked the shrine in 1521. Movable stones were looted by Augustinians, arriving in 1537, for their temple, but the majestic stairs, terraces, and platforms, quarried at different levels, were a fixed part of the earth. A Cyclopean stage overhanging the valley is identified by an altar and pillar bases as the longest, strangest pre-Conquest temple known. The masterpiece is the Temple to the Sun God, which the Aztec Warrior Knights of the Jaguar and Eagle clans tended. Its door is a carved likeness of the Earth Monster's mouth, symbol of eternal evil these Knights were sworn to battle ceaselessly. From the floor of this temple rise relief carvings (still part of the hill's matrix) of the pelts and heads of the Knights' mascot-gods, the jaguar and the eagle. The carved mountain faces at Mt. Rushmore in the U.S. are pygmy concepts beside this deep but artistic reshaping of a hill. If possible, visit this site during the village *fiestas* of Holy Week and September 16.

CHALMA is a few miles beyond, end of the road. The sanctuary of the dark-skinned, life-sized crucified Cristo, the Lord of Chalma, rises dramatically at the dead end of the single village street in the narrowing triangular cleft between the deep gorge of the Chalma River (a Mexican Ganges—pilgrims bathe in its waters) and rocky precipice to which clings a two-storied Augustinian monastery with unusual guest house cloister, an arched front piazza. Above this is the cave, now a chapel, where the idol of Oztocteotl

(Azt., "Cave God") attracted pilgrims from untold centuries until, after Augustinian monks arrived and found the inhabitants deaf to their preachings, one morning the old god lay in fragments beside his empty pedestal. Over him stood the crucifix now in the church. Won by this miracle, the Indians accepted the new faith. The cave was purified, refurnished, and rededicated to the new patron as the Chapel of San Miguel of the Cave. Rivaling Guadalupe, pilgrim attendance soon had to be controlled and the annual geographic schedule is still the custom for pre-Lenten visits: pilgrims from Otomí and Aztec villages of the Central Plateau, January 6; Zapotecans from Oaxaca, February 2; throngs from Morelos, Guerrero, Tlaxcala, Puebla, the first Friday in Lent. There are no rules for attendance during week-long *Pascua Chica* in May. Here, in the atrium, pagan dances are still performed to primitive drum and flute music in ecstasy not often seen at more accessible shrines.

BACK TO C.N. 55. First town beyond Tenancingo is sprawling VILLA GUERRERO; its Sunday market right on the road is *fiesta*-gay. (Side trips from here to several fascinating villages near old mines, the loveliest SULTEPEC—also accessible from Toluca-Nevado road.)

IXTAPAN DE LA SAL (Azt., "Near Salt Mines") is a popular playground-spa of Mexico City vacationers and foreigners, as well as a mecca for health-seekers.

Hotels: Ixtapan—expensive, elegant. Moderate are Hotel Kiss, Posada de Don Manuel, Bungalo Lolita, many others.

TOTANICO, last charming village before Las Grutas and Taxco road, with mineral pools. Pretty, unique baskets and trays are woven here.

BACK ON THE TOLUCA–MEXICO CITY HIGHWAY from these villages, the way continues scenic. Near the Desierto de Los Leones stands an obelisk commemorating a victory of Cura Hidalgo y Costilla. A short distance away is a post of interpreter guides, who give information gratis and paid guide service. For Mexico City, turn to the left via Lomas de Chapultepec, Chapultepec Park, and the Paseo de la Reforma.

FROM NOGALES TO MEXICO CITY

VIA THE WEST COAST HIGHWAY (C.N. 15)

THE WEST PACIFIC COAST or INTERNATIONAL HIGHWAY, C.N. 15, is U.S. Westerners' gateway to a superlative tropical winter holiday. An unhurried traveler can happily spend a week or a month en route to Mexico City, via Guadalajara, about 1,550 miles from Nogales, and still regret postponed side trips and stop overs. Vacationing and loitering must be scheduled for good weather months between mid-November and early spring. Only quick through trips to the Capital with overnight stops at air-conditioned hotels are possible during summer's humid heat, so intolerable many hotels close. September storms rarely delay traffic, as road repair service is quick and efficient. Inquire about local roads before leaving the highway—*at all seasons and everywhere.* The adventurous or lucky owners of jeeps can visit innumerable fishing villages with their enchanting beaches with some kind of lodgings, makeshift or primitive, or get through to inland villages, mountain-guarded mine towns and hunting grounds.

Between Nogales and Guadalajara, C.N. 15 crosses the rich mining, fishing, agricultural states of Sonora, Sinaloa, and Nayarit into Jalisco.

NOGALES, Sonora, opposite Nogales, Arizona, is the most friendly entry port. The town is in a nest of metallic hills, among the walnut (*nogal*) groves for which it is named, in a cheese-making ranching district. Here Geronimo was prisoner, in the building that is now a restaurant, La Caverna. The two Nogales celebrate spring with a flower festival in May.

Hotels: Fray Marcos de Niza and Olivia. Both comfortable.

First baggage inspection 4 miles beyond Nogales; the second at the thermal spa, Imuris, almost 40 miles south.

MAGDALENA, is an agricultural, mining center with

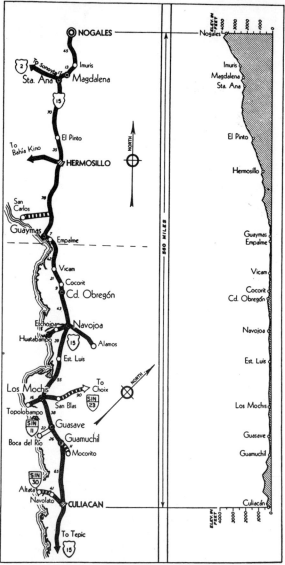

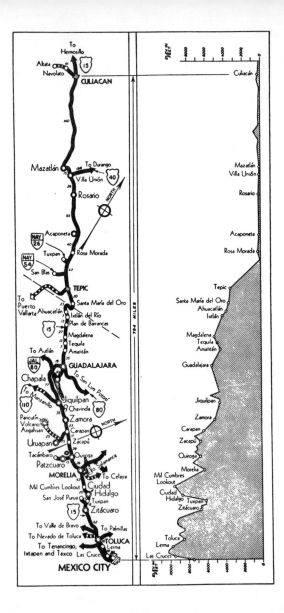

several small hotels. During its annual gala *fiesta*-fair, October 4, to honor the mircale-performing image of San Francisco, Papago Indians usually dance the *pascola*.

Side trips: Cananea copper mines and mission town, San Ignacio de Caborca, on C.N. 2 (new highway from Tijuana which connects with C.N. 15 at Santa Ana).

BENJAMIN HILL, junction of *Ferrocarril Pacifico* and *Sonora-Baja California* railways. Just south is Federal Agricultural Inspection post.

EL OASIS, 29 miles beyond, has a gas station and a restaurant. Last baggage inspection. The landscape beyond is cactus-punctuated.

HERMOSILLO (Er-mo-see-yo; Span., "Little Beauty"), ancient Pitic (Yaqui, "Where Two Rivers Meet") of the great Yaqui people, settled by Spaniards in 1742, is the pretty, modern, busily expanding capital (Alt. 77 ft., Pop. 96,122) of Sonora. A popular winter resort, it is friendly to tourists, who may ignore the parking meters in the main streets. Exhibits in the strikingly modern State Museum and Library building on the State University campus, built in 1942, include the controversial mummy of the Yecora man, possibly 12,000 years old. The patio of the partly Moorish-style Palacio de Gobierno is a garden spot guarded by stately twin laurels. Good shops; lively municipal market and several new neighborhood ones.

Excursions: Visits to High Life Brewery; Rodríguez Lake; Puerto Kino by C.E. 16, and other beaches. Rocky, snake-infested Tiburon Island, across the shark-thronged waters from Kino, was until recently the waterless refuge of the last Seri Indians, a most primitive but daring fishing people, eating their catch raw, knowing no farming; the women painting their faces in archaic designs. Coveting gasoline motors, most of 275 Seris have moved to crude huts on the mainland beaches so that the males, fishing for sharks, can sell the livers for gasoline.

Accommodations: Hotels—Gandara, De Anza, Moderno, Kino, Posada México, and San Alberto. Motels—Bugambilia, La Siesta, El Encanto.

Sample the local tripe and corn stew, *el menudo*.

GUAYMAS (Goo-wy-mas), the romantic Sonora winter resort, famous for its superb game fishing and the beauty of its bay, is an expanding commercial fisheries port where the U.S. maintains a space-communication station. Guaymas was settled by the Guaymatas Indians, a branch of the Yaquis, for whom the town is named; it was explored by Spaniards 1535 and a Jesuit mission was established by Father Kino around 1700. It was really settled by Spaniards in 1769. Free port. Had a stormy past as a depot for Sonora's gold and silver awaiting sea shipment; frequently raided by pirates of many nationalities, the last battle was in 1854. A rolling peninsular barrier screens the beach resort from the port town on Guaymas Bay, where old Spanish-Moorish houses, aloof in their gardens, are overlooked by upstart modern apartment buildings.

Accommodations: In the resort area on Miramar Beach on the spectacularly beautiful, island-dotted, mountain-ringed Bacochibampo (Yaqui, "Sea Serpent") Bay, are many comfortable hotels (most elegant and expensive, Playa de Cortés) and all water sport facilities. There is a fall fishing tournament and on May 10, as birthday homage to ex-President Abelardo Rodríguez, a water-sports *fiesta*. Motels on the highway: Guaymas Inn, Flamingos, Armida, Marlin —all relatively dear in winter. Escalante Trailer Park is on the beach.

Diversions: Shell collecting and clamming, fun to some, serious business to others. Horseback riding; fine hunting in hills.

Excursions: Hacienda de Aranjuez; old San José de Guaymas Mission; the parakeet-haunted realm of Saguaro Forest; Yaqui villages at the foot of Yaqui Sierra Bacatete. Now progressive farmers are marking their prowess with high wheat-growing records. Their proud hunting culture endures in the complicated choreography of the Deer Dance at *fiestas* such as at Vicam, on St. John the Baptist's Day, June 24, or during Holy Week.

CIUDAD OBREGÓN is named after the late Sonorense General Alvaro Obregón, the first of the Revolutionary Reconstruction presidents (1920-24), whom the Yaquis helped win many a battle. It is a prosperous, growing city, with many cotton gins, granaries, a conglomeration of adobe huts and modern buildings, its dusty streets full of trucks and automobiles.

Accommodations: Hotels—Colonial, Imperial, and San Jorge. Motel—Costa de Oro.

NAVAJOA is a fast-growing town, with plane and train connections and roads leading to interesting places; a paved one leads 23 miles to secluded Huatabampo and 11½ more to the lovely port Yavaros. Near here are the Mayo Pueblas. The Mayos, of Yaqui stock, are gentler people. Chiefly farmers, they weave heavy one-piece *serapes*. Their deer dance, similar to the Yaqui one, is performed at their chief May *fiestas*.

Motels: Del Rio and El Mayo. The Merendero Restaurant is quite satisfactory.

ALAMOS, 32 miles from Navajoa. Between wooded crags a fine paved road climbs a trail worn by silver- and gold-laden burros and mining barons' lordly carriages to an upland valley, where this mellowed portrait of colonial New Spain is preserved as a national monument. Here in 1541 Coronado's army camped among the cottonwoods (*alamos*). The early feverish, raw mining settlement was gradually refined by the hills' wealth into a splendorous, populous (Pop. 30,000 in 1790), eighteenth-century city. As ore seams thinned out and market prices declined, Alamos too declined (present population less than 3,000); its decay was halted recently by retired Mexicans and foreigners who restore and cherish old mansions (the youngest building is over a century old). The humblest homes wear the narrow, grilled windows of old Spain and have blooming patios. Winding cobbled, almost untenanted, streets; gracefully crumbling walls and pillars; exquisite traceries of wrought-iron balconies and ornaments belong to a vanished golden age. The serene façade of the cathedral, surmounted by a graceful bell tower and dome, broods over the typically arcaded Plaza de Armas. A favorite stroll ends among the cemetery's marble, ornately grilled mausoleums.

A branch of the National Museum of Popular Arts and

Crafts (open 8 A.M. to 12 noon; 1 to 5 P.M.; no entrance fee) has tasteful exhibits of Mexico's best folk art. The sole industry is the collection and exportation of "jumping beans," larvae-infested seeds of local shrubs.

Accommodations: Motel Álamos, on outskirts, discordantly modern. Hotel Portales, a mansion on the Plaza, delightful, moderate. Expensive, de luxe Casa de los Tesoros is open October to May.

Diversions: Rock and gem stone collecting; hiking and hunting in the hills; picnicking and bathing at Rio Cuchujaqui; watching Mayo Indian women at La Uvulama handmold pots and fire them primitively; exploring abandoned mine-smelter towns. One of the latter, La Aduana, comes to life every November 20-21 for the Mayo Indian festival of the miracle-working Virgin de Balvernara at its old church, where, centuries ago, prospectors were supposedly led to a rich silver lode by the apparition of the Virgin, disguised as a beautiful woman snared in the spiny arms of the gigantic old cactus still growing from its wall.

Los Mochis (Cahita, "Land Turtles"), Sinaloa, is 3½ miles east of C.N. 15, nearly 100 miles south of Navajoa. A flourishing farm center of the area irrigated by the great El Fuerte River Basin system, Los Mochis has the largest Pacific Coast sugar refinery and is a shipping point for tomatoes, chick-peas, cotton.

Accommodations: Comfortable stopover is Hotel Santa Anita or Motel Chapman (no restaurant).

Excursions: El Fuerte, an old Nayarit mining town 50 miles away, has lovely Colonial mansions. Soon to be linked to Alamos, when cobbled Camino Real is paved. The thriving mountain-encircled fishing port of Topolobampo has a sugar mill and a shrimp-packing plant; it offers exciting sport fishing on local commercial craft. (Best lodgings in Los Mochis.) Terminus of the new Chihuahua Railroad, the town is slated for port modernization, expansion.

Guasave, plane stop. Restaurant, gasoline. From here there is a 22-mile trip on an all-weather road to Boca del Rio for camping, swimming, fishing on a Gulf beach.

Guamuchil is named for the mesquite-like tree—the

cottony packing around the seeds in the twisted pods is edible. Just off C.N. 15, Guamuchil has gas, a restaurant, and a hotel.

CULIACÁN (Alt. 216 ft., Pop. 84,602), capitol of the wealthy mining state of Sinaloa, perpetuates in its name ("The God Coltzin's Place of Worship") the prolonged thirteenth-century sojourn of the migrating Náhuatl-speaking Colhua during their arduous trek to the Valley of Mexico. The Spaniards settled in Culiacan shortly after the Conquest, and Cortés and Alarcan sailed from here for Baja California in 1537. It was from here, too, that Coronado led out his army to seek fabled Quivira and the Seven Golden Cities of Cibola. He had entered Culiacán in a brilliant sham battle, and after several days of feasting, left in his golden armor, mounted on a white steed, followed by grandees in shining steel and Indians in bright *serapes* and feathers, with banners flying and drums beating. Here he led back, two years later, the tattered, half-starved survivors of the ill-fated quest, having found the mythical cities to be nothing more than Indian adobe pueblos in what is now the U.S. Southwest.

Despite its long-standing role as a mining center and more recent one as the busy nexus handling farm product exports, Culiacán retains a languid Colonial—or tropical—air, fostered by its situation in the verdant basin of the Culiacán and Fuerte Rivers. It is a pleasant city to ride in or stroll about, especially along the river boulevard, where the best restaurant, Merendero, stands—its new night club sister is on the heights.

Excursions: CARRIZALEJO ARROYO, baths; YMALA, hot springs resort a dozen miles away with petroglyphs on nearby canyon walls; good ocean swimming and fishing at EL DORADO, about 40 paved miles away, and at ATLATA, almost as far (only 30 miles of road are paved); hunting in nearby mountains.

Accommodations: Air-conditioned San Luis Hotel in town. Hotel Mayo has air-conditioned rooms. Motels on highway—San Luis and Tres Rios.

MAZATLÁN (Azt., "Place of the Deer") (Pop. 74,934) is a

popular beach resort the Mexicans fondly nickname "Pearl of the Pacific." An active commercial fishing port, the town supports shrimp-packing plants as well as the Concordia textile factory, El Robles sugar mill, and other industries. Internationally known for its annual fishing tournaments, deep-sea fishing is a year-round sport. The people are pleasure-loving and the place is noted for its pretty girls and gay carnival mood, accented by the flowers and palm trees.

No traces of the now extinct pre-Conquest Chibcha Indians' settlement or the early Spanish port, at which a Manila galleon touched each year, distract pleasure-seekers. Pirate raids, successive seizures by filibusters and U.S. troops have left no scars on the sun-filled city on its tapering peninsula, 25 miles below the Tropic of Cancer, about opposite the tip of Baja California. The Palacio Municipal guards a small legacy of historical mementos. Twin gold-tiled spires surmount the Basilica of the Immaculate Conception on the Plaza de la Republica, a latecomer started in 1875.

Modern engineering has added to the peninsula the blunt nose of Creston Island, which flanks La Bahia, the bay where the local fishing fleet rides at anchor. From its height of 515 feet the tall lighthouse, El Faro, lights ships 30 miles off shore. Close to its base is Playa Sur, the South Beach local people frequent.

The west-coast beach, the visitor's playground, is split by the jutting Cerro de Neveria, which is translated as Icehouse Hill, but known locally as Ice Cream Parlor Hill. A continuous boulevard with four sectional names (Paseo de Centenario, Olas Altas, Paseo Claussen, and Avenida del Mar) runs inland past the Cerro and serves the whole waterfront, tidily separating beach territory from the string of hotels, shops, and restaurants.

Beaches and Accommodations: The older, most popular beach tract, closest to the port's center, Olas Altas (High Waves) Beach, backs up to the Paseo de Centenario and Olas Altas. On the inland side are the established favorites —Hotels Freeman, Belmar, and La Siesta, all moderate; the latter has a fine restaurant. Copa de Leche, a large and showy restaurant, is on this stretch also. Beyond the Cerro the boulevard, here called Paseo Claussen (furnished apartments for rent around here) and then, as Avenida del Mar, curves northward around beautiful Playa Norte (North Beach) to distant Playa Las Gaviotas (Sea Gull Beach), to coil back to C.N. 15. On the last beach is the large, new Hotel Playa Mazatlán, usually called La Playa. North Beach's newer accomodations include Hotels de Cima and Eldorado, modernistic Motel Las Arenas (Sands), Agua Marina, and Las Palmas—all moderate; air-conditioned rooms higher priced. In town inexpensive hotels include Milton, Central, and Avenida, and Motel Posada Colonial —its dining room famed for shrimp specialties. Town eating spots include Los Comales (good Mexican menu), Joncol, and Doneys.

Diversions: Aquatic sports; fishing; trotting along Paesó Centenario in a two-wheeled *araña* (small fringed surrey); boat trips to bird-thronged island, Palmito de la Virgin, and other islands; loitering along commercial docks; watching shifting rainbow hues of Mazatlán's famed sunsets. Highlight of *fiestas* is week-long, pre-Lenten carnival.

VILLA UNIÓN is at the junction of C.N. 15 with the spectacular cross-country mountain highway, C.N. 40, from Durango.

ACAPANETA is the starting point for a horseback trip into the State of Nayarit, home of the Cora and Huichol Indians, whose textiles, music, and *fiestas* are most interesting.

SAN BLAS, Nayarit, is the coast terminus of paved C.E. 46, a 23-mile ride from C.N. 15, turning west about 160 miles south of Mazatlán, through the tangled beauty of palm-guarded jungle swamps to skirt coastal mangrove-fringed lagoons. A cluster of creeper-covered ruins shrinking into the hillside is the pathetic remains of the Spanish shipbuilding port where 20,000 people lived less than 200 years ago. Today's almost tree-canopied fishing village (Pop. 1,597) is, between summer invasions of Tepic-Guadalajara vacationists, a beachcomber's haven.

Accommodations: Pleasant, moderate Hotel Bucanero, a block from the plaza, is handy to good seafood meals at the Beachcomber and Torino's. Hotel Casino Colon on un-trammeled Matanchen Beach and Playa Hermosa on Bor-rego Beach will do. Rates moderate.

Diversions: Swimming, deep-sea fishing, boat trips along estuaries to a banana plantation or a run up the Conchal Laguna among white lilies and herons.

TEPIC (Hard Stone) (Alt. 3,027 ft., Pop. 53,955), capital of Nayarit, was founded as a Spanish mission-outpost in 1524 at the foot of extinct volcano Sangangüey on both banks of the Rio Compostela. Now a modern city with a few Colonial streets and an excellent archeological collection in its State Museum. *Fiesta*, May 3.

Accommodations: Hotels—Imperial, Sierra de Alicia. Motels—Loma, Cora. All modest.

Excursions: To waterfall on outskirts on Tepic River; to swim and fish at Pacific beach hamlets—Los Cocos, Las Conchas, Miramar; to another former Spanish mission-out-post, COMPOSTELA (Camp of the Apostle), founded 1535 and named for the Spanish city in Coruña, a tranquil town in the coffee-growing, mining valley of the Rio Compostela. Here the Fiesta of Santiago (St. James), patron of the 1539 red *tezontle* (volcanic stone) church, is July 25. Tourists may get permits to visit the Federal prison on Maria Madre Is-land, largest of Islas Marias, west of Tepic. It is a short plane flight to Puerto Vallarte (see p. 81).

IXTLAN DEL RIO is 5 miles south of Tepic on C.N. 15 at the entrance to dramatic mountain gorge country; bleak rocky areas overhang tropically clad ravines. A mile from town is the archeological zone of the same name, containing the ruins of a conspicuous round building with a row of unique cross-shaped loopholes, probably dedicated to the Wing God. Considered post-Classic, about 1,000 years old.

TEQUILA (Nahoa, "Mescal," *maguey* liquor) is 58 miles beyond in the State of Jalisco, where sap contained in the hearts of several small species of *maguey* plants is distilled into Mexico's best-known hard liquor. One may visit distil-leries. Let the uninitiated sample cautiously. Stock up on small souvenir bottles.

GUADALAJARA (Arabic, "Rocky River," named for

74

Spanish city) (Alt. 5,220 ft., Pop. 734,346), capital of Jalisco, founded 1530, is second only to Mexico City in size and importance, now undergoing a drastic face-lifting. Much of the Colonial center has been sacrificed, but important old buildings still stand, and many low houses, grilled windows, and patios filled with plants and singing birds remain.

Accommodations: Hotels—moderate are Fenix, Del Parque, Morales, Roma, Frances—the latter is a recently remodeled monastery—many others. Motels—Camino Real, Campo Bello, Chapalita, Malibu, Tropicana, many more.

Restaurants: De luxe Copa de Leche, Juárez 414; Chamberi, Juárez 426, Mexican and continental food; Copenhagen, Cazadores, Parador Germano, Cadillac. Inexpensive good Mexican restaurants abound on small streets off Juárez. Guadalajara has many special recipes—chicken and pork dishes, specially seasoned *enchiladas* and *tacos*. *Pozole,* a pork and hominy dish, is differently spiced than elsewhere. *Aguas frescas* (see p. 13) of countless flavors are sold even in street-crossing tunnel arcades; *tepache,* a pineapple one, is popular. Alcoholic favorites naturally start with *tequila* (the most refined *tequila* is crisp, almond-flavored *pechuga almendrado*), and hot or cold *ponches,* flavored with fruit or nuts, are also popular.

Although typical regional dishes are served in hotels and restaurants, they are more savory in small hole-in-the-wall restaurants. The legendary Doña Valentina has been succeeded by her daughter; the restaurant is now located in front of the Santuario. You will be served simply, but the food is good. And while you eat you can listen to music by itinerant *mariachis*.

Amusements: To sample the night life of this provincial city, ask your hotel for the best current club or dance spot and what cultural events are on the calendar, especially at the Teatro Degollado, which has concerts by local and visiting symphony orchestras as well as occasional plays. There are band concerts in parks and plazas, and neighborhood *fiestas* scattered through the year. The annual State Fair in December features bullfights, cockfights, and baseball and soccer games for the sports-minded traveler. *Mari-*

75

achi orchestras enliven many public spots. Be sure to see the *Jarabe Tapatio,* the lively regional folk dance. Excursions galore.

Shopping: Mercado Libertad, the airy modern public market, has a large arts and crafts section. Private shops

Folk Dance at Charro Festival—Mexico City

abound. You can visit many workshops and buy on the spot. For addresses of best and newest shopping spots, see *Guadalajara Tourist News* and local *News Week*. Arte Indigena, Lopez Cotilla 265, and Todo Típico, Juárez 599, both carry objects of good taste. Telas Domus, Hidalgo 1378. Sportswear for both men and women—dresses, *rebozos,* shirts, neckties, curtain material. The Avolos, Catalan 314, is the best for handblown glass in blue, amber, amethyst. (For pottery, see TLAQUEPAQUE.) Helena, Juárez 424, crafts and gifts.

Bookstores: Libreria International, Av. 16 de Septiembre 179, also has a modern art gallery. American Book Store, Libreria Font, Libreria Printania, and Libreria Alhambra carry books in English.

U.S. Institutions: American Consulate, Av. 16 de Septiembre 489; Biblioteca (Library) Benjamín Franklin, Lopez Castillo 594; El Instituto Mexicano-Norteamericano, Tolsa 300; and American Society Office, Tolsa 300.

Art Galleries: Casa de la Cultura, a gallery run by the state, shows the art of Jalisco. The Teatro Degollado has frequent art exhibitions.

Palacio de Gobierno, the State Capital, on the west side of the Plaza de Armas is a handsome Churrigueresque building, with a fine patio. On the walls and dome of the main stairways are frescoes by the late, internationally famous José Clemente Orozco, showing the noble figure of the Cura Hidalgo y Costilla and others, to symbolize the good and the bad in politics. Above, in the Hall of Sessions, is another fresco by Orozco, completed just before his death, in 1949. The central figure is again Hidalgo, with his decree freeing all Indian slaves, which he signed in this very palace in 1811. Other important historical figures are with him—Morelos, Juárez, Carranza.

The Cathedral (1561-1618) on the Plaza de Armas is a curious mixture of Oriental and Spanish styles, its golden Byzantine domes visible for miles around. Ornate interior, with carved doors and choir seats, paintings. Murillo's "Assumption of the Virgin" hangs in the Sacristy. The curious coffin near the altar is the tomb of Bishop Mendiola, who died in Zacatecas, in the 18th century. Tradition says the mule bearing his coffin was lost and later appeared at the cathedral door, upon which it knocked three times. The church authorities took this as a holy sign that the coffin was to be kept there. Now it is quite worn out, for those who wish the sainted man to work miracles for them knock on it three times.

Churches: Santa Mónica, on the street of the same name, has the most beautiful façade in the city. It is elaborately carved in an ornate Plateresque style and has a huge statue of St. Christopher with the Christ Child. El Carmen has an interesting interior with paintings by native artists. San Francisco (1550), on the old plaza of the same name near the railroad station, is of early massive construction. The Sanctuary of Guadalupe is especially interesting during the Novena to the Virgin of Guadalupe. (December 9-18), when all Guadalajara turns out to pray, eat, and promenade. San Juan de Dios and Mexicaltzingo are also popular churches.

Hospicio Cabañas, Cabañas Street near the main plaza, is an orphanage and home for aged women. It also houses a girls' industrial school, a huge building with over twenty lovely patio gardens. The lofty neo-Roman chapel, now serving as a lecture hall, is magnificently decorated in fresco by José Clemente Orozco. The ceiling vaults contain an allegory of the natural elements in brilliant colors. The sea, earth, and fire are symbolized by the heads of men, the lat-

Detail from "Man of Fire," Fresco by Orozco—Hospicio Cabañas, Guadalajara

Detail from "Man of Fire"

ter in flames. And on the walls in sober colors are historical figures and events showing Cortés and his followers on splendid lifelike horses, and modern warriors.

La Universidad, Plaza Universidad, founded 1791 in a former Jesuit church and monastery, is a fine college. The summer school, emphasizing fine arts, attracts foreign students. The frescoes by Orozco in the main building illuminate man's creative quests and achievements. Siqueiros and Cuevas painted the chapel frescoes.

State Museum, one block from the main plaza, shares a former seminary (1701) and stately patio with the State Library (open only 10 A.M. to 1 P.M.). Has astounding, badly arranged collections of primitive artifacts, folk art, heirlooms of many types, oil paintings by Murillo, Villalpando, Artega, and others. Check with your hotel as to the hours during which the museum is open.

Museo Taller José Clemente Orozco (museum-work-shop), Aurelio Aceves 27, near the Arch across Av. Vallarta at the city's west entrance, contains a few paintings of this native son, probably Mexico's greatest muralist, and some touching personal effects. It was built for Orozco as a studio while he was still living in Mexico, but he died (in September, 1949) before he could enjoy it. Open daily except Monday—10 A.M. until 2 P.M. One *peso* entrance fee.

El Penitenciaria. Visitors are admitted to this humane penal institution. Prisoners' handicraft for sale.

Excursions: TLAQUEPAQUE, an old pottery town 5 miles east, was once renowned for delicate handmade ware. The current factory output is largely nightmarishly colored and designed "novelties." Hunt for the artistic pieces still made —then revive your spirits with refreshments and *mariachi* music in the patio of the plaza shop block. Local blown glass is still tasteful. Watch blowers at work in one of Calle Independencia shops and visit the Glass Museum on same street. A Sunday rendezvous for city people to eat barbecued meats, drink beer, and hear *mariachis*. Picturesque *fiesta* with dances and fireworks on June 29.

TONALA, 1 mile off C.N. 80, a few miles beyond. In this ancient pottery village, families proudly resist vulgarization and mechanization. Their special fine *debujo de petatillo,* a lovely basket-weave design, is exemplified in a variety of articles. Their animal figurines are soft-hued, imaginative.

ZAPOPAN (Azt., "Among the Zapotes," fruit trees), an Indian village Guadalajara has overgrown, is now a western suburb. Famed for its tile-domed, Plateresque-fronted seventeenth-century Franciscan church and monastery and an image of the Virgin, brought to Jalisco from Spain by a Franciscan friar in the sixteenth century, credited with many miracles, and deemed a protectress from the perils of lightning. For centuries it has been customary for her worshippers to carry her in pomp, accompanied by dancers, on a round of brief visits to other local churches during the rainy season. She returns October 4 to her own shrine—her reception a fervent, exuberant *fiesta*.

BARRANCA DE OBLATOS, near the city, is a hikers' excursion. At the bottom of the canyon, 2,000 feet deep, is a rushing river and rich vegetation. Juanacatlan Falls, on the Santiago River, off Chapala Road, is the largest in Mexico.

CHAPALA is a famous old resort town, 30 miles from Guadalajara on Lake Chapala (paved road). Lovely villas in gardens, stately trees, and flowers. But with the receding of the waters of the lake, bathing is no longer a feature. Hotel Monte Carlo, a villa in charming gardens, is pleasant for lunch or a visit.

AJIJIC, a picturesque old fishing village, is on a narrow strip of land between the hills and the lake. The charming Villa Tzintzuntzan is the home, weaving workshop, and sales headquarters of Neill James, who is introducing the culture of silkworms in Ajijic. Posada de Ajijic is a pleasant inn. Modest.

JOCOTOPEC, beyond Ajijic, is also a fishing village, where good heavy *serapes* are woven. Pleasant to stay at La Quinta. Reasonable rates.

PUERTO VALLARTA, Jalisco, a delightful village on the Pacific Coast, is fast gaining a reputation as an ideal inexpensive vacation spot. No train, no paved road, not even a good dirt one, but a pleasant flight over the mountains via Mexicana de Aviación, less than two hours' flying time from Guadalajara (still faster from Tepic). Vallarta is picturesquely built on a hill, has an ideal climate, and is free of insects. *Fiestas*—the important one for the Virgin of Guadalupe, December 12, with a colorful procession, *charro* stunts, and fireworks on the sea.

Accommodations: Hotels—Las Campanas, Oceano, Río Tropicano, Paraíso, and Rosita—modest or moderate. Posada Vallarta—new, de luxe. Furnished apartments for rent. Cottages at Posada de la Selva. Restaurants—Flamingo, Delmar, and Patio are excellent.

COLIMA (Alt. 1,657 ft., Pop. 44,860), quiet, pleasant capitol of Colima, is 136 miles from Jiquilpan, Michoacán, where C.N. 15 joins C.N. 110. An old city, its Indian predecessor Cajitlan (Azt., "Pottery-making Place") was founded in the eleventh century and occupied by the Spaniards in the sixteenth century. Colima is dominated by two volcanic peaks, the 12,275-foot high Volcán de Colima, nicknamed "Fuego" (fire) for its occasional hint of flame, and quiescent snow-tipped El Nevado. On the main plaza, a quaint cathedral and *portales* and bandstand. The *fiesta* in November is gay. Hotel Casino is inexpensive, Motel Colima best stopover.

CUYUTLAN BEACH, en route from Colima to Manzanillo on C.N. 110, is the place where the famous towering *ola verde* (green wave) comes rolling in ominously—to break harmlessly and ebb from the white beach.

MANZANILLO, Colima (Pop. 16,591), one of the oldest and most important Pacific Coast ports, is slowly being rebuilt on its steep escarpments after a 1959 tidal wave and typhoon. There are always foreign ships in its deep harbor, yet it is a remarkably orderly, tranquil town. Reputed to be the site of the pre-Conquest capital of the Coliman tribe, then called Tzalahua (Azt., "Place Where Cloth is Stretched to Dry") and twisted by Spaniards to *Salagua* (Salt Water.) Its present name is an alleged corruption of the poisonous tree, *manchineel.* Cortés founded a shipbuilding center here in 1526; fishing boats are still made of good tropical woods.

The curving sweep of beach from town to Santiago Peninsula, its palm backdrop erased by the 1959 storm—and for hardy swimmers only—is lined with hotels, motels, and cottages for rent with a great range of furnishings, services, and prices—mostly from modest to moderate. In town the Colonial Hotel and Foreign Club have good seafood restaurants. Superb shellfish at street stands and along waterfront.

BARRA DE NAVIDAD, on the tropical golden sands of the Bay of Navidad (Christmas) is 38 miles north of Manzanillo on paved C.E. 200. (This highway is part of the projected Pacific Coastal route steadily being extended north to reach Puerto Vallarte before long. It has now been connected with the cross-country highway from Tampico.) Has an unusually fine hotel, Malaque, Am. Pl. and moderate, as is Motel El Dorado, on an enchanting miniature bay 5 miles away. North of here, 18 miles by sailboat or speedboat, and accessible by unfinished C.E. 200, is the newly invaded golden beach of LOS ANGELES DE TENACATITE. Provision-bearing campers can rent thatched-shelter sleeping quarters and enjoy the Eden the new road will destroy.

Another excursion from Guadalajara will take you on C.N. 80 (link between Central and Pan-American Highways from Monterrey via San Luis Potosí) to LAGOS DE MORENO, near junction of C.N. 80 with Central C.N. 45. 30 miles away from that junction is SAN JUAN DE LOS LAGOS. Both towns are rewarding to visit. Many households of San Juan, the more colonial of the two, are busy workshops; the female members continually sew and embroider or do drawn work, make aprons, tablecloths, handkerchiefs, dainty blouses—the latter sold all over Mexico. The men of the family are the salesmen, many traveling ones.

Local Virgin de la Candelaria (Candlemas), close in popularity to Guadalupe, attracts adoring multitudes several times a year. The great festival from January 5 to February 5, includes her own day (Candlemas—February 2). Here, during Holy Week, is held the largest Lenten fair in Mexico—still a thronged, tumultuous medieval fair with reveling and worship centered around the Virgin's shrine in the parish church, a most electrifying congress of the devout. Route 80, going west from Guadalajara, will be a shortcut to the coast when the last stretches are improved and paved, and will join the Gulf at Tampico to the Pacific at Manzanillo.

GUADALAJARA TO MORELIA: The West Coast Highway, C.N. 15, follows Lake Chapala for some miles, enters State of Michoacán before Jiquilpan (junction with Manzanillo C.E. 110), runs through pine woods, and skirts Lake Patzcuaro. Has many on- and off-the-road attractions.

JIQUILPAN (Azt., "Where Indigo Plants Grow") is an interesting old town and the birthplace of ex-President Cárdenas. The library, formerly a nineteenth-century chapel, has Orozco murals.

JACONA, lovely garden village.

ZAMORA (Pop. 31,991), busy farming center, was founded as a Spanish garrison to subdue Chichimeca. Has 2 old churches. Modest hotels Fenix and Mendoza are satisfactory. After passing Tangancícuaro, 10 miles beyond, turn for a pleasant side trip to Lake Camecuaro.

CARAPAN is the first village in La Canada de los Once Pueblos (Ravine of the Eleven Villages), along the Rio Duero. The practical missionary, Don Vasco de Quiroga—*Tata* (Father) Vasco then and still to all Mexicans—helped these villages survive, as he did many Michoacán towns, by teaching each to specialize in and perfect one craft. Carapan is a laquering town from which C.E. 39 leads south over wooded hills to CHERÁN (splendid sixteenth-century church) and ARANZA (*serapes*) to PARACHO, which is, as its Tarascan name says, "Home of Instrument Makers"—of violins, guitars, and so forth—but as truly a town of music makers, cradle of Michoacán folk song. The men are the carvers—making furniture, household articles, toys, polished trays and bowls of fine wood. The women weave *rebozos*. Fascinating, unspoiled *fiesta* begins August 8. The next town is *serape*-weaving CAPACUARO.

URUAPAN (Oo-roo-*ah*-pahn; at first, "Hurapan." Name is enigmatic, but *pan* is Aztec for "place") is an old laquering community and garden city (Alt. 5,500 ft., Pop. 45,580) in a ring of pine-clad slopes. There is conflict over the date of the Spanish settlement—from 1531 to 1541—by a Franciscan monk, Fray Juan de San Miguel, as San Francisco Uruapan. Delightful to linger here and "unwind" at one of the small, modest hotels—Progreso, Mi Solar, Mansion Tarasca; at Colonial Casa Maravillas (House of Wonders); and eat gourmet fare at Restaurant El Cupatitzio. Stroll through the market streets of the three plazas (busiest day —Sunday). Visit the Regional Museum, La Guatapera (a 16th-century hospital that has a lovely patio and a chapel with a noteworthy carved façade). At the edge of the town are *huertas,* or public gardens, beautiful with tropical vegetation, through which the River Cupatitzio (Singing Waters) flows, making music as it rushes over stones and falls, its high banks covered with ferns.

Excursions: Picnic at the Falls of Tzaráracua (Tarascan, "Sieve," literally apt, for spray flies from holes in the rocks), 6 miles from the main plaza—road paved. Climb to scenic heights—Balcon de Diablo (Devil's Balcony) and Cruz Barrida (Swept Cross). Go down to Tierra Caliente (Hot Country) to the melon fields around Apatzingán (Hotel Tapachula is best); the area is being remade by such projects as irrigation under the Commission of Tepalcatepec (Azt., "Hill for Broken Pottery"). Visit the volcano Paricutín, born in farmer Dionesio Pulido's corn field, February 20, 1943, terrifying him at his plowing as the earth began to smoke and shake beneath him. Now the largest crater, 4,000 feet high, on a base more than a mile in diameter, surmounts a vast, fantastically wrinkled lava field and ash heaps—below them buried villages and ranches. The homeless (over 5,000 people) interpreted this natural catastrophe as punishment for their sins. The village, as one of the "Eleven Villages" (formerly Parangaricutiro) had been assigned the manufacture of bed coverings by Don Vasco; thus their patron saint became officially San Juan de las Colchas (St. John of the Counterpanes). The survivors of the catastrophe carried the miraculous image of their saint to Los Conejos (The Rabbits) near Uruapan and tend him still with excessively penitent reverence. His chief festival is September 14.

Highway C.N. 15 again, en route to Quiroga.

Juancito produces lovely, unglazed pottery.

Zacapu (Stony Place) (Pop. 22,241) has a Franciscan parish church, begun 1540, with a notable Plateresque entrance. A mile away at Malpaís are *yacatas* (Tarascan, "pyramid-temples"). In Comanja, the pottery established by Vasco de Quiroga is still working. Chipicuaro is a lovely spot, with a small tree-shaded beach and hotel, at foot of Lake Patzcuaro; it is an archeological area. Santa Fé de la Laguna, where "Tata" Vasco founded a hospital in 1540, is a pottery town. The church contains a chair and other Vasco relics.

Quiroga is a junction with C.N. 41. Its highway streets are lined with shops selling wares of the Eleven Villages and neighboring towns—Santa Ana pottery, Paracho guitars, etc. Be wary—don't buy cheap cleverly painted substitutes as Uruapan lacquer! The patron saint's *fiesta* is

November 13—dances, fireworks.

SIDE TRIP TO PÁTZCUARO, 14 miles south of Quiroga on C.N. 41.

TZINTZUNTZAN (Tarascan, "Hummingbird"), between Quiroga and Pátzcuaro, 5 miles south of the junction on C.N. 41. Former Tarascan capital on Lake Pátzcuaro, the town has shrunk from its pre-Conquest population of 40,000 to about 1,200; its early lordliness has been reduced to a handful of villager's whitewashed adobe homes. A Christian church stands on the site of the Tarascan Palace in an atrium of olive, ash, and cedar trees planted by Franciscan missionaries over four hundred years ago. The church was burned out in 1944, but its adjoining monastery remained intact and both are a perfect setting for the local Passion Play. Folk dances enliven the *fiesta* of Cristo Rey, known locally as Señor del Rescate (the Redeemer), February 1-7, as well as the February 22 pottery fair.

The roadside in front of the atrium is lined with stalls of local diversely patterned and colored but always charming, even whimsical, pottery; woven wheat straw and reed articles; furniture. Buy local fabrics at the weavers' homes. Half a mile above town are five *yacatas* of the old Tarascan capital. Don't buy caretaker's idols as antiques.

PÁTZCUARO (Alt. 7,180 ft., Pop. 14,281), on the hill slopes above Lake Pátzcuaro, deserves its Tarascan name of "Place of Delights." Upon the arrival of Don Vasco de Quiroga, 1540, the Tarascan city here began the transformation to a Spanish town, still markedly Colonial in architecture, but inately Mexican in character.

The town is pleasant, with plazas a block apart, from which the cobbled streets run up and down hills. The largest plaza, shaded by century-old ash trees, is the scene of the Friday and Sunday markets, to which Indians come from all the lake and hill villages, with pottery, lacquer, copper vessels, textiles, fruit, and vegetables. Many of the women wear regional costumes, consisting of embroidered blouses with red or black woolen skirts—rolled, pleated, or folded—and held tight by narrow woven sashes. Purely local are their heavy silver and coral jewelry; chief motifs are hollow silver fish and crosses.

Accommodations: Hotels—Posada de Don Vasco, halfway between the town and lake. Colonial-style, semi-resort, with gardens, outdoor and indoor games. Tuesday and Thursday evenings folk dance of *Los Viejitos* (see CUCUCHUCHU). Posade de la Basilica, in the town near the basilica, small and pleasant, moderate to expensive. Motel Albergue Toliman, across from Don Vasco, same management, new, expensive. El Gordo, restaurant near the railroad station, serves the local small white fish.

Shopping: Local products are sold in plazas' shops—best selection at Casa Cerda, Dr. Coss 15, near Plaza Grande. Fabrics, *rebozos,* smart embroidered clothing, etc. are available at Vicki's on the pine-lined avenue entering town. She ships to the U.S.

Architecturally Colonial, but Mexican in character, the most important of the several interesting churches is La Colegiata, which was to have been the Cathedral of Michoacán before Morelia was selected as the seat of the See. It dominates the town from its beautiful location on the hill and has a very handsome wrought-iron fence. A statue of Nuestra Señora de la Salud (Our Lady of Health), of miraculous fame, is there. It was made, of an exceedingly lightweight maize paste of a yellowish color, by the Indians, probably at the request of Bishop Quiroga; but the legend is that an Indian found it floating in a canoe on Lake Pátzcuaro. Her merry *fiesta* starts December 8; her worshippers bring novel goods to market then. The nearby church of La Compañía de Jesús was built by Don Vasco in 1546. The urn containing his ashes is guarded in a steel safe behind the main altar.

The San Francisco church and convent, of simple, massive lines, has several maize-paste saints. The small Guadalupe sanctuary, with its sculptures by Tresguerras of Faith, Hope, and Charity, around the belfry, is very harmonious. In the cemetery is a tiny chapel, highly Indian in construction, called El Humilladero, the name based on the legend that Caltzontzin, the last Tarascan king, was humiliated there. On a hill, at a short distance from the center, stands

El Calvario, a small chapel reached by a path, flanked by the stations of the cross. The view from there of the lake and countryside is magnificent, but surpassed by the one from El Estribo.

The interesting house called La Casa del Gigante derives its name from a huge sculpture of a giant in the patio. The new modern theater on the plaza was formerly an Augustinian convent. In the Bocanegra, Public Library, next door, an interesting fresco by Juan O'Gorman stresses the Colonial church's goodness to the Indians.

The houses are of one story, solidly constructed with projecting roofs that furnish shade to the leisurely pedestrians. The ancient wells, scattered throughout the town, are always alive with maidens and women who come to chatter and gossip. Then they fill their jars and walk gracefully away, balancing them on their heads.

The fine examples of *mesones* on Calle Nacional, beyond the Colegiata—great yards paved with cobblestones, with stalls for burros and horses and places for the men to spread their *petates* to sleep on—are always full of peasants and their animals from all parts of the state.

The former school of Vasco de Quiroga, a very fine old house, is now a Museum of Popular Art and Archaeology, and the exhibition rooms—a chapel with votive offerings, kitchens, dining room, and others—are furnished in sixteenth-century style. The objects were collected and arranged by a native artist, Rodolfo Ayala. Outstanding is a collection of nearly four hundred old lacquer bowls, called *bateas*.

Excursions: Many interesting places can be visited from Pátzcuaro by car. SANTA CLARA DEL COBRE (on paved C.N. 120) is the source of hand-hammered copper vessels—the industry initiated here by Don Vasco. The town rings with the rhythmic hammering of about two dozen smithies. This charming tree-decked village with a pink church holds a copper fair August 12-15.

Only a jeep should try the 14 miles to Lake Zirahuen; the shore village of COPÁNDARO DE GALEANA is on a second-class bus line from Morelia. You can take the paved road to

TUPATARO, with its noteworthy church, and over the hills to picturesque TACAMBARO.

LAKE PÁTZCUARO, 13 miles long, 30 miles in circumference, and 6,717 feet above the sea, is the highest navigable lake in Mexico, very picturesque with its island and shore villages. Tourists can hire gasoline launches by the hour or fishermen's dugout canoes. Check the weather, as the water often becomes rough in the afternoon.

JANITZIO, on the slopes of a hilly island, is internationally famous. Its inhabitants are proud fishermen; their festooned "butterfly" nets are in evidence everywhere, either drying or being woven. An air of great activity pervades the hilly, twisting, cobbled streets and the lake shore.

Pátzcuaro Fisherman with Butterfly Net

Crowded houses, sturdy, with projecting tile roofs, straggle down the hill like spilled blocks. The summit is crowned by a huge, unsightly hollow cement statue of the patriot hero, General Morelos, designed by Guillermo Ruíz. Fifty frescoes of Morelos' life, the work of Alva de la Canal, decorate the stairwell to the head—here is Morelos' death mask. Open all day—small admission.

The village church, overlooking the lake and surrounded by a cemetery, affords a perfect setting for the unique festival of the Day of the Dead (November 2), for which the village is famous. On the night of November 1, at about midnight, families carry food and table linen, flowers, chiefly *zempasuchil* (marigold) pieces, and *pan de muerto* (the "dead's bread"), twisted in odd knots or in animal and human shapes, to adorn the graves of their dead. Women and children sit about the candle-lit graves; men group themselves to be choristers and sing *alabanzas,* hymns of praise, at intervals, until the watch ends at dawn. A fantastically beautiful scene.

LAKESIDE VILLAGES: Fifteen on the shore, more tucked among sloping hills, each has individual charm and practices a craft "Tata" Vasco taught—over 400 years ago! Men and boys of the farming village CUCUCHUCHU perform the rollicking dance of *Los Viejitos* (The Old Men), dressed in

Butterfly Fishermen at Janitzio

90

Los Viejitos—Cucuchuchu

their simple white cotton shirts and trousers (sometimes the latter's cuffs are embroidered), wide-brimmed, gaily beribboned hats, a small *serape* slung over one shoulder. They wear wooden masks of exaggeratedly old faces, and shoes in order to intensify the varying rhythms they beat with wooden canes. If no regular *fiesta,* ask the hotel to arrange a special show.

IGUATZIO (Tarascan, "Place of Coyotes") is on the mainland but a mile from Cucuchuchu by water. Agricultural and picturesque. The sixteenth-century church has a fine primitive stone carving of a Tarascan man and woman paddling a canoe. The annual *fiesta* takes place on October 4, with dances and fireworks. *Yacatas* nearby.

JARACUARO. The music-loving people of this orchid-growing hamlet have a good string orchestra and compose and play Tarascan music. Chief industry: palm leaf hats.

ERONGARÍCUARO is on a rugged dirt road with bus service. Sunday mornings boatloads of Indians and their goods—foods and crafts—pull ashore for old-time barter market. Money is always acceptable. Visitors should stock up at Vicki's home workshop (she has been the Mayor here!) and Elena Gordon's weaving sheds—her fabrics are the finest in Mexico, simple designs to elegant metal-threaded ones.

Wild Duck Hunting: The natives' autumn-winter sport. The season opens just before the Day of the Dead, as wild duck is a special dish for the occasion. Hundreds of canoes set out, gradually closing in on the ducks in ever-smaller circles. As the frightened ducks start to fly, the natives harpoon them with spears, thrown with great skill.

MORELIA (Alt. 6,334 ft., Pop. 100,258) was founded on the fertile, temperate plain of Guayangareo, around an Indian Matlatzinca village of the same name, by the first Viceroy, Don Antonio de Mendoza, in 1541, and named Valladolid for his Spanish home; it was renamed for native son, Father José Maria Morelos y Pavon on September 12, 1829; capital of Michoacan. Least remodeled of Colonial cities, protected by law from drastic building deformation, every stroll through its clean streets reveals mementos of former grandeur. Traditionally a custodian of culture since Bishop Quiroga's Colegio Primitivo y Nacional de San Nicolas was transferred here from Patzcuaro, it has been the birthplace of many notable Mexicans besides Morelos: Melchor Ocampo, Santos Degollado, Augustin de Iturbide (ignored locally as he abused his victories to make himself —briefly—emperor of Mexico), poetic revolutionary painter, Alfredo Zalce, still resident here—his frescoes are in the State Museum and Palace.

Accommodations: Hotels—Villa Montaña Villa and San José, comfortable retreats in Santa Maria Hills, are highly priced, but offer excellent services and food. In town: Hotel de la Soledad (Vicki of Pátzcuaro has a branch shop here) in a remodeled Colonial building, exceptional for moderate rates; Virrey de Mendoza, only fair, moderate; Alameda, across street, higher. Small, drab but clean, cheap hotels open off the plaza under the *portales*. Motels—in an emergency try Morelia Courts, El Parador.

Churches: The lordly, soft-colored Baroque and Churrigueresque cathedral (1640-1744) and its regal towers brood over the city's parklike Plaza de los Martíres; the remodeled interior lacks beauty. Guadalupe Church, near the aqueduct, has an almost rakish exterior and ornate gilded altars and ceiling. Nearby is the narrow tranquil, romantic square, Parque Azteca, a spot to dream in, among old statuary, at twilight. Not to be slighted are Nuestra Señora del Socorro, El Carmen, Convento de la Compañía, San Francisco, and La Iglesia de las Rosas, in front of the delightful Jardín de Rosas. The internationally known Boys Choir of the Escuela de Música Sagrada de las Rosas (first school of music in New Spain) may be heard during rehearsals and, occasionally, in the cathedral.

Public Buildings: San Nicolas College, its stately patios decorated with Marion Greenwood's modern frescoes. Cura Hidalgo was once its rector. The former Jesuit church and monastery (1681) is now the State Library and an industrial school. Casa de Morelos, Av. Morelos 232, is a museum of the patriot's personal effects and other historical objects. Murals by Zalce and Federico Cantú decorate the eighteenth-century palace that is the State Museum, exhibiting pre-Cortésian relics, Colonial weapons, furniture; Colonial, religious, and contemporary art. Some rooms are furnished in the olden manner. The State and City "Palaces" are notable Colonial edifices. Most churches and landmarks are strolling distance from the central plaza. The City Market (market days, Thursday and Sunday) is behind the cathedral. It is pleasant to stroll about a mile along the handsome (1789) aqueduct and most delightful to loiter up and down the Calzada de los Penitentes (Avenue of the Penitents), a pedestrian's cobbled promenade between low stone walls, a medieval approach to Guadalupe. It is no longer a path for remorseful sinners to traverse on their knees, but a poetic lane for lovers, poets, weary souls seeking tranquility. From its exit, crossing under the aqueduct, the stroller enters the Bosque Cuauhtémoc or saunters over to Parque Juárez.

Shopping: Intriguing stalls on shady main plaza,

market, and shops offer fine embroideries and peasant-style regional blouses, *rebozos,* and all Michoacán handicraft. Candy stalls line the *portales,* selling delicious local fruit paste, *ates,* caramel wafers, *morelianas,* and many others.

Fiestas: May 18, founding day, and September 30, Father Morelos' birthday, are most splendid.

Excursions: To delightful villages nearby. Wood carvers of suburban Santa María de Guido have an August 15 fair. There are mineral baths at COINTZIO, off the highway on a gravel road. Drive via C.E. 25 to two old lake villages—CUITZEO, where there is a handsome Plateresque Augustinian church and convent, with an immense open chapel, a beautiful cloister, and sixteen unusually fine choir stalls in the sacristy; and YURIRIA, a little farther on, 2 miles off the road on Lake Yuriria (from Yuririapundaro, "Lake of Blood"). The latter has an enormous medieval 1550 church-monastery, which has a unique Gothic rib-vaulted cloister and was built by Pedro de Toro. It was designed as a fortress to protect the Tarascan town from attacks by the Chichimecas, who were only subdued in 1589. Open 9 A.M. to 1 P.M. and 4 to 6 P.M.

FROM MORELIA TO TOLUCA the road continues through the valley but soon begins to climb and then follow thirty miles of gorgeous mountain scenery—forests, ravines, waterfalls, wild flowers—through the Parque Nacional, 9,900 feet above sea level. At El Mirador de Mil Cumbres (the Lookout over a Thousand Peaks) the view is breathtaking. Nearby is the Parque Nacional de Atzimba, 9,900 feet above sea level. Then there is a descent into a tropical valley and the old town of Tuxpan, on the Tuxpan River, with all its rich vegetation.

SAN JOSÉ PURUA, on a branch road at Km. 182, has a de luxe mineral spa hotel, Agua Caliente—good, modest. Nearby is the Rancho Agua Blanco, a small ranch hotel, in a lovely village.

ZITACUARO is an agreeable little city, with Colonial houses. The climate is temperate, and the Hotel Agúilar quite comfortable. The road goes on through pleasant country and drops into the Toluca Valley.

For TOLUCA and surroundings, see the end of CENTRAL HIGHWAY (p. 66).

MEXICO CITY

MEXICO CITY, always referred to simply as **Mexico** (which was the name of an Aztec god and chief and means "In the Moon's Navel"), is the capital of the Republic. It is situated in the Anahuac Valley, on the Central Plateau, at an altitude of 7,350 feet above sea level—the highest major city in the world and the oldest metropolis on the American continent. In June, 1962, the metropolitan area had 5,-364,000 inhabitants. The city is built on the site of the Aztec capital Tenochtitlan (Azt., "Where the *Nopal* Is on the Stone"). Called "The City of Palaces" because of its many palatial edifices, it now has as many handsome modern buildings. It is the seat of the federal government, the National University, and the largest financial institutions.

Ixtaccihuatl (White Woman)

Due to its elevation and peculiar situation in a large bowl-shaped valley, Mexico City has only two seasons—a dry and a rainy one. The rains usually start in May and last into October. It generally rains in the late afternoons and the mornings are warm and sunny even in the winter. The coldest months are December and January.

The large valley in which the city is situated is dominated by two snow-capped volcanoes—Ixtaccíhuatl (Azt., "White Woman," pro. Ees-ta-*see*-uatl) and Popocatépetl (Azt., "Smoking Mountain," pro. Po-po-ke-teh-petl)—which rise spectacularly to an altitude of more than 17,000 feet. On the southern side is a high mountain range, in the center of which is the beautifully wooded Mt. Ajusco.

In pre-Conquest times the two volcanoes were worshipped as deities. The most romantic of the old legends states that Ixtaccíhuatl, the beautiful daughter of an aging Aztec emperor, was offered in marriage by him to the war-

Amecameca with Popocatépetl in Background

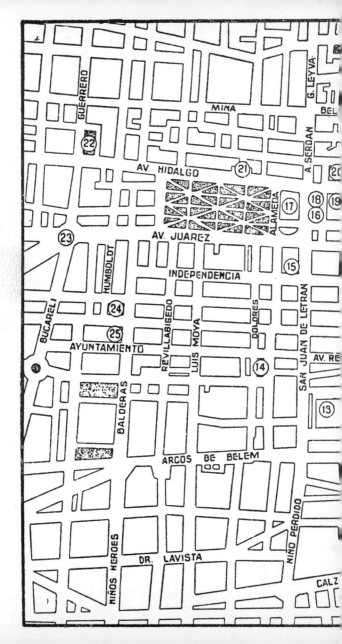

1 NATIONAL PALACE
2 NATIONAL MUSEUM
3 CATHEDRAL
4 AZTEC RUINS
5 NATIONAL PAWNSHOP
6 PREPARATORY SCHOOL
7 MINISTRY OF EDUCATION
8 SAN LAZARO STATION
9 PENITENTIARY
10 NATIONAL BANK OF MEXICO
11 NATIONAL CITY BANK
12 NATIONAL LIBRARY
13 LAS VIZCAINAS

14 SA
15 W
16 BA
17 FI
18 PO
19 M
20 FE
21 FL
22 SA
23 EL
24 Y.
25 Y.
26 CA

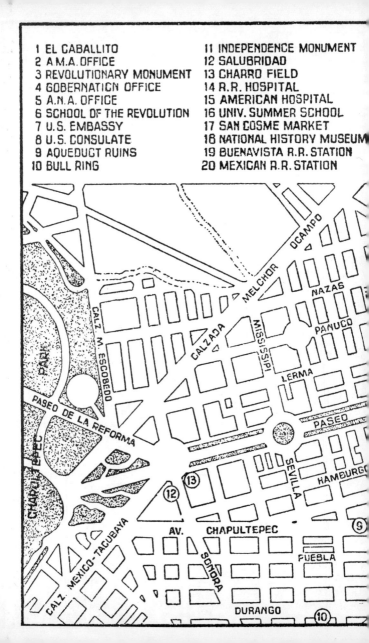

1 EL CABALLITO
2 A.M.A. OFFICE
3 REVOLUTIONARY MONUMENT
4 GOBERNATION OFFICE
5 A.N.A. OFFICE
6 SCHOOL OF THE REVOLUTION
7 U.S. EMBASSY
8 U.S. CONSULATE
9 AQUEDUCT RUINS
10 BULL RING

11 INDEPENDENCE MONUMENT
12 SALUBRIDAD
13 CHARRO FIELD
14 R.R. HOSPITAL
15 AMERICAN HOSPITAL
16 UNIV. SUMMER SCHOOL
17 SAN COSME MARKET
18 NATIONAL HISTORY MUSEUM
19 BUENAVISTA R.R. STATION
20 MEXICAN R.R. STATION

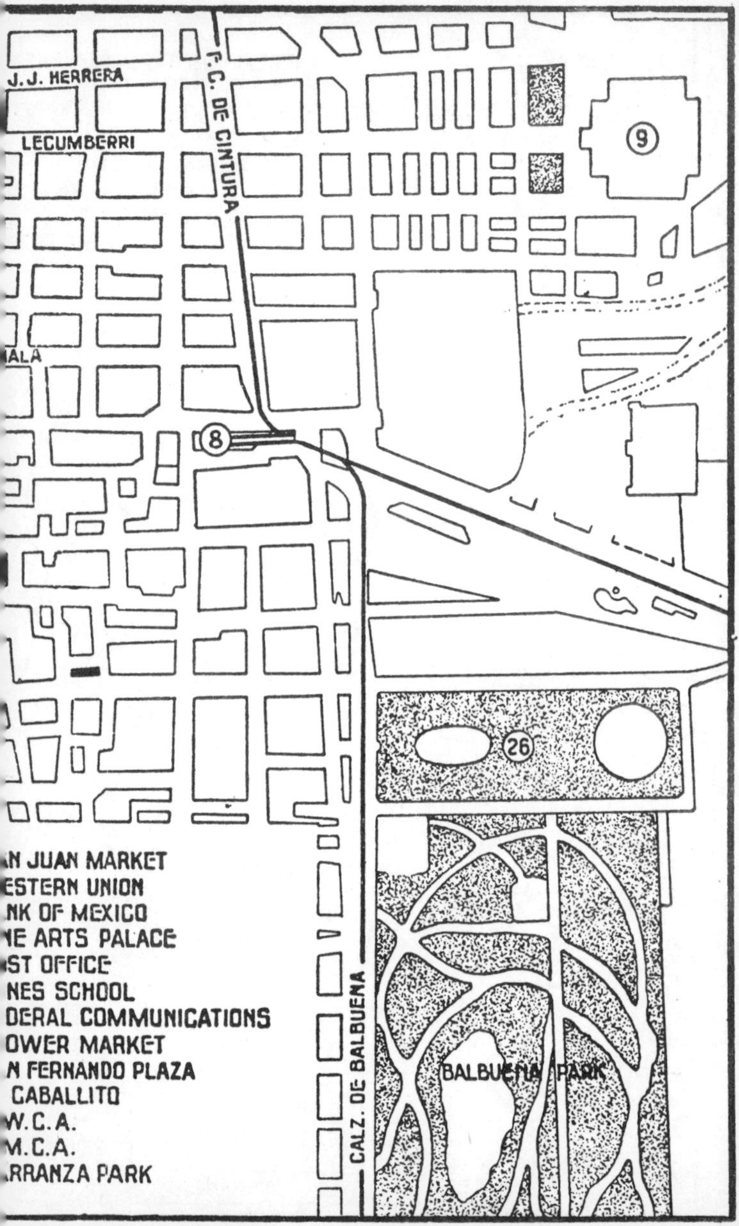
J. J. HERRERA
LECUMBERRI
F.C. DE CINTURA
9
ALA
8
26
CALZ. DE BALBUENA
BALBUENA PARK
N JUAN MARKET
ESTERN UNION
NK OF MEXICO
IE ARTS PALACE
ST OFFICE
NES SCHOOL
DERAL COMMUNICATIONS
OWER MARKET
N FERNANDO PLAZA
CABALLITO
W.C.A.
M.C.A.
RRANZA PARK

rior able to vanquish the enemies who threatened his kingdom. Among the warriors who went to fight was Popocatépetl, who for years had loved Ixtaccíhuatl. He returns triumphant from the long and bloody war. But his rivals had falsely sent news of his death, which caused the Princess to languish and die. In his profound grief, Popocatépetl built a great pyramid to hold his beloved Ixtaccíhuatl, and another close by where he stands bearing a torch to illuminate her perpetual sleep.

An equally interesting Aztec legend refers to the founding of Tenochtitlán, or Mexico City. The war god Huitzilopóchtli appeared to the chief priest of the nomadic Aztecs, who were seeking a place in which to settle, instructing them to continue searching until they found an eagle with a serpent in its beak, perched on a cactus growing from a rock. This they found on an island on Lake Texcoco, where they built their capital, filling in parts of the lake for the purpose. Thus it is that Mexico's emblem consists of the eagle, serpent, and *nopal,* or prickly pear, and that many of its streets were canals long after the Conquest.

HOTELS

Mexico City has hotels for every taste and budget, the higher priced ones catering chiefly to tourists. All good hotels have English-speaking personnel, restaurants, and bars, and many have tourist bureaus and shopping arcades. To locate apartment hotels, furnished apartments, or rooms, inquire locally and follow the ads in the English-language daily, *The News.*

DE LUXE HOTELS: Expensive. (See p. 11)

Alameda, Av. Juárez 50. Central; has pool.

Alffer, Revillagigedo 18, 141 rooms. New, handsome; roof garden with putting green.

Ambassador, Humboldt 3. New, central.

Bamer, Juárez 22, 150 rooms. Elegant, modern; garage.

Continental-Hilton, Reforma 166, 400 rooms and suites.

The decor, almost entirely of native crafts and designs, and the charming public rooms almost warrant the high rates. Belvedere Room on roof for night of pleasure.

Del Paseo, Reforma 208. New, studio rooms, some with beautiful views of Paseo de la Reforma; swimming pool by which one may breakfast.

Del Prado, Juárez 70, 600 rooms. Shops, snack bars; Nicte-Ha cocktail lounge, movie.

El Presidente, Hamburgo 135, new, studio rooms (some with terraces). Fancifully designed and decorated.

Jardín Amazones, Rio Amazones 73. Garden, pool, night club.

Monte Cassino, Genova, 56. Good restaurant.

María Isabel, Paseo de la Reforma near Angel Statue. Modern, elegant.

Premier, Milan and Atenas.

Reforma, Paseo de la Reforma at Paris, 300 rooms.

San Francisco, Luis Moya 11.

Tecali, Mariano Escobeda 736, suites only. Elegant.

First-Class Hotels: Modest to moderate

Arizona, Gomez Farias 20. Small, modern.

Cortés, Hidalgo 85, 22 rooms around lovely patio in Colonial mansion.

Cristóbal Colón, Colón 27. New, central, pleasant.

Del Bosque, Melchor Ocampo 323, 80 rooms. Good.

Diligencias, B. Dominguez 6. New, central.

Emporio, Paseo de la Reforma 124, 70 rooms.

Francis, Paseo de la Reforma 64, 100 rooms. Good.

Frimont, Jesús Teran 35. Simple, moderate.

Geneve, Londres 130, 450 rooms. Garage; very popular.

Guadalupe, Revillagigedo 36. Moderate to expensive.

Guardiola, Madero 5, across from Sanborn's.

Hunter, Villalongin 12, at Insurgentes and Reforma.

Small Hotels: Modestly priced.

Lincoln, Revillagigedo 24, 40 rooms. Good restaurant.

Luma, Orizaba 16, 140 rooms. Garage; pleasant.

Majestic, Madero 73, 77 rooms, some on the Zocalo.

Maria Cristina, Lerma 31, 78 rooms. Popular bar.
Marlowe, Independencia 17. Roof garden.
Meurice, Marsella 288, 40 rooms. Swiss restaurant.
Moneda, Calle Moneda 8, opposite National Palace. Modest.
Montejo, Paseo de la Reforma 240, 54 rooms. Pleasant.
Prince, Louis Moya 12, 120 rooms. Good restaurant.
Regis, Juárez 77, 350 rooms. Good, inexpensive suites.
Ritz, Madero 30, 150 rooms. Popular bar; very good.
Romfel, Revillagigedo 35, 200 rooms. New, air-conditioned.
Saratoga, Alvaro Obregon 38. Central; garage.
Vasco de Quiroga, Londres 15. Moderate; in the new shopping and restaurant center.
Virreyes, José Maria Izazaga 8. In the old section.

Consult your local AAA for good motels on the outskirts.

Posadas and Pensiones
Am. Pl. or serving only breakfast, conveniently located, homey, helpful to visitors. Good ones include: the two Casas Chavez, at Florencia 36 and Lerma 26; Casa de Huespedes, Carlos J. Finlay 14.

RESTAURANTS

Mexico City is a gourmet center for Mexican, U.S., and continental cuisine. Reputable restaurants have high standards of quality and cleanliness. Some serve a dinner (*comida corrida*) of conventional courses from 1 to 3 P.M.; a very few offer a supper menu (*cena*); the majority offer only *à la carte* service. Very modest ones still have a *10 peso comida corrida.* Many Spanish ones provide gargantuan meals for 11 or 12 *pesos;* modest-priced dinners begin at 12 to 20 *pesos; à la carte* orders always higher. The following feature cosmopolitan menus:

De Luxe Restaurants: Expensive.
Alex Cardini, Av. Morelos. Italian.
Ambassadeurs, Paseo de la Reforma 12. International;

elegant décor and service.

Delmonico's, Londres 87. Specialty—steaks. Music.

El Lago, Nuevo Bosque de Chapultepec. Elegant.

Focolare, Hamburgo 87. International; pleasant.

Jena, Morelos 110. International; very good.

La Calandria, Insurgentes Sur 1217. Elegant. Colonial.

La Cava, Insurgentes 37. Music; international.

La Ronda, Genova 39. International.

Mauna Loa, Hamburgo 172. Polynesian-Chinese food; lovely Islands' décor, including live flamingos and a family of kangaroos.

Muralto, top floor Latino Americano Tower; 1 P.M. to 2 A.M. Prices include superb view.

Pabellon Suizo, Plaza Miravalle 17. Good European.

Parador, Niza 17. Good; Spanish specialties.

Normandia, Lopez 3.

Quid, Puebla 154. Small, intimate; international. Charcoal-broiled meats, crêpes suzettes, entertainment.

Rivoli, Hamburgo 112. Continental décor and food.

Semiramis, Florencia 37. Middle Eastern cuisine; music.

Villa Fontana, Reforma 240. Popular for its violinists.

1-2-3 Restaurant, Liverpool 123. International.

Hotels Monte Cassino, Marlowe, Prince, and Lincoln have good restaurants, the latter noted for its seafood.

RESTAURANTS FEATURING MEXICAN FOOD:

Café Tacuba, Tacuba 28. Pleasant and inexpensive.

Circulo Sureste, Bucareli at Lucerna. Good Yucatēcan food.

El Refugio, Liverpool 166. Among the best.

Fonda Santa Anita, Insurgentes 1098 and Humboldt 48.

Fonda del Recuerdo, Bahía de la Palmas 39. Vera Cruz food, music; low prices.

La Flor de Lis, Huichapan 21. Light supper dishes.

Las Cazuelas, Columbia 69. Popular; *mariachi* music.

Margo, Nazas 73. Yucatēcan. Very good; inexpensive.

MODERATELY PRICED RESTAURANTS:

Bavaria, Insurgentes 953. Hotel Pennsylvania. Squabs!

Bellinghausen, Londres 95. Good simple food.

100

Café de Flore, Reforma 8-10. Sidewalk cafe and restaurant. Good coffee and pastry. Meals 9 A.M.-11 P.M.

Café Concierto, Niza 68. Arabian. Coffee-grounds fortune readings.

Capri, Julio Verne 83. Superb Italian food, wines.

Cardini, Insurgentes Sur 523A.

Carmel, Genova 70A, and **Kineret**, Génova 34. Kosher-style food.

Casino Espanol, Isabela la Catolica 29-31. 2-4 P.M.

Centro Castellano, Uraguay 16, just off San Juan de Letrán, up one flight, and **Centro Vasco**, Madero 6, elevator to 3rd floor and roof in arcade beside Sanborn's, serve low-priced (11-12 *pesos*) midday, many-coursed Spanish dinners.

Convento, Fernandez Leal 96, Coyoacan. Tranquil Colonial house. *À la carte*.

Coyote Flaco, Francisco Sosa. Superb 18-*peso* lunch in historic house in Coyoacan; patio annex. Do not miss!

Czardas, Atoyac 93. Middle European; gypsy music.

Borda, Pasaje Borda on Madero 27. Lunch only.

Casa del Virrey, 31 Revillagigedo. Meats broiled in the Argentine manner.

Embassy, Calzada del Desierto 67. Good lunches in lovely garden; Italian specialties *à la carte*.

Fontana Rose, Nápoles 17. Popular Go-Go spot. One of many.

Hosteria de Santo Domingo, Belisario Dominguez 72. Reputedly the oldest in the city; Mexican specialties.

Lar Gallego, 71 Lerma. Excellent Spanish cuisine, very popular—best to go at off-hours.

La Loraine, San Luis Potosí 132. French.

Mansión San Angel, Av. Revolución 54, San Angel. Inside moderate-priced restaurant and a large garden; art gallery.

Passy, at Amberes and Reforma. Lunch (1 to 6); garden

Perigord, Yucatán 33. Excellent French; pleasant.

Prendes, 16 de Septiembre 10. Popular for seafood.

Shirley Courts, Sullivan 166. American; all you can eat at midday for 18 *pesos*.

Tío Luis, Cuautla 43. Middle-European; home-style.

Yi Yen, on Hamburgo. Cantonese; good.

SNACKS AND LIGHT MEALS

Sears coffee shop stays open until 1 A.M. El Refugio has an open-late annex. Hoyo 19, Reforma 432, Insurgentes S. 738, open late. Sorrento, Balderas 36, is inexpensive.

Most espresso shops serve light meals and stay open late. They are usually found in the Niza-Londres area. Several pleasant older cafés can be found on Calle José Azueta and streets parallel to it just off Juárez. Sanborn's on the Reforma is open late; also Pam Pam at 123 Reforma. Cafe Suizo, Londres 142, serves good cake. Café Konditorei, Genova 61, serves open Danish sandwiches and salads and pastries; good coffee.

TAXIS

Taxis in Mexico City and elsewhere in the Republic are cars of all makes—some owned by their drivers. Hail a cruising taxi when its windshield displays the sign *libre* (free). Cars waiting around the larger hotels usually ask fancy prices. Insist on the meter rate. Telephone a taxi-stand, a *sitio,* when cabs are scarce. *No tipping,* except for extra helpfulness, beyond leaving driver small change from a *peso.* Meters on cruising taxis start at one *peso* and 50 *centavos.* Pay 50 *centavos* or one *peso* above the reading for *sitio* taxis.

On several main streets, taxis called *peseros* give jitney service, picking up passengers for a *peso* fare for any length drive along a route. *Peseros* from the Zócalo serving the Reforma, sometimes Insurgentes, start in front of the cathedral, go along 5 de Mayo and Av. Juárez to Reforma. They can be identified by driver's signal—extended forefinger of left hand. Taxi hire without guide-interpreter service, 20 *pesos* an hour in Mexico City (may be more or less elsewhere), 35 *pesos* an hour beyond the Capital's limits.

AMUSEMENTS

There need never be a dull moment for anyone in Mexico City, as there are amusements and entertainments for every taste. In addition to those found in other major cities, there are the exotic, typically Mexican ones such as bullfights and *charreadas,* or rodeos.

The daily, English *News* and free *Daily Bulletin,* distributed at hotels, cover most events. Mexican, Spanish-language newspapers have complete movies, theatre, concert, sport, and lecture ads and announcements.

BALLET: Mexican modern and folklore ballet has won international acclaim. The Ballet Folklorico, directed by Amalia Hernandez, is preserving pre-Conquest indigenous dances in stylized choreographies of great beauty; other Bellas Artes ballet groups are as excellent. There are low-priced week night and Sunday morning performances at the Palacio de Bellas Artes and elsewhere on other dates. (Try to get a monthly calendar of dances and all other events sponsored by the Instituto de Bellas Artes.) Don't miss visiting foreign ballet groups.

BOXING AND WRESTLING are increasingly popular in Mexico. Most ring events are held in the Arena Mexico, on Dr. Rio de la Loza No. 94—wrestling on Thursday nights and boxing on Saturdays. Occasionally a very good card is given. Also at the Arena Coliseo, Peru 77. Boxing on Wednesdays and Saturdays, wrestling on Tuesdays and Fridays.

BULLFIGHTS: The season begins in October and lasts through March. During the rest of the time there are fights (*novilladas*) by young apprentices called *novilleros*. During the regular season in Mexico City, they take place every Sunday afternoon, at 4 P.M. The ring is divided into *Sol*, or that part in the sun, and *Sombra,* or that which is in the shade. Seats in the *Sombra* section cost almost double.

Bullfights are held in the Plaza Mexico, Ciudad de los Deportes, Insurgentes. Tickets are on sale there on the days of fights and before that at their ticket office, Izazaga 27. Good seats are best secured through your hotel or tourist agency and cost several dollars. Seats in *Sol* may be had for 50 cents. Tickets may also be bought on the day of the fight at the ticket offices of the plaza and from scalpers, who generally have very good reserved seats and charge only 20 per cent above cost, as permitted by law.

Bullfights were introduced into Mexico by the Spaniards shortly after the Conquest with such splendor that they appealed to the imagination of the Mexicans and have continued to be popular down to the present time. Even now they are brilliant and colorful, with elements of beauty similar to those of a ballet—the costumes and the movements of the *toreros.* The audience of *aficionados,* or fans, is in itself a spectacle. Their reactions are expressed noisily and enthusiastically. The most celebrated *torero* is not spared if he is clumsy or shows fear, he is jeered with insults and a bombardment of seat cushions; when he exhibits unusual skill, he is rewarded with wild applause, and flowers and hats are thrown into the arena. Then the audience, fluttering white handkerchiefs and shouting, demands of the authorities that he be given the bull's ears and tail; sometimes he is carried on the spectators' shoulders into the streets.

The *torero* or *matador,* the chief actor, wears a beautiful and costly costume—short, skin-tight trousers, a white linen shirt, a handsome hand-embroidered jacket, and a black pointed hat, called a *montera;* always pink stockings and black ballet shoes. This costume, called *traje de luces,* weighs 18 pounds and is planned for protection as well as for show. The *caleta,* or braid, is worn to protect the base of the skull. Before going into the ring, the *torero* prays either at home or in the chapel in the *toreo,* to La Macarena, protectress of the *toreros.*

The favorite tunes played by the band at bullfights are gay *pasos dobles,* or two-steps. At ten minutes to four, the band strikes up "La Macarena," named after the Virgin. This is greeted with cheers from the fans because it is so popular.

When anything especially fine is done during the *corrida,* or fight, the band plays a Spanish piece called "La Diana," considered as a cheer.

The bullfight follows a very old ritual, everything being done according to exact rule and custom. First the man representing the Spanish *alguacil,* or constable, mounted on a spirited horse, crosses the arena to the judges' box to ask permission for the fight to commence. He then backs out of the ring and returns leading the *paseo de las cuadrillas,* or parade. The *matadores* walk abreast, each followed by his own *cuadrilla* of two or three helpers and two mounted *picadores;* last come the ring attendants, called *monosabios,* or wise monkeys, in white suits with red caps and sashes, who remove the slain bulls. After the parade disbands, all leave the ring, the bugle sounds, and the bull is admitted.

Matador and Bull

As the bull rushes in, he is excited by helpers from opposite sides of the ring to give the *matador* the opportunity to judge his speed and method of attack. Then the *matador* begins a series of graceful passes with his big cape, the first of which are called *veronicas* after the woman who washed Christ's face, always ending with a downward sweep over the bull's face. Next enter the *picadores,* on horses which are heavily padded to protect them from the bull's horns. When the bull attacks the horse, the *picador* tries to push him off by planting the *pic*—a long pole with a short barb—into the heavy shoulder muscle. Each bull has to charge the horses three times and each *matador* in turn takes him away with a series of passes called *quites*. It is in the *quites* that the *matadores* do their fanciest cape work, each one trying to excel the other in the beauty and daring of his passes, some of them becoming classic and bearing the names of their inventors.

If the bull is unsound or cowardly, or for any reason refuses to fight, the crowd demands that he be taken out and another substituted. This fault is usually obvious as soon as he enters the ring and he must be taken out before he charges a horse. To remove the bull from the ring, trained oxen are brought in, who surround him and lead him out.

After the *quites* are finished, the bugle sounds for the *banderilleros* to come into place the *banderillas*—short gaily-adorned sticks with small hooks at one end which pierce the skin and hang on. The *banderillero* sights the bull, runs to meet him, leaps lightly into the air, leaving a pair of *banderillas* in the thick shoulder muscle to the left of the center. Some *matadores* place their own with great skill and beautiful movements.

Next the bugle announces the *faena,* the last and most dramatic phase of the fight. The *matador* enters the arena alone, holding a sword in his right hand covered with the *muleta* or small blood-red cape. The *faena* reveals the caliber of the *matador,* as the passes with the *muleta* are the most difficult and dangerous. When ready for the kill, the *matador* incites the bull with the sword in his right hand and makes the sign of the cross over his left arm, which is holding the *muleta* close to the ground in order to make the bull lower his head. As the bull charges, the *matador* leaps to meet him, his body poised for the thrust between the horns which sends the sword into the small area between the shoulder blades and the heart. The moment the bull falls, a helper gives him the *descabello*, or *coup de grace*, with a small dagger.

CABARETS: The following are first-class:

Capri, Juárez 79. Dancing; floor show.
Chanteclair in the Hotel Reforma. Elegant; good music.
Club de las Artistas, Vertiz 118.
La Fuente, Insurgentes S. 890.
La Jacaranda, Genova 56. Beautiful club; dancing.
Los Globos, Insurgentes S. 810.
Kalénova, next to Plaza de Toros de Cuatro Caminos.
Roca, Insurgentes S. 1168. Jazz is one attraction.
Run Run, Reforma and Insurgentes S., opposite Vista Hermosa Hotel.
Señorial, Hamburgo 188. Tops in everything, even prices.
Terrazza Cassino, Insurgentes S. 953. Good food and talent.
Versailles, in the Hotel del Prado. Good food and interesting décor; features international night-club talent.
The Del Paseo roof, the Bamer Roof Gardens, and the Continental Hilton Belvedere share several characteristics: they offer handsome views of the city after dark, are elegantly decorated, not too crowded, serve good food at almost any hour, and are almost as expensive as those back home.

MODERATELY PRICED PLACES:

Amanecer Tapatío, corner Obrero Mundial and Nino Perdido. *Mariachis.*

Club Babalú, Bolívar 73A. Existentialist fun.

Catacumbas, Dolores 16. Dancing in the almost total dark among waiters dressed as monks.

Gitanerias, Oaxaca 15. Literally a three-ring flamenco circus, winding up with confetti and streamer-throwing.

Guadalajara de Noche, Honduras 17. *Mariachi* music.

La Gran Tasca, Morelos 77. Spanish entertainment and food.

Plaza de Garibaldi opens off San Juan de Letrán. A gathering place of *charro*-costumed male players and singers of Mexican songs. Best-known among plaza night spots, Tenampo Bar asks ridiculous prices. Try any of the others. *Mariachis* will also play to you in your car, in the Plaza Park or elsewhere. Prices moderate. Great day here is November 22, Santa Cecilia Day, patroness of musicians. Sign of the times is new curfew: midnight on Sunday, 1 P.M. week nights. Can't take the *mariachis* home with you for a party any more, day or night, unless three neighbors agree.

For jazz enthusiasts: Restaurant 33, Av. Juárez 20; Manolo's, Lopez 1, corner of Av. Juárez; and out at Regus Bar, Hotel Insurgentes, Insurgentes S. 1668.

FRONTÓN (JAI ALAI): This spectacular game is well worth seeing. Almost as much fun is the constant, rapid betting in the audience. Every day except Monday, from 6 P.M. on, in Frontón Mexico, on the Plaza de la Republica.

HORSE RACES: The Hipódromo de las Américas, beautifully situated just outside the Lomas de Chapultepec. Races are held every Thursday, Saturday, and Sunday at 2 P.M., from October to April. Tourists pay only admission tax at the Tourist Gate. Visit the Jockey Club.

MOVIES: Mexican films are internationally popular. There are numerous first-class, neighborhood and central, modern movie theaters, which exhibit Mexican, U.S., and European films. The University Ciné Club and cultural institutions of several nations exhibit the world's best films, old and new. The annual film festival is a great event.

MUSIC: Mexico City has a reputation for good musical events, many free, especially at the Casa del Lago in Bosque de Chapultepec, at the National University and in public parks; the others are extremely low-priced. Indoor and outdoor symphony concerts by Orquesta Sinfónica Nacional, A. C., and the University's Symphony Orchestra. Opera, both national and international in season. There are madrigal singers and other choral groups. Vocal and chamber music concerts by Mexicans or foreign artists are frequent. Lively band concerts of popular or classical music are regular Sunday morning features in the Alameda and other parks. See newspapers for current ones.

OUTDOOR SPORTS: There is swimming, but only in pools in hotels and private clubs or the warm thermal waters of *balnearios* in pleasant gardens on the Calzada Ignacio Zaragoza (former Calzada Mexico-Puebla) outside the city. The largest is Deportivo Bahía. Agua Caliente, at No. 846, has motel accommodations, too.

One can arrange to play golf at Churubusco Country Club, Calzada de Tlalpan; a little farther out at Club de Golf, La Hacienda; and Chapultepec Golf Club. Tennis at Churubusco Country Club and Club Deportivo de Chapultepec, Calzada Mariano Escobedo at Calle Victor Hugo. Polo at Campo Marte, Chapultepec Park, Reforma, behind Auditorium. Sunday matches in season.

Soccer season, June-December; football, first Saturday in October to end of November; baseball, end of March to end of September.

HIKING AND CLIMBING: There are many good treks from the outskirts to Desierto de los Leones (see p. 62), Ajusco Peak, villages beyond Xochimilco. Before tackling the volcanoes or any hard climbs, consult Club de Exploraciónes de México, J. A. Matéas 146, Mexico, D.F., Tel. 19-52-46, which inaugurated the well-attended annual international ascent of Popocatépetl on the Sunday nearest Columbus day to celebrate the desire for world peace. Check at Y.M.C.A., Av. Ejercito Nacional 253, Tel. 45-72-25, about local sports and group excursions, if you are a member.

HUNTING AND FISHING: See PREPARATIONS FOR YOUR TRIP (p. 17). Get local advice from Asociación de Caza y Pesca del Distrito Federal, Buenavista 8-2, Tel. 21-05-78; another office, Km. 14½, Toluca Highway, Tel. 20-07-19.

109

THEATER: Mexico City has few commercial legitimate playhouses. The largest, most modern is *Teatro Insurgentes,* Av. Insurgentes Sur 1578. Smaller ones include *Sala Chopin,* Insurgentes and Puebla; *Ofelia,* Glorieta Ejercito Nacional and Thiers; and *5 de Diciembre,* Lucerna and Lisboa. Little theaters, where professionals or amateur groups produce classic and contemporary plays in English, Spanish, and French, abound.

Three institutions are patrons of fine theater. The *Instituto de Belles Artes* sponsors plays in its Palacio, at el Nuevo Teatro Fabregas, Donceles 27; Teatro de Periodista, Filomena Mata 8; at the Lago de Bosque, Teatro Granero; and, for children, Recreo Infantil del Bosque, the last three within Chapultepec Park (the last two behind the National Auditorium); at other theaters, auditoriums and in public squares. The *Dirección General de Difusión Culturales* of the National University sponsors drama in the auditoriums of many faculty buildings on its campus, at its theater, El Caballito, Rosales 26, and elsewhere. The *Federal Social Security Department, I.M.S.S.,* supports two theaters, Xola at the corner of Av. Xola and Nicolas San Juan, and Hidalgo, corner of Hidalgo and 2 de Abril, opposite Alameda Park.

Teatro Clásico de México stages dramatic pageant plays, classical drama of all lands in Colonial patios, church atria or plazas, on the steps and summits of pre-Columbian temples—unforgettable open-air spectacles limited to the nonrainy season and worth traveling far to see—even if one doesn't understand Spanish. Puppet shows are given inside and in public squares, usually on Sunday.

Music halls offering variety shows (vaudeville and "girl" shows, even burlesque) include Teatro Lirico, Calle de Rep. de Cuba 46; Teatro Blanquita, Plaza de Aquiles Serdan 16; Teatro Follies, C. Leyva 41.

Newspapers carry announcements of current programs, and hotel desk men will help you. The National Auditorium advertises a full schedule of entertainments and exhibitions, some free and the rest inexpensive. The Sunday morning (11 A.M.) performances are varied and often quite unusual.

RODEOS, or *charreadas,* are held every Sunday morning at the Rancho del Charro, Av. Ejercito and Calle Schiller, Colonial Chapultepec-Morales, and several other spots. There the *charros* in their picturesque costumes engage in fancy riding, rope tricks and lassoing, similar to those of the American cowboys. The *charros,* however, are not cowboys, but well-to-do ranch owners or city people who enjoy the sport.

Riding horses are for rent at the ranchos where all the information riding enthusiasts need can also be obtained.

SHOPPING: The tourists' favorite sport need only be limited by one's souvenir budget. (See THE FOLK ARTS, p. 285.) For places to go wild in Mexico City see the Directory, p. 157. While some merchants are amenable to bargaining,

Charro before Performance

others are tired of it and adopt a take-it-or-leave-it attitude.

THEATRICAL FOLK DANCES: You can see theatrical folk dances at the Mexican Folklore Center, Londres 15, every Friday at 9 P.M., and at Riveroll's, Colon 35, every Friday at 9 P.M. Dances and costumes are stylized for the stage, but they give one an idea of the authentic folk dances and provide colorful performances.

MISCELLANEOUS CULTURAL INTERESTS: Museums (see the Directory, p. 155), square and other dances, library services, intensive language courses, photo and art exhibits, concerts, talks on a wide range of themes by experts—these and related activities, sometimes several the same night, are sponsored by the following and other organizations: U.S. Biblioteca Benjamin Franklin; Librería Británica, Villalongin 32; institutes sponsored by English, French, Italian, U.S., and other nations as well as by Mexico's National University and many institutes and government departments. Not every one gets listed in newspapers. Consult CULTURAL RELATIONS INSTITUTES (p. 154) and ask around.

In the Tizoc Room of the Hotel Vasco de Quiroga, Londres 15, a program of professional Mexican folk songs and dances is presented on Fridays at 8:15; cocktails and dinner service begin at 8 P.M. Cameras allowed.

Look down on the city, 10 A.M. to midnight, from the Latino-Americano Tower Observatory, Madero and San Juan de Letrán, for 4 *pesos*. Cameras allowed.

Signs Posted in Mexico City

SIGHTSEEING

No matter how one enjoys shopping, amusements, cultural activities, and sports, everyone comes to Mexico as a sightseer. Some, armed with this book or another, enjoy exploring by themselves. Others, anxious to get a glimpse of as much as possible with a minimum of time lost arranging time-schedules and transportation, wisely use local guide and tour services. The person who would welcome informative guide help, but wants more comprehensive insight into aspects of Mexico than any walking encyclopedia of a guide can dispense to a group of people of disparate interests, should sample the following specialized excursions, chiefly to points of interest in Mexico City.

The most accurately informative, friendly excursions to historic and archeological spots, art galleries, and museums, and the most inexpensive (usually costing no more than your bus fare and lunch), conducted by professional archeologists, art authorities, and historians, almost every Sunday of the year in the urban area, are sponsored by the Instituto Nacional de Antropología y Historia. Pick up current program at the office, Córdoba 45, or phone for information. Someone is sure to speak English if the tour leader does not. Longer excursions, sometimes for several days, at fantastically low prices, are adjusted to long weekends or national holidays. They were initiated to show Mexicans their capital and country but visiting foreigners are more than welcome to share this privilege. Every outing is an entry to acquaintanceship with Mexicans who share your hobbies and enthusiasms.

Local excursions, similar in scope and purpose but less frequent, are sponsored by the Institutos Anglo-Mexicano and Mexicano-Americano.

Street Names - Colonias - Plazas

In Mexico City streets bear names, often changing one or more times along their way, especially the old streets, where formerly every block bore a different name, related to occupations, events, legends, etc. Madero, which becomes Juárez at San Juan de Letrán, used to be called Calle de Los Plateros because of the silversmiths who had their shops there. In recent times the old names have been changed to unrelated new ones, such as those of Revolutionary heroes and events and dates, Latin-American republics, states, Mexican and foreign cities, scientists, writers, poets, musicians, lakes, trees, and flowers. All that survives of the old custom of naming blocks is that each one has a number— 1a, 2a, or first, second, or whatever it may be, followed by the street name.

Outside of the business center, the city is divided into *colonias,* or districts, and in each one the streets bear related names. In the *colonias* Roma and Juárez, for example, they are of foreign cities—Londres, Berlin, Manchester, and others; in the very poor Colonia de la Bolsa one sees the names of Bach, Beethoven, and other great musicians on the street plaques.

The plaza, or square, is a Mexican institution, a center of life. Every town has a main one around which are located the principal church, government buildings, and *portales,* or arcades, with stores and stands; in addition every *colonia,* or neighborhood, has its own. The plaza is not only a place for business but also for pleasure—band concerts, promenades, *fiestas.*

THE ZÓCALO AND VICINITY

Mexico's main plaza, La Plaza Mayor de la Constitución, is always called the "Zócalo," a name derived, perhaps, from an Indian word or from the French *socle,* meaning foundation (of the never-completed monument to Mexican independence), or the Spanish *zócalo* for its colonnaded, roofed, sidewalk market. Occupying the site of the great, religious-political center of Tenochtitlán, capital of the Aztec Empire, 1275-1521, the Zócalo has been the chief stage of almost 700 years of Mexican history, the scene of sieges and battles, of revolutions, of the rise and fall of emperors and presidents, of religious pageants and royal processions, of bloodshed and rejoicing.

The Zócalo, shorn of its flowering garden plots in a recent, too drastically utilitarian modernization crusade, is an immense barren paved plaza, framed by stately Colonial-style buildings, kindled into breathtaking majesty on the nights that their façades are electrically illuminated. Guarding but a few landmarks of the civic and religious splendor of Tenochtitlán, capital of the Aztec Empire, 1325-1521, the area within a quarter-mile radius of the Zócalo is a living museum of 300 years of history of New Spain's Colonial Capital which travelers hailed as the City of Palaces (more truly a city of churches). In these neighboring history-laden streets, some as narrow as medieval passages, hundreds of edifices, survivors of centuries of use and misuse, exhibit the finest details of Colonial architecture: Gothic, Classic, Renaissance unfolding into Plateresque, softened and brightened by the Mudejar (Moorish), developing into the Baroque and ultra-Baroque or Churrigueresque, retreating back to the severer neoclassic. These adopted seventeenth- and eighteenth-century European patterns were affected by close trade contacts with the Orient and subtly stamped by indigenous creative artistry. With the exception of the Tecpan on the Plaza of Tlaltilolco, no building of the sixteenth century in this area escaped the destruction of the savage floods of that era. All had to be rebuilt, some many times.

Except by government permission, no building in this area can be pulled down or remodeled. Private landlords, incapacitated by small returns due to rent freezing, have been unable to keep up their properties. So dilapidated, semi-ruined mansions house shabby offices, stores, and workshops or are doleful *vecindades* (slums). Their harmonious proportions, carved stone and wrought-iron or fading tile decorations lend them an aura of romantic melancholy. But dynamic Mexican genius is about to arrest further decay. A corps of scholar-researchers is making a street-by-street historical, anthropological, sociological investigation of *every* building, an undertaking of tremendous scope directed by *arquitecto* José Gorbea and due to terminate soon. As knowledge accumulates, preparations to preserve and restore *all* important buildings, eradicate the slums, and permit only that new construction which will harmonize with the stately beauty of the past are being made; some restoration work has already begun.

Visitors should not miss the opportunity to see this ancient quarter as it is today—its seignorial mansions, churches, chapels, and scattered oases of *plazuelas*. Buildings wear worn tiled plaques recording efforts of dedicated Spanish monks and priests to aid their Indian converts on a worldly plane by founding schools and hospitals. Of some ancient structures only fragments remain—a tiled dome, a fountain, carved doors and window frames, and niches, some occupied by charming statues of guardian saints. Others retain entire cloisters and patios, halls of convents and monasteries—some now schools and libraries. Wall

Cathedral and Sagrario Metropolitano—Mexico City

Detail from Sagrario Metropolitano

markers define sites of still older buildings and historical events such as the capture of the last Aztec emperor, Mexico's warrior-hero, Cuauhtemoc.

Visitors who want to become familiar with this treasury of Colonial architecture and absorb centuries of history by associating with its landmarks can make their headquarters in hotels in the vicinity: the Majestic, overlooking the Zócalo and a part of its history; the more modest Moneda, across from the National Palace, on Calle Moneda in the building where the first printing shop on this continent was installed in 1539 (much rebuilt less than a century later); one of the newer modest hotels on Pino Suarez, the street running south from the Zócalo; or Hotel Virreyes, J. Izazaga 8, across from the 1750 chapel of Purísima Concepción and the restored fountain of Salto de Agua; or hotels on Calle Republica de Cuba near Santo Domingo Church and Plaza. Brief and repeated strolls between major sight-seeing sorties, in early morning or twilight hours—or on a moonlit night, any time when foot and car traffic is less bothersome, is an aesthetically satisfying trip into Mexico's rich inheritance.

LA CATEDRAL (The Cathedral) is on the north side of the Zócalo, slightly southwest of the site of Tenochtitlán's greatest temple or *teocalli* (house of God), shrine of the Gods of War and Rain. As the mark on the crypt floor below the cupola indicates, it partly covers the site of the Tzompantli, holy rack on which skulls of the sacrificed were exposed. The largest church on the continent, its cornerstone was laid, 1573, slightly north but close to the Iglesia Mayor (Large Church), the first church—not chapel—of New Spain, which was finished in 1525. Dedicated in 1667 to the Asunción de María, the cathedral was finally completed in 1813. The labor of building, as well as one-third of the cost, exceeding three million *pesos,* was contributed by the local people, numbers of whom died each day because of the long hours of unaccustomed, strenuous work. The architectural harmony of the cathedral is remarkable in view of the fact that during the long period of construction many architects and sculptors worked on it.

Repairs of earthquake damage and reconstruction, begun in 1943, continue. A handsome new high altar replaces the too heavy, unsafe one built 1842-1850 by Lorenzo Hidalgo; its famous life-size saints now line a crypt passage. Removal of an ornate tomb slab opened an entrance to underground chambers and tombs. This slab is incorporated in the door of the crypt chapel, where archbishops and cardinals are buried in wall tombs. The remains of Mexico's famous first archbishop, Zúmarraga, are in one of these, not in front of the altar in the ponderous memorial tomb, decorated with twined serpentine scrolls meeting at an ancient stone visage of a god he expelled from Mexico.

The exterior of the building is a combination of Doric, Ionic, and Corinthian styles, freely treated. The three figures which decorate the facade—Faith, Hope, and Charity—and the large dome were the work of the famous Spanish architect-sculptor Manuel Tolsa. The Doric interior is elaborated by ornamental motives from other styles. Noteworthy are the principal dome and the double row of Doric columns, which have not suffered from alterations as have other parts of the interior. The fourteen chapels which flank the aisles contain splendid examples of Churrigueresque carving. The Altar de los Reyes, copied from a Churrigueresque chapel in the cathedral in Seville, Spain, by Balbas, the artist who executed the original, is the finest in the building. It has several paintings by J. Rodriguez Juárez, whose masterpiece, "The Adoration of the Kings," is directly over the altar. Another notable and much frequented altar, Del Perdón, behind the choir, contains Churrigueresque decorations and a large painting of the Virgin, the origin of which is the subject of various legends.

The choir, situated in the center of the building between the two organs, is elaborately carved. In the sacristy are many fine paintings and chests filled with costly vestments. The Chapter Room, on the opposite side, is also hung with splendid paintings.

THE SAGRARIO METROPOLITANO, next to the cathedral, was built 1749-1769 by Lorenzo Rodríguez, in the form of a symmetrical Greek cross, as the capital's first parish church. Doric columns support an octagonal dome. The exquisitely carved southern and eastern facades are in the best Mexican Churrigueresque style. Repair of structural earthquake damage and unfortunately devised interior decoration are in progress. Only its exterior remains warm and beautiful.

In the lawn behind, at the south side of a sunken formal garden, is the Pozo de Cortés, reputedly the well where

Spaniards watered their horses in 1521. In the narrow garden plot plaza between the Sagrario and the old building of Calle Seminario, a tiled plaque at the base of the pleasing fountain monument to the Apostle of the Indians reads, in Spanish, "Stranger, if you love virtue, stop and venerate. This is Fray Bartolomé de las Casas, Father of the Indians."

NATIONAL PALACE (El Palacio Nacional). This block-square building flanks the entire east side of the Zócalo. Its present aspect dates from 1692, at which time it was practically rebuilt following an attack upon the building by a rebellious Indian mob. Some of the material of the Palace of Moctezuma, over which the present building was erected, was used in its construction which, with alterations, continued for over two centuries. Its architectural style is a restrained Colonial-Baroque and its exterior is faced with *tezontle,* a red volcanic stone. In 1927 a third story was added. The building has three main entrances which lead to a series of spacious patios. In a peaked niche above the central entrance hangs the Dolores Parish Church bell that Cura Hidalgo used to call Mexicans to arms against Spain in 1810. It is rung to honor that liberating "Grito" at 11 P.M. every September 15.

In the palace are the executive offices of the President, of Hacienda, the National Treasury, and the Archivo General de la Nación (General Archives of the Nation), housed in the south patio, a treasure-house of scarcely investigated historical documents. On the walls of the main staircase in the central patio are the famous frescoes painted by Diego Rivera in 1931—a crowded, dramatic, panoramic history of Mexico from the pre-Conquest era to the social upheaval of the 1930's. Of the projected economic history on the second-floor balcony walls, begun in 1943, only the vivid recreation of pre-Hispanic peoples' industry and trade and a single panel of the conquering Spaniards' exploitation of these peoples were finished before Rivera's death in 1957.

The palace has several large and elaborate salons, the most regal that of the Ambassadors, containing portraits of Mexico's outstanding presidents. In the Hall of the Constitution is a large allegorical painting of the Constitution of

1857. In the rear patio, just beyond the doorway of Hacienda's great public library (a memorial to Miguel Lerdo de Tejado and open to all visitors), is the entrance to a tree-shaded garden—a fragment of the land Moctezuma's great zoological park occupied. A bowered retreat of the Empress Carlotta, it is the recess ground of children of widowed federal employees attending their special primary school in adjacent palace rooms.

The Recinto de Juárez (Precinct of Juárez) opens off the north patio, the stairway just left of the bronze statue of President Benito Juaréz. A most revered patriotic shrine, the library and simple living quarters of that noble friend of Abraham Lincoln are of special interest to U.S. visitors.

The building is open daily during office hours and there are guides to show one through. Entrance to the salons is in the southwest corner of the second floor of the main patio. Walk up the main stairway past the frescoes and turn to your right.

ARCADES OF THE TRADESMEN (Portales de Mercaderes): On the west side of the Zócalo, opposite the National Palace, are these busy arcades, reproductions (one of this century) of the earliest built in 1524, when the Colonial government granted permission to the adjoining stores to build a wide portico over the sidewalk as protection against the rain and sun. The class of merchandise sold—cheap jewelry, notions, food, and drinks—has changed.

PALACE OF JUSTICE (El Palacio de Justicia), on the southeast corner of the Zócalo, handsome modern-Colonial, was completed in 1941. Above the main stairway are frescoes by José Clemente Orozco, depicting false and true justice. In the first-floor hall is a huge fresco by George Biddle (1944), with sculptures by Helene Sardeau, his wife, on the subject of war and peace.

CITY HALL (Palacio del Ayuntamiento): The two handsome buildings on the south—originally a single structure but cut through to create the broad Calle 20 de Noviembre —face the cathedral. The original, begun by Cortés in 1522, built of stones of Aztec buildings and sold to the Spanish Crown by his heirs, was destroyed in the Indian riots of

1692 and was rebuilt in 1720. In 1909 a third floor and some exterior Colonial-style decorations were added. In the façade are state shields formed of tiles. The library contains many remarkable documents pertaining to the history of Mexico.

NATIONAL PAWNSHOP (Monte de Piedad): North of the Arcades, across from the cathedral. Founded in 1775 by the Conde de Regla, Pedro Romero de Terreros, wealthy owner of the Real del Monte mines at Pachuca. The building is the original one, a very fine restrained Colonial-Baroque, but additions and some interior alterations have been made from time to time.

The pawnshop was founded as a philanthropic institution for the benefit of all social classes in distress, and, for a long period, loans were made without interest. Borrowers generally made gifts and were expected to offer prayers in the chapel in the building. Reasonable interest is now charged, and the public is treated with courtesy. The institution, which is a part of the Public Charities of the Federal District, also operates a sound savings bank, which does a large business. Auctions of unredeemed pledges are held monthly, and thousands of articles of every description are on sale daily at plainly marked prices. It is often possible to purchase valuable items at moderate cost.

Almost directly across the street, outside the cathedral fence, looking west down Calle Cinco de Febrero, is the monument to the celebrated Portuguese cosmographer, Enrico Martínez, who in 1607 built the deep cut of Nochistengo to drain the Valley of Mexico.

MUSEO NACIONAL DE ANTROPOLOGÍA (National Museum of Anthropology), Chapultepec Park. On these premises once stood a stately Baroque edifice built in 1731 as the Royal Mint (Casa de Moneda), later known as Moneda No. 13. From 1839 to 1841 it was the home of Madame Calderon de la Barca, author of *Life in Mexico*. A museum since 1866, it was moved in 1964 to a new site in Chapultepec Park on the Paseo de la Reforma opposite the Zoo and will be reopened as the Museo de las Culturas.

To visit a museum of anthropology is to contemplate a series of chapters in the history of mankind, but this unique museum, already acclaimed as a model, re-creates in vivid detail countless centuries of Mexican history as well as a contemporary chapter. It is so open, so accessible that only small, fragile objects—and not all of these—are kept behind glass. No one object is singled out; each has its own claim to attention. The finest examples of plastic art of past centuries mingle with objects of modern folk art. Ranging from ancient jewelry and weapons to figures of gods—such as the dramatic monolith of Tláloc re-erected outside the entrance—and wheeled toys, the exhibits assembled here may repel or delight, but they are not soon forgotten.

The vast structure merits attention not only for the scholarly quality of its exhibits but also for its blend of ancient and modern styles, native and foreign materials, and for the sense of spaciousness and freedom of movement.

Entrance to Museum of Anthropology, Chapultepec Park.

A tour of the museum is a walk of more than 3 miles. Landscaped woodlands contrast with expanses paved with volcanic stone from Durango and flagstones from Querétaro. As visitors approach the museum, via an avenue of Cyclopean length and breadth leading to the wide marble threshold, they cannot help but appreciate the museum's massive strength and sense the momentous aesthetic experience awaiting them within. Mortar is used so carefully be-

*Aztec Calendar Stone—National Museum of
Anthropology, Mexico City*

tween the blocks of volcanic stone that the walls seem to be built stone upon stone, as the early Mexicans built. The exterior echoes the simplicity of Teotihuacán. White marble has been brought from Carrara, Italy, for the façade, and marble of shifting colors—gray, orange, and red—from Santo Tomas, Puebla, decorates the walls.

The doors open into the cool tranquility of an enormous, high-ceilinged lobby. The great Patio and the exhibition *salas* may be glimpsed through a glass partition. From some of these *salas* may be seen related structures and sculpture in the garden. At the right of the entrance are rooms containing current exhibitions and special displays. The great pillared fountain catches the eye at once. Its umbrella is an ingenious device for aiding visitors to proceed dry-shod from the lobby to the various exhibition halls during the rainy season. The walls of the lower floor of the museum are stark; the upper walls, made largely of glass, are decorated with aluminum grillwork.

Aztec Goddess of Life and Death—
National Museum of Anthropology

A pillared "umbrella" fountain is a striking architectural feature of the Patio.

Thoughtful planning makes it possible to visit exhibits in chronological or geographical order if desired. Twelve *salas* occupy three sides of the Patio level. These include a hall of Introduction and *salas* portraying Middle America, Early Man, the Pre-Classic period, Teotihuacán, Toluca, and Mexica (Aztec). In the south wing are *salas* containing exhibits of Oaxaca, the Gulf Coast area, Maya territory, and northern and western Mexico. You might prefer to begin your first tour in the Hall of Indigenismo and proceed through the *salas* of northern cultures; the exhibits representing the Lowland and Highland Mayas, and the Huastec and Totonacs of Veracruz, ending with the exhibit which includes the fascinating variety of cultures of Oaxaca. Ethnographic exhibits of contemporary cultures occupy the top floor, including rooms portraying the culture of the Coras, the Huichols, the Purepecha, the Otomí-Pames and that of the peoples of the Puebla area.

The museum also contains a library and reading room, research laboratories and the National School of Anthropology. On a floor below the entrance-hall area are offices, an auditorium seating 350, and a restaurant and cafeteria.

Schedule and Services: Hours, Tuesday through Friday,

*At one end of the Patio is a pool with a snail-shell sculpture,
a symbol of the "fair god," Quetzalcóatl.*

10 A.M. to 2 P.M.; 4 P.M. to 8 P.M.; Saturdays, Sundays, and
holidays, 10 A.M. to 6 P.M. Closed Mondays. Entrance fee,
Tuesday to Saturday, 3 *pesos;* Sunday, 1 *peso.* Restaurant
and cafeteria service: Tuesday to Friday, 10 A.M. to 9 P.M.;
Saturdays, Sundays, and holidays, 10 A.M. to 7 P.M. Cameras
may be checked at far left of entrance. Permits to enter with
cameras vary from a fee of 2 *pesos* for a simple camera to
a fee of 30 *pesos* for a movie camera.

Guided Tours: Inquire for free guide service at counter
next to checkroom. Knowledgeable guides, all of whom
have some background in archaeology and anthropology,
speak English, French, and German. No tipping. Tours set
out as soon as five or six visitors congregate, from 10 A.M.
on until the museum closes, except Sundays; then only during morning hours. An hour's tour encompasses an average
of only 3 *salas,* long enough for a single visit for the average
pair of feet. Wear your most comfortable walking shoes. To
absorb the major aspects of three varied cultures in a single
hour is no easy task. After a brief respite, another guided
tour or a "poke-around" on one's own may be in order.

Illustrated orientation hour in lecture theater given
daily at 12 noon. Admission fee, 2 *pesos.* Commentary,

spoken slowly and clearly in Spanish, accompanies sequence of slides and exhibits of large-scale models. Sound effects and music add to impact. This visual survey is invaluable in helping the non-Spanish-speaking visitor to the National Museum of Anthropology to understand and appreciate Mexico's remarkable past.

CHURCH OF LA SANTÍSIMA TRINIDAD: Two blocks beyond the Academy, on Emiliano Zapata (the eastward continuation of Calle Moneda), corner of La Santísima. Built 1750-1786 by Lorenzo Rodríguez on the site of a 1570 chapel. Noteworthy Churrigueresque style, with an elaborately carved façade. Many primitive artistic features of the adjacent cloister have survived frequent alterations.

CHURCH OF LA SOLEDAD: At the end of Soledad Street, three blocks east on E. Zapata to broad Circunvalación and one south, in a colorful neighborhood of the poor. The Virgin of the Soledad, housed in a niche in the façade of the church, is the protectress of the people of the underworld. In the early days, thieves were often apprehended here as they came to do homage to the Virgin. Special devotion is now paid here to the sad black Christ who protects from poisoning, *el Señor del Veneno*.

CHURCH AND PLAZA OF LORETO: Three blocks north of La Santísima, on Calle Santísima at the corner of San Ildefonso. A delightful, well-kept plaza, surrounded by the churches of Loreto and Santa Teresa and old Colonial buildings. The Loreto church, completed in 1816, resembles the French churches of the same era. It has a beautiful dome and a handsome façade. Unfortunately, the church has been sinking unevenly, and leans considerably to the east.

CHURCH AND CONVENT OF LA ENSEÑANZA: Donceles No. 104, near Argentina. This small well-preserved and beautiful Baroque church, dating from 1754, is one of the loveliest in the city. The unique façade is exquisitely carved and the adjoining convent, with its *fine* patios, now houses the Civil Courts of the Federal District.

CHURCH AND CONVENT OF S. S. PEDRO AND PABLO: On the corner of San Ildefonso and Carmen. A remarkable example of an early single-nave church (1603). An unusual feature is the heavy tower, strangely located near the rear of the edifice. The church is now a public lecture-hall, with wall decorations by Roberto Montenegro. The adjoining convent, of severe and heavy construction with spacious patios, now houses a high school and barracks. In and near the main stairway, entered at Carmen No. 60, are some interesting frescoes by Roberto Montenegro, portraying the reconstruction following the Revolution, homage to the popular arts, and a scene of the festival of the Cross.

RUINS OF THE AZTEC TEMPLO MAYOR (Escalerillas): Corner of Guatemala and Argentina, across from the rear of cathedral on Calle Seminario. The entrance is through the Museo Etnico (Ethnic Museum), which has fine models of ancient dances still preserved in the Republic and a detailed reproduction of the heart of Tenochtitlan. Believed to be a fragmentary part of the Teocalli, or Great Temple of Huitzilopochtli, the ruins consist of a series of stairways, a platform, and many carvings.

MINISTRY OF EDUCATION (Secretaría de Educación Pública): West side of Calle Argentina, between Obregón and Venezuela, 3 blocks north of the cathedral. A fine, modern building completed in 1922. It houses the principal federal offices of the Department of Education, to which visitors may go for information.

Frescoes by Diego Rivera and other Mexican painters on the walls of the great patios and balconies are now faded and awaiting restoration; murals in several of the offices are difficult to visit.

NATIONAL PREPARATORY SCHOOL (Escuela Nacional Preparatoria): south side of San Ildefonso between Rep. Argentina and Carmen. The school, affiliated with the National University and authorized to confer Bachelor degrees, is housed in a splendid Baroque structure. Built in 1749, it was for some time the Jesuit School of San Ildefonso. In this building, as well as in the Ministry of Education, are some of the finest frescoes in Mexico, principally the works of the famous artist José Clemente Orozco. They are sadly time-worn, but scheduled for restoration.

Permission to visit the Salon El Generalito should be

obtained from the office in the building. This room contains some remarkable carved seats and a pulpit taken from the Convent of San Augustín, now the National Library. The designs are of Biblical scenes, executed by Indian artists.

Also in the building, with an entrance on Justo Sierra, is the Anfiteatro Bolívar with decorations around the stage by Diego Rivera (1921). The subject of these murals, done in encaustic, is Creation. In the rear lobby are murals by Fernando Leal of scenes taken from the life of the great liberator, Simón Bolívar.

PLAZA DEL 23 DE MAYO (formerly Santo Domingo); two blocks north of the Zócalo, between Calle Republica de Cuba on the south and Av. Republica de Brasil on the east. On the west side are the very old Arcades of Santo Domingo, housing public scribes who now prefer the typewriter to the classic quill pen. On the southwest side are the offices of the Federal District Treasury, in what was formerly a splendid Colonial mansion. In the center of the plaza is a statue to Doña Josefa Ortiz de Domínguez, who was on the side of the Mexicans in the War for Independence. Another statue, near the church, is of Doctor Manuel Carmona y Valle, who introduced European methods of anaesthesia.

CHURCH OF SANTO DOMINGO: North side of plaza. Built in 1737 to replace the former church destroyed by a flood, it is one of the best examples of Mexican Baroque in the Republic. The carving on the façade and on the doors is beautifully wrought. The cruciform interior is large and lofty. The church contains twelve chapels, with interesting images of saints. The Churrigueresque altars, at one time very elaborate, still reveal much of their former splendor.

NATIONAL SCHOOL OF MEDICINE: On the northeast side, on Av. Brasil, is a severe Colonial building, formerly the Tribunal de Santa Oficio (Holy Office of the Inquisition) and headquarters of the Dominicans; and until recently the National School of Medicine (now in new quarters in University City). The patio is notable for its very fine stairway and an unusual unsupported arch.

CASA DEL CONDE DE SANTIAGO CALEMAYA, a few blocks

south of the Zócalo at Pino Suárez 30, on the corner of Republica de Salvador, one of the most beautiful mansions of Colonial times, is now the Museo de la Ciudad de México. Built on the site of the 1528 residence of Cortés' cousin, Licenciado Juan Gutierrez Altamirano, it has two Baroque floors, a monumental entrance, canon gargoyles, and a handsome patio and fountain. The huge head of a serpent in the street-corner wall belonged to the old Coatepantli, the serpent wall fencing off Tenochtitlan's Great Temple. Buildings were torn down across the street to prepare a garden stance, Rinconcito de Jesús (Little Precinct), from which to admire this edifice. Opening across from it on Salvador is a picturesque L-shaped passage, Callejón del Marqués, where a cross once marked the tomb of Cortés.

HOSPITAL DE JESÚS NAZARENO, is on the corner of Av. 20 de Noviembre and Republica del Salvador, four blocks south of the Zócalo. The oldest hospital in the New World, run today by Sisters of Charity. It was founded by Cortés in 1527 on the spot where Cortés and Moctezuma first met. The building was renovated in 1938. The patios and rooms are now hospital offices, with the original cedar panels and beams, in the heart of the a modern office building. In the adjoining church (built in 1570 and rebuilt in 1601-29, with Baroque doors) Conqueror Cortés is allegedly buried. The choir ceiling was decorated by José Clemente Orozco with religious motifs, including the Four Horsemen of the Apocalypse.

IN THE VICINITY OF THE FINE ARTS PALACE

The Palace of Fine Arts, because of its conspicuous location, is the logical starting point for exploring the interesting places in this district as well as other areas nearby.

PALACE OF FINE ARTS (Palacio de Bellas Artes): A huge ornate, white marble building, designed and started by the Italian Amado Boari in 1905. Construction was halted by the Revolution and the interior has been done in quite another style, with handsome marbles and beautiful woods from various parts of the Republic.

131

The Palace of Fine Arts—Mexico City

The palace houses a theater and a museum. The theater was intended for opera and similar functions, for the elite, and hence seats only a few thousand persons. Now it is used for concerts, opera, plays, and large public meetings. The stage is spacious and has a glass curtain by Tiffany, designed by a Mexican painter, Dr. Atl (Gerardo Murillo), depicting the two volcanoes—Ixtaccíhuatl and Popocatépetl. As the curtain has to be raised by machinery, it is not always used. However, there are special exhibitions of it Sunday mornings between 9 and 10 for 4 *pesos*.

El Museo Nacional de Artes Plásticas was inaugurated in the palace, September 18, 1947, for the exhibition of ancient and modern sculpture, paintings, prints, Colonial church art, and modern handicrafts. The exhibits are changed periodically, but among the paintings that are there permanently are those of the best nineteenth-century artists—José Maria Estrada, Clavé, Landesio, José Maria Velasco. Among the prints is a good collection of José

Detail from Diego Rivera fresco—National Palace (page 120)

Guadalupe Posada (1851-1913), Mexico's greatest engraver. And there are always the works of the modern Mexican artists and occasionally an exhibition by some foreign artist.

On the left, or west wall, on the third floor, is a fresco by Diego Rivera, completed in 1934. The subject is "Man at the Crossroads, Looking with Uncertainty but with Hope to a Better World." This fresco contains the social ideology of the artist and is a reconstruction of the one previously destroyed in Radio City, New York, because the owners of Rockefeller Center did not agree with the artist's point of view.

On the east, or opposite, wall is José Clemente Orozco's fresco (1934), expressing the chaos of the modern world. Two frescoes are by David Alfaro Siqueiros. The subject of one is democracy and the other, Cuahtemoc. On the walls below are two huge frescoes by Rufino Tamayo (1953), one depicting the destruction of the old order by the Spaniards and the other, Mexico of today.

Open daily from 10 to 5:30; Sundays 10 to 2. Authorized English-speaking guides will show you through for a small fee.

On the top floor are permanent exhibits of modern and contemporary Mexican paintings.

THE ALAMEDA: West of the Palace of Fine Arts, a large and magnificent park, filled with stately elm and ash trees and lit by mercury vapor lights. Dating from 1592, it covers the place where victims of the Inquisition were burned. It has figured prominently in revolutions and in other phases of Mexican history. During the nineteenth century, as the gathering place for promenades and celebrations of the aristocracy, it was fenced around to prevent the entry of the common people. It has undergone many changes, although the trees and a splendid old fountain still remain. Many tile benches, statuary, and fountains have been added. During the day it is full of people of all classes and in the evenings the park benches serve as a trysting place for romantic couples. It is interesting on Sundays, when the place is full of adults and children enjoying themselves. Often there are band concerts.

The semicircle of white marble is a monument to Benito Juárez, the great Mexican patriot and president who instituted the Reform Laws. It was erected in 1910 to commemorate the first centennial of Mexican Independence and is characteristic of the flamboyant heroic style of that period.

MAIN POST OFFICE (Casa de Correo Mayor): Across from the Palace of Fine Arts, at the corner of Tacuba. Constructed in 1904 by Amado Boari, in Spanish Gothic style with Plateresque embellishments. Stamp Museum on top floor.

ENGINEERING COLLEGE OF THE NATIONAL UNIVERSITY (Facultad Nacional de Ingeniería): On Tacuba near the post office. Only a few departments of engineering studies remain here; the others are in University City. This handsome building was designed by Manuel Tolsa, famous architect and sculptor, in 1779. Of neo-classic style, it is harmonious with the typical Colonial architecture of the city. The patio and stairway represent Tolsa's best work. The chapel and Salón de Actos preserve the original decorations. In the next patio are the offices of the Secretariat of Agriculture.

NATIONAL CHAMBER OF DEPUTIES (Camara de Diputados): On the northeast corner of Donceles and Allende. This body corresponds to the U.S. House of Representatives. The building is elaborate but without particular interest architecturally. Visitors are frequently admitted to the galleries while the Chamber is in session.

EXPRESS OFFICE OF THE NATIONAL RAILROADS, corner of Donceles and Republica de Chile, is another magnificent example of a Colonial-Baroque seignorial mansion, with a red *tezontle* façade adorned with elaborately carved gray stone. The flattened corner is sculptured in the Churrigueresque manner, and there is a handsome niche. Inside is an unusual stone railing.

On Donceles there are many other fine Colonial buildings with unaltered façades, now commercial premises.

CINCO DE MAYO STREET: Extends from the Fine Arts Palace to the Zócalo, and was opened in 1859 on the lands of the Profesa Convent after the Reform Laws abolished church ownership of property. Named for the date of the Mexican victory over the French, it is a wide street, unlike others in the same district.

AVENIDA FRANCISCO I MADERO, named after the leader of the 1910 Revolution (formerly Calle de Plateros, or Silversmiths). Business street, with many fine Colonial buildings, former carriage promenade of the city aristocracy.

CHURCH OF LA PROFESA, corner Madero and Isabel la Católica, was founded by the Jesuit Order in 1595. The monastery of the church was torn down after the passage of the Reform Laws. The architecture is a fine example of Mexican Baroque, with an interior of pleasing proportions.

BANCO NACIONAL HIPOTECARIO (National Mortgage Bank), Madero No. 32. A modern building, with frescoes by Fermín Revueltas dealing with industry and commerce.

ITURBIDE PALACE, Madero No. 17; the home of Mexico's first emperor, 1823; a Baroque mansion, with a handsome *tezontle* façade and a stately patio, flanked by arched corridors. Now occupied by shops and offices.

CHURCH OF SAN FRANCISCO, across from La Casa de la Condesa. Established in 1524 by the first 12 Franciscans to arrive on Mexican soil. Of its two-block square grounds and buildings there exist now only the church and adjoining chapel; historically the most interesting in the Republic. The church, on which work continued for two centuries, has a fine Churrigueresque facade and handsome Baroque doors which date from the early 18th century. Parts of the original edifice were built of stones taken from the Aztec Teocalli. The interior, severe and lofty, is being radically remodeled.

SAN FELIPE DE JESÚS, adjoins the church of San Francisco. Completed in 1897 and dedicated to the patron saint of Mexico City—San Felipe, who was born in Mexico in 1575 and suffered martyrdom as a missionary in Japan. It is in the severe decadent Roman style.

HOUSE OF TILES (Casa de Azulejos)—Sanborn's, Madero 4. A fine example of Mexican Mudejar style. It was constructed at the end of the 17th century by a descendant of the House of Orizaba who, according to legend, was a spendthrift. His father taunted him one day—"You are no good; you'll never build a house of tiles." His answer was this beautiful building, with its white and blue tile façade, sculptured gray stone doorway and niches. For a long time it was the home of nobility; under the Díaz dictatorship, it housed the famous Jockey Club; now it is the popular Sanborn Restaurant and stores. On the wall of the stairway is an Orozco fresco, entitled "Omniscience."

NATIONAL LIBRARY (Biblioteca Nacional): Corner of Uruguay and Isabel la Católica. Completed in 1692, the church and headquarters of the Augustinians, the building was remodeled as a library. An imposing building with a handsome façade, containing a fine bas-relief of San Augustín.

The Library has about 200,000 books in all languages, priceless documents and manuscripts, ecclesiastical chronicles, and first editions of century-old books, published in Mexico and Spain. Attached to the library and now a part thereof is the old Church of the Third Order, shaped like a Greek cross, rare in Mexican architecture.

CASA DE LA CONDESA SAN MATEO VALPARAISO (now Banco Nacional de México): Corner of Isabel la Católica and V. Carranza. A Colonial-Baroque mansion, with a handsome façade, ornamented with sculptured stone mouldings.

COLEGIO DE NIÑAS (School for Girls): Corner of Bolívar and V. Carranza. Founded by Franciscans in 1548. The church is now the French colony's Lady of Lourdes; the school a theater abandoned in handsome melancholy. On the tiny plaza across from the church are an ornamented clock and amusing old fountain, upon which is perched the figure of a frog playing a mandolin.

CHURCH OF SANTA VERACRUZ, Avenida Hidalgo 23, on the north side of the Alameda, with a *tezontle* façade and very fine towers, adorned with Churrigueresque carvings. Established in 1568 and rebuilt in 1730, it was formerly one of the fashionable churches, to which the Virgin of Los Remedios was brought in elaborate procession to Mexico City. Has a marked slant due to sinking earth.

CHURCH OF SAN JUAN DE DIOS, Hidalgo 47, faces the

above across a flagged court in front of part of old Convent Hospital, still a hospital for women. The Baroque exterior is richly carved and the interior contains four large murals. The miracle-working image of San Antonio de Padua is covered with silver votive offerings. He is the healer of broken hearts, constantly visited by those seeking love or suffering from it.

CHURCH OF SAN HIPÓLITO on Hidalgo, corner of Zarco. Founded in 1525 to commemorate the final victory of the Spaniards over the Aztecs, on the site where Cortés lost several hundred men in his retreat from the city. The church was rebuilt in 1602, the work continuing until 1739. It has a notable tiled dome and a simple but good exterior. In the unique cornerpiece of the atrium wall is a large Aztec stone, carved with a legend relating to the Conquest.

CEMETERY OF SAN FERNANDO, along Hidalgo, corner of Guerrero, on the plaza of the same name, is where some of Mexico's heroes are buried—Juárez, Guerrero, Zaragoza, and others. The Church of San Fernando has a massive Baroque façade. On the tiny plaza stands a statue of the patriot Vicente Guerrero. Visitors are admitted to the cemetery.

AVENIDA JUÁREZ: This western continuation of Av. Madero runs from San Juan de Letrán past the Alameda to El Caballito monument, bordered by many fine shops. Calle Dolores, a side street off Juárez and terminating at the San Juan Market, is a Chinese neighborhood.

MUSEO NACIONAL DE ARTES INDUSTRIAS E POPULARES, with exhibits and sales rooms of folk arts, in the old Corpus Cristi Church, at No. 44.

EQUESTRIAN STATUE OF KING CHARLES IV, familiarly referred to by Mexicans as El Caballito, at corner of Reforma and Juárez. It is of bronze and weighs 30 tons.

THE NATIONAL LOTTERY, in the modern building near El Caballito, belongs to the Public Charities, and is administered with scrupulous honesty. Profits are used for the support of many worthy institutions—hospitals, clinics, orphan asylums, schools, and others. Drawings are held thrice weekly at 8 P.M., on the dates indicated on the tickets, and are open to the public, who may also examine the system for selecting the winning numbers.

MONUMENT TO THE REVOLUTION OF 1910 (Monumento de la Revolución): Stands at the end of Av. Juárez, beyond El Caballito. It is of marble and stone, with four huge arches supporting an immense copper dome, 250 feet high. Below the dome on each corner are gigantic allegorical sculptures—the one in the southeast corner representing Independence; on the northeast, Reform; on the southwest, Agrarian Laws; on the northwest, Labor Laws. The architect was Carlos Obregón Santacilia and the sculptors were Frederico Canesi and Oliverio Martínez.

CALLE BUCARELI: An important arterial street, south from El Caballito. The Chinese clock was a gift by the Chinese to the Mexican government when it celebrated its first century of independence from Spain. Two blocks east from the Chinese clock is La Ciudadela, a fine Colonial building, dating from 1700, which houses the Escuela de Diseño y Artesanias (School of Designs and Crafts), branch of the Federal Institute of Fine Arts; entrance, Balderas 125.

The park in front was the scene of the fighting between opposing government forces during the Decena Trágica of 1913, when President Madero was killed.

INSTITUTO INDIGENISTA INTERAMERICANO, Niños Heroes 139. Library and exhibition of handicrafts. Open daily to 2 P.M.

PASEO DE LA REFORMA begins at El Caballito, runs 2 miles to Chapultepec Park, and is being extended northeast to the Plaza of Tlaltelolco. It was completed in 1866, at the behest of Maximilian, with tree-shaded walks and *glorietas,* containing monuments and gardens. Its once aristocratic dwellings are now almost completely dislodged by modern office buildings, hotels, restaurants, shops, and residences.

MONUMENT TO CUAUHTEMOC. On the plaza where Insurgentes crosses Reforma. He was the last Aztec emperor who valiantly defended his people against the Spaniards. The carved archeological motifs around the base and the heroic bronze statue of Cuauhtemoc make it the finest monument in the Republic. On the morning of August 13,

Modern Buildings on Paseo de la Reforma—Mexico City

ceremonies including Conchero dances remember the fall of
Tenochtitlan and Cuauhtemoc's capture. On August 21,
only Conchero dancers close the *octavo,* customary celebra-
tion attached to Mexican religious holidays.

MONUMENT TO INDEPENDENCE, completed in 1910, is the
150-foot high white marble column, surmounted by a
gilded angel, who fell in the earthquake of 1957, but has
since been restored. The bronze figures around the base represent Law, Justice, War, and Peace. In homage to the
soldiers who died in battle, floral offerings are placed near
the constant flame that burns in their honor.

THE SEGURO SOCIAL, or Social Insurance building, near
the graceful Diana Fountain, was completed in 1950. It is
made almost entirely of glass, and makes a brilliant landmark at night.

THE FEDERAL HEALTH DEPARTMENT (Salubridad), near
entrance to park south: a handsome modern building com-

pleted in 1929. Visitors are admitted to the Salón de Actos, containing frescoes by Diego Rivera, with female nudes portraying Life, Health, Purity, Continence, Science, and Wisdom. On the second floor are four large stained-glass windows of the four ancient elements designed by Rivera. In this building are the offices of the Secretary of the Health Department and Public Charities.

CHAPULTEPEC PARK AND CASTLE (Azt., "Hill of the Grasshopper") at the end of the Paseo, occupies a sacred pre-Conquest area, the holy retreat of Emperor Moctezuma, whose old stone "bath" is close to the tree-lined drive. Waters from the hill's spring ran to Tenochtitlan in a great viaduct. It has many lovely walks, shaded by century-old *ahuehuete* trees, pines, eucalyptus, and others, with such romantic names as Calzada de los Filósofos, Poetas, and Artistas. Institutions within the park's borders include the zoo, a children's playground, huge Auditorio Nacional, theaters, sport fields and stadium, a lake with boats for hire and on its shore La Casa del Lago for concerts and plays.

The castle, begun in 1785 on the site of an Aztec fortress as a summer home for Spanish viceroys, was not finished until about 1840, when it was made the nation's

Charros along Paseo de la Reforma

141

Military Academy, a few years before U.S. intervention. It was captured by U.S. troops in 1847. The boy cadets—in whose honor the white marble monument at the base of the hill in front of castle was erected—fought until the last one living wrapped the Mexican flag around him and jumped to his death rather than give up the flag. Enlarged and beautified in 1866 to be, briefly, the imperial residence of Maxi-

Monument to Boy Heroes in Chapultepec Park, Mexico City

milian and Carlota, it was later the residence of Mexican presidents until President Cárdenas made it the National Historical Museum and selected the modest house among pine trees at the park's southwest corner, Los Pinos, to be Mexico's "White House." Among the hill's rocks are caves and some former Aztec shrines. On the south side is the Tribunal.

MUSEO NACIONAL DE HISTORIA (National Museum of History) in the castle. Many *salónes* with objects of great interest, especially of the Colonial period, among them weapons, banners, ceramics, furniture, old carriages. One room is devoted to jewelry, fans, and other adornments of the Colonial period, and there are some good paintings. In the front of the building are exhibited the suite of Maximilian and Carlota and rooms used by the presidents of Mexico, as originally furnished.

Open daily from 9:30 A.M. to 5 P.M.; Sundays from 10 A.M. to 2 P.M. To the left of the semicircular monument to the heroes of 1847/48, a bus runs up the hill every 15 minutes.

Just before the entrance to the Castle, at the top of the hill, a shaded walk leads to an exciting new museum of the political and historical development of Mexico.

CAJA DEL AGUA DE LERMA (the Lerma Water Box), where the water comes in from the Lerma Reservoir, is just above Los Pinos. Diego Rivera has painted the walls of the Caja with frescoes (which are partly covered by water) of sea life and sirens. He also designed the huge, magnificent Tlaloc, Aztec rain god, in front of the building.

ESCUELA DE ORIENTACIÓN, a modern primary school adjoining the stadium, contains some mural decorations by Roberto Montenegro.

INSTITUTE OF CARDIOLOGY (Instituto de Cardiología): a part of Centro Medico Nacional, Av. Cuauhtemoc 330, inaugurated in 1944 and considered the best in Latin America. In the entrance hall are frescoes by Diego Rivera, dealing with the history of cardiology.

MINISTRY OF PUBLIC WORKS (Secretaria de Obras Publicas, abbr. SOP), beyond the Centro Medico between Xola and Casas Aleman. A modern building with huge mosaic exterior murals designed by Juan O'Gorman. The theme is "A hymn of praise to the Fatherland." Get road information here.

FUENTE DEL SALTO DEL AGUA, at end of Arcos de Belén, is a reproduction of the carved stone fountain (eighteenth century) where the aqueduct from Chapultepec Park terminated. Ruins of that colonial aqueduct extend along Avenida Chapultepec near Valladolid. Across from the fountain is the Chapel of Purísima Concepción (1761).

COLEGIO DE SAN IGNACIO, or LAS VIZCAINAS: On Vizcainas Street, one block east of San Juan de Letrán. An immense Baroque building erected in 1751 as a vocational school for girls, part of it is still used for one. Although seriously deteriorated from lack of upkeep and parts of it are tenements, it is one of the best examples of the Colonial-Baroque style in the city and has a fine chapel. It is faced with *tezontle,* and the principal façade displays splendid stone carvings.

CHURCH OF REGINA, corner of Vizcainas and Bolívar. A severe seventeenth-century edifice, containing some of the richest and best preserved Churrigueresque altarpieces in the city.

NORTH OF THE ZÓCALO AND ALAMEDA

CHURCH OF SANTA MARIA LA REDONDA: From Av. Santa María la Redonda (a name for part of the northward extension of San Juan de Letrán), opposite the Plaza de Garibaldi. Turn west into Calle Pedro Moreno one block to the pleasant plaza and the church, named either after a famous Virgin of Rome or its rounded (*redonda*) west side, shaped to conform to the contour of the island it was built on. Reconstructed from a 1524 Franciscan monastery and almshouse, and enlarged to be a school for Indian children about 1598, the church was finished in 1677. In a circular niche above the entrance is a splendid sculptured figure of the Virgin; her day of *Asunción,* August 15, is celebrated merrily in the plaza and adjoining streets.

PLAZA DE SANTIAGO DE TLALTELOLCO, to the end of Av. Santa Maria la Redonda and to the right or from the center of the city by bus or streetcar on Isabel la Católica. Having undergone a stupendous re-creation of its pre-Conquest and Colonial appearance, it now forms, together with the enormous contemporary housing project of the adjacent district of Nonoalco, a complex of three historical eras.

Peer of the Zócalo in age, and of more historical significance, this great plaza was once the temple-shadowed market center of the independent island city-kingdom of Xaltilulco, settled in 1337 by dissident Mexica from Tenochtitlan, a community their intense commercial enterprise soon made flourish. Absorbed into the Aztec empire in 1473 by the more politically aggressive Tenocha of the sister island-city, Tenochtitlan, to which it was connected by a causeway, Tlaltelolco became the sensitive nerve of the Aztec economic and political regime as the District of the Pochteca. Traveling merchants, who penetrated every corner of the realm and far beyond, and the emissaries and tribute-gatherers of the Empire traveled unarmed and fearless, with the small canes which identified their role, at the head of a caravan of produce-burdened slaves. In this plaza the combined Tlaltelolco and Tenocha forces made a last desperate stand against Cortés.

Immediately after the Conquest, this district, where 60,000 people daily bought and sold in the arcade-surrounded marketplace that Cortés described as twice the size of Salamanca, was made the segregated living quarters of all natives (except house slaves and servants), in which, after toiling all day to erect the new city of Mexico on Tenochtitlan's rubble, the Indians were confined at night. The first

145

Spaniards to live here (1524) were the Franciscan monks—a notable early convert instructed by them was Juan Diego (see p. 162).

Planned by Fray Juan Bautista and supervised by Fray Juan de Torquemada, the typically early Franciscan fortress-church and monastery of Santiago was begun between 1531-1534. Almost simultaneously was begun the Colegio Imperial de Santa Cruz, inaugurated January 6, 1536, to educate Indians, the first school (primary to college, bestowing bachelor degrees in law, logic, and many other subjects) of higher learning in this continent, a century older than Harvard, also founded to educate native Americans. Many illustrious native scholars—Latinists, logicians, doctors, etc. —were educated here, and Independence hero General Mariano Matamoros was a student.

The church has been carefully restored and the adjoining monastery-school is almost completed as a Colonial historical museum-library. North and west of the church in spacious grounds are reconstructed parts of Aztec pyramids, walls, and platforms.

The plaza, a small tree-shaded park, has been fenced in and decorated as a replica of the San Marcos Plaza of Aguascalientes.

Toward the southeast limits of the area, almost lost among the new apartment houses, is a small museum, not yet opened, which was built to incorporate the long buried arches discovered when the old vocational school was torn down. These are considered by many to be part of pre-Conquest Tlaltelolco's market buildings which became the *Tecpan,* the post-Conquest seat of the Indian governors the Spaniards used to control native peoples till the late seventeenth century. Oral tradition locates the Aztecs' last stand on this spot.

CHURCH AND PLAZA OF LOS ANGELES: On Lerdo, 1 block west of Av. Santa Maria la Redonda. Santuario de Nuestra Señora de Los Angeles was built on part of the site of the sixteenth-century Capuchin church and convent, which was destroyed to make Lerdo Street in 1831. Now a neighborhood church of the poor. The Virgin housed therein is said to have appeared upon the water flooding the city, causing them to subside. Her festival and fair begins here on August 2, after which it continues at the Church of Santa Maria la Redonda.

MARKETS

Modern urbanism has erased the picturesque medieval-fair atmosphere of district public markets. New sanitary buildings, with such services as nurseries for children of women venders and chemical sprinkling systems to disinfect vegetables and fruit, now stand where formerly a welter of colorful, variegated street stalls and wandering hucksters provided lively drama. The following still have charms for visitors:

CHAPULTEPEC FLOWER MARKET at the Tacuba entrance to Chapultepec Park.

JAMAICA, at the continuation of Av. F. Marazan and Calzada Morelos, the largest wholesale vegetable, fruit, and flower depot. Not long ago it was the landing stage of Xochimilco garden stuff at the end of the famous Viga Canal, which is now covered over and part of Av. de la Viga, on which produce comes in by truck. Its dazzling merchandise and almost brawling bargaining merits a pre-breakfast visit between 5 and 8 A.M.

LAGUNILLA (Little Lake, because it was built on filled-in lake land), one of the earliest, largest markets, is in three separate buildings. The section on Allende (continuation of Bolívar) and Ecuador, a few blocks north of Zócalo, sells leather goods, some crafts, and toys. Open Sunday, when the traditional open-air market on nearby Calle República de Paraguay is open. Book-lovers' mecca; all kinds of antiques. The sellers know current prices (may even

147

overestimate values) and turn deaf ears to bargain hunters until—and only sometimes—near closing time. Often real "finds."

MERCED, named for the great Merced Church-Monastery, (built between 1634-1700) is still the economic heart of the almost intact, typically Colonial, Barrio de Merced—eighty blocks of seventeenth-, eighteenth-, and nineteenth-century houses, churches, and squares—protected against drastic change as a "Zona Tipica" by the Department of Colonial Monuments. These streets are hectic in the morning as produce trucks unload and sell to waiting retailers. Shops of certain blocks are wholesale depots of only one vegetable or fruit. Visitors should dodge their way through these crowded streets and squares to catch a glimpse of old-time trading in the shadow of the nobly proportioned, beautifully decorated old edifices before the trucks are banished and streets become quiet thoroughfares and their old buildings are cleaned up and mended to retain the face of the past but not the vigorous pulsing life of bygone centuries. Street stalls have gone. The market itself has been removed to huge buildings beyond the broad avenue of Anillo de Circunvalación. Visit the flower market and the basement handicraft section opening on Calle Ciprian. Be sure to visit the Cloisters of Merced Monastery, Calle Uruguay 170, where a primary school camps out in rude plank rooms on a balcony supported by the finest carved pillars in Mexico.

RODRIGUEZ MARKET, between Venezuela and Colombia, east of Carmen. A model market, named after ex-President Gen. Abelardo Rodriguez. Constructed around the old Carmelite Convent. The upper floor houses a theater and offices of the Civic Department of the Federal District. The patio, corridors, and stairways of the market have been decorated by a group of artists with modern frescoes, with subjects related to agriculture and the life around the market.

SAN JUAN MARKET, one of the oldest, now occupies several scattered buildings. The flower market (Luis Moya and Ernesto Pugibet) is a floral outburst not to be bypassed. Visitors should leave some cash reserves at the hotel before

148

inspecting the 126 stalls of its Mercado de Curiosidades, corner of Arco de Belén and Doctor Valenzuela (one block from the Salto de Agua fountain at the end of San Juan de Letrán). Don't lose your head—many trashy or machine-made articles are mixed with genuine handiwork. Bargain to your heart's content. If male salesmen forget their manners, please report to the Tourist Bureau.

SONORA MARKET, east on Fray Servando Teresa de Mier, just beyond Cine Sonora, small, wholesale, and retail, selling toys, pottery, and herbs. Among heaps of plastic toys are handmade wood and straw ones, delightful miniature household articles, clay whistles, banks. Truly cheaper by the dozen, one item can cost a *peso,* a dozen 2½ or 3 *pesos.* A good place to stock up on Christmas stocking trinkets.

TEPITO MARKET, north of Zócalo, via Argentina to Calle de Fray Bartolome de Las Casas to the plaza of the same name (site of an Aztec marketplace). Nearby is the old (the present 1734 building is on the site of the 1682 one) San Francisco de Tepito Church, now wearing a coat of ghastly yellow paint, but with Baroque harmony shining through. This former Thieves Market is now respectable in new conventional market buildings.

UNIVERSITY CITY

UNIVERSITY CITY (Ciudad Universitaria) (11 miles out via Insurgentes on Mexico-Cuernavaca Highway).

The National University of Mexico is the oldest, yet the most modern in North America. Founded in 1551, its spectacular new 50-million-dollar University City was inaugurated in January, 1954.

Construction was started by ex-President Miguel Alemán, an alumnus, in 1950. More than a hundred architects, numerous engineers, designers, sculptors, and artists, and some ten thousand laborers worked feverishly for two years but were unable to finish everything before the end of his term, December, 1952. So the last details and inauguration devolved upon Alemán's successor, President Adolfo Ruiz Cortines.

As soon as the doors were opened, some of the faculties began moving in. Formerly scattered about the city in European fashion, they now enjoy a U.S.-style campus, complete with all facilities.

The colorful University City rises in open country on the Pedregal, an ancient lava plain strewn with grotesque black boulders in striking constrast to trees, grass, and flowers. Its architecture is exotic, yet symbolic of modern Mexico—a blending of Indian, Spanish, and modern, its elements integrated in all aspects, even to the decorations and landscaping.

The buildings that are plainest in appearance have interiors of the finest Mexican marbles and woods. But not many are plain. The science group has seven amphitheaters that form a rippling contour and the engineering buildings are decorated with a series of concrete domes with tiny glass

Juan O'Gorman Mosaic—Library, University City

150

Siquieros Mosaic—Administration Building, University City

apertures. Above all the others rises the glass-sheathed Administration Tower, its metallic color offset by red panels and bands. There is a mural by Siqueiros of the students returning the fruits of their studies to the nation. Another mosaic mural, the work of Chavez Morado, appears on the Science Building, depicting the god and sources of science.

At one side of the campus, near the Olympic swimming pool, are the *frontón* ball courts, in the form of truncated pyramids with thick lava walls, reminiscent of the Ciudadela at San Juan Teotihuacán. On the opposite side of the highway lies the Olympic Stadium, its façade shaped to re-

151

semble the mouth of a crater, with a sculpture painting by Diego Rivera, portraying the history of Mexican sports from the days of the Mayas down to the present. The situation, form, and colors of this immense stadium, with a seating capacity of over a hundred thousand, make it the most extraordinary of its kind in the world.

But the most prominent and original of all the buildings is the library, by Juan O'Gorman, architect and artist. It is square with straight lines and a ten-story, windowless tower, all covered with colored mosaics, depicting the history of Mexican culture from pre-Conquest to modern times. The surface of this unique mural measures 4,700 meters and the number of stones that went into it is estimated at seven and a half million. The north wall portrays the prehistoric epoch, the south the Spanish, and the east and west the modern, the latter showing the blending of the three. The stones seem to become brighter as they age. Already they are a symphony of rich colors.

DIRECTORY OF MEXICO CITY

This directory is intended for rapid consultation and includes only items of special interest. Others may be found in the Anglo-American and classified telephone directories.

AIRLINE OFFICES:
   Aeronaves de Mexico, Reforma 46. Tel. 35-49-00.
   Aerovias Guest, Reforma 46. Tel. 35-49-00.
   Air France, Reforma 76. Tel. 46-91-40.
   American Airlines, Juárez 117. Tel. 35-94-70.
   Eastern Airlines, Reforma and Morelos. Tel. 35-78-50.
   KLM, Reforma 37. Tel. 35-10-00.
   Lineas Aéreas Picho, S.A., a feeder line operating in the states of Michoacán, Guerrero, and Colima.
   Mexicana de Aviación and Pan American World Airways, in same office, Av. Juárez 82. Tel. 18-12-60.
   TACA International Airlines, Reforma 52. Tel. 46-88-07.
   Western Airlines, Reforma 51. Tel. 46-90-40.

AMERICAN (U.S.) INSTITUTIONS:
   American Society, Av. Insurgentes S. 105.
   Benjamin Franklin Library, Niza 53. Open from 9 to 8; Saturday until 2.
   Chamber of Commerce, Lucerna 78.
   Club, Plaza Santos Degollado 10. Restaurant and bar.
   Embassy—Consulate and Embassy offices, corner of Reforma and Danubío. Embassy residence, Niza 53.
   Hospital, American British Cowdray, Victor Hugo 79. Tel. 25-09-52.

ART GALLERIES (Sales and Exhibitions):
   Central de Publicationes, Juarez 4.
   Galería Antonio Souza, Reforma 334-A.
   Galería de Arte de Coleccionistas, Reforma 325, ground floor.
   Galería Arte Contemporaneo, Amberes 12.
   Galería de Arte Mexicano, Milan 18.
   Galería de Arte Moderno, Roma 21.
   Galería de Artes Visuales, Varsovia 52.
   Galería Bryna, Reforma 404.
   Galería Genova, on inside plaza off Londres.
   Galería May Brooks, Genova 65-B.
   Galería Mexicana, Ramón Alcazar 8. Rivera paintings.
   Galería 1577, Av. Hidalgo 107.
   Galería San Angel, Galvez 23, Villa Obregón. Art gallery, bookstore, lending library, auditorium.
   Galería Tuso, Hamburgo 68.
   Museo Orozco, Hamburgo 113.
   Salon de Plastica Mexicana, Havre 7.
   Turok-Wasserman Gallery, Amazones 17.

ART SCHOOLS—Open to foreign students:
   Escuela Nacional de Artes Plásticas, Academia 22.
   Escuela de Pintura y Escultura, San Fernando 14.

BOOKS AND PERIODICALS:
   American Book Store, Madero 25.
   Antigua Librería de Robredo, corner of Guatemala y Argentina.
   Belles Artes, Juárez 18-D.

153

Central de Publicaciones, Juárez 4. Also inner plaza, off Londres.

Libreria Britanica, Villalongin 32; branch, Av. de Paz 14, San Angel. Current British books.

Libreria de Cristal in Alameda Park; many city branches.

Libreria Francesa; next door to Ambassadeurs Restaurant, on Reforma. French books and periodicals.

Libreria Herrero, Cinco de Mayo 4.

Porrua Hnos. y Cia., Argentina 15, and Juárez 18.

Bus Lines:

See page 22 for border connections. Consult your travel agent or hotel for domestic bus service. Lines include: Autos Pullman, Plaza de Buenavista 9; Autobuses de Oriente, Buenavista 9; Estrella de Oro, Fray Servando Teresa de Mier 74; and eight-passenger jitneys, Netzahualcoyotl 163. For local city ones, see telephone directory under *Camiones Urbanas para Pasajeros,* pp. 138-39, yellow section.

Consulates and Clubs (See also American Institutions):

British Embassy, Lerma 71.

Canadian Embassy and Consulate, Melchor Ocampo 463.

Country Club of Mexico, Churubusco, Calz. de Tlalpam.

Lions' Club (Club de Leones), Ures 23. Tel. 25-35-26.

Polo Club, Chapultepec Heights.

Rotary (Club Rotario), Londres 15.

University Club, Reforma 150.

Y.M.C.A., Av. Ejercito Nacional 253. Tel. 45-72-25.

Y.W.C.A., corner of Articulo 123 and Humboldt.

Cultural Relations Institutes:

The three following have classes in the official languages of their countries, also lectures on Mexican cultural subjects; musicals and art exhibitions. Each institute has its own library.

Instituto Anglo-Mexicano, Maestro Antonio Caso 125. (English-Mexican.)

Instituto Francés-Mexicano, Nazas 43. (French-Mexican).

Instituto Mexicano-Americano, Hamburgó 115. (Mexican-North American).

GLASS FACTORY

Avalos Hnos, Carretones 5. Fascinating exhibit.

INSTITUTIONS OF HIGHER LEARNING:

Escuela de Verano y Intercambio Universitario (Summer School and University Exchange of the National University of Mexico), Ciudad Universitaria de Mexico, D. F.

Apply to the Ciudad Universitaria de Mexico, D. F., for information about entrance credits, degrees, etc.

University of the Americas, Mexico-Toluca Highway Km. 16, beyond capital limits. Spanish literature, Latin-American culture, Mexican art, archeology, anthropology, and folklore.

MUSEUMS:

El Anáhuacalli, Calle Museo, in San Pablo de Tepetlapa, just beyond Coyoacán, off the main artery Av. División del Norte.

Galería Taurina of Celerino Velazquez, Calle Monclova 50. Open 9 A.M. to 8 P.M. Free.

Instituto Indigenista Interamericano, Niños Heroes 139. Open 10 A.M. to 2 P.M. except Sundays. Free.

Museo Casa de Venustiano Carranza, Lerma 35. Open 10 A.M. to 5 P.M. except Sundays. Free.

Museo de Armas, Secretaría de la Defensa Nacional, Lomas de Sotelo. Open Mon. to Fri. 10 A.M. to 2 P.M., Sat. 10 A.M. to 1 P.M. Free.

Museo de Arte Moderno, Chapultepec Park. Entrance near Bolívar Statue. Open 10 A.M. to 5 P.M. every day. Admission 1 *peso*.

Museo de C.E.D.A.M. (Club de Exploraciones y Deportes Acuáticos de México), Museum of Marine Archeology, Carlos B. Cetina.

Museo de Figuras de Cera (Wax Figures), Argentina 21A. Open 9:30 A.M. to 5:30 P.M. Admission 1 *peso*.

Museo de Geología, Plaza de Santa María de la Ribera. Open 8 A.M. to 2 P.M. on week days. Free.

Museo de Historia Natural in New Chapultepec Park, off Av. Constituyentes. New building. Magnificent scientific displays and wild-habitat exhibits. Open 10 A.M. to 5 P.M. daily except Monday. Admission 1 *peso*.

Museo de la Ciudad de México, in handsome Colonial palace of Condes de Santiago de Calimaya, corner of Pino Suárez and República de El Salvador, kittycornered from historic Hospital de Jesús and the restored Church of Jesús where Cortés is buried.

Museo de las Culturas (Casa de Moneda), Paseo de la Reforma, opposite the zoo.

Museo Dinámica, Tepexpan 14, Barrio de Niño Jesús, Coyoacan.

Museo Etnológico, corner of Seminario and Guatemala with Ruinas de Zona Pre-Hispanica de Santa Teresa. Open 9 A.M. to 5 P.M. daily. Admission 1 *peso*.

Museo Nacional de Antropología, Chapultepec Park.

Museo Nacional de Artes Industrias y Populares, Corpus Cristi church, at No. 44.

Museo Nacional de Artes Plásticas, Palace of Fine Arts.

Museo Nacional de Banderas Historicas, Palacio Nacional. Open 9 A.M. to 2 P.M., except Sundays.

Museo Nacional de Historia, Chapultepec Castle. See page 143.

Museo Nacional de Pedagogía, Av. President Mazaric 526 (corner Bernard Shaw St.). Open Mon. to Fri., 8 A.M. to 2 P.M.; Sat. 8 A.M. to 1 P.M. Free.

Museo Postal, Correo Mayor, San Juan de Letrán. Open 9 A.M. to 1 P.M.

Observatorio Meteorologico, Av. Observatorio 192, Tacubaya. Open 8 A.M. to 2 P.M., except Sundays. Free.

Pinacoteca Virreinal de San Diego, Calle Doctor Mora 7, facing western end of Alameda Park. Supreme examples of Colonial paintings displayed fittingly in former monastery headquarters of Spanish Inquisition.

Stamp Museum, top floor, Post Office.

PHOTO SUPPLIES:
American Kodak, Madero 43.
La Ansco, 16 de Septiembre 13.
Calpini, Madero 34.
Photo Regis, Juárez 80.

156

PUBLIC AGENCIES AND SCHOOLS:

For information on health, social service, etc., apply to the Dirección de Cooperación Interamericana de Salubridad Pública, Secretaría de Salubridad y Assistencia, Paseo de la Reforma y Calz. de Tacubaya. For information on public schools and education, apply to the Secretaría de Educacíon Pública, Argentina y Gonzalez Obregón.

RAILROAD OFFICES:

Ferrocarriles Nacionales de Mexico (National Railroads of Mexico), information office, Calle Gante 9, off Madero. Helpful and courteous staff. Excellent quarterly train schedule and price bulletin. Expendio de Boletos (Ticket Office), Bolívar 19, corner of Cinco de Mayo; Tel. 13-57-18. Open weekdays only, 9 A.M. to 1 P.M. and 3:30 to 5 P.M.; Saturdays, 9 A.M. to 1 P.M. or at Gran Estación Central de Buenavista (Buenavista Grand Central Station). Open daily, Sundays, holidays from 6 A.M. to 9:30 P.M.; Tel. 47-89-72. Tickets sold at both places for Ferrocarril Mexicano-Puebla trains and for trips to Yucatán, the national railway system connecting at Coatzacoalcos with Ferrocarril del Sureste, S. C. T., for Campeche and Merida. Oficina de Equipajes (Baggage Office) at Buenavista Grand Central Station.

Ferrocarril de Chihuahua al Pacifico, Baja California 245-901; Tel. 12-83-35.

Southern Pacific (Ferrocarril Sud-Pacifico de Mexico) Czda. Tlalpan 1956-6; Tel. 49-22-02.

SHOPS:

There are three main shopping centers for Mexican arts and crafts, novelties and antiques, furniture and candies, modern art and pre-Columbian artifacts (or good copies), glassware, silver, jewelry, leather goods, objets d'art and bricabrac, old books and straw toys, imported articles, etc., etc., etc. The first and oldest begins at the Portales in the Zócalo and runs west along the main arteries (Tacuba, Cinco de Mayo—one-*peso* cab to Reforma route), Madero, 16 de Septiembre, and connecting cross streets. The trail continues up Av. Juárez to the Caballito (across the Alameda are the Hidalgo old bookshops) to meet Reforma and on to the smart tourist section of hotels, shops, galleries, and eating places—from snack bars to the most de luxe restaurants—in the Niza-Londres-Genova-Hamburgo-Amberes neighborhood. Here are glitter, lure, and many genuine values, but the discriminating should not start buying before visiting lovely old San Angel, the new center of antique and handicraft shops and art galleries. Lower suburban expenses, hence lower prices. On Saturdays, from 10 A.M. to 8 P.M., the gayest place in the city is Bazar Sábado, Plaza de San Jacinto (superb lunches and pastry, too), a pioneer in attracting creative, sophisticated Mexicans as well as non-Mexicans to sightsee, eat well, and meet friends or make new ones while selecting the best contemporary art and handicraft treasures from all over Mexico.

A newcomer, Mansion San Angel, Av. Revolución 54, is a village in itself. A restaurant (moderate) indoors; a large garden one in the shadow of the Carmen Monastery; a bar; galleries of antiques and modern art; and almost a score of attractive little shops carrying all known arts and crafts. Prepare to spend hours. Another newcomer is El Centro de Arte y Artesania, Amargura 4.

Albus, Av. Juárez. Also Londres 118. Crafts, clothing.

Aries, at entrance to Del Prado Hotel, leather goods.

Artes de Mexico, Amberes 61-A. Fabrics, decorative accessories, copies of Colonial furniture. Essentially wholesale, but retail sales made, also by mail.

Baretto's, Revillagigedo 29. Unusual folk-craft objects.

Casa Cervantes, Juárez 18. Good assortment of dishes, glassware, Oaxaca tablecloths and napkins, peasant dresses.

Los Castillo, Juárez 76, mezzanine. Amberes 41. Famous jewelry.

Chimalpopoca, Luis Moya 19. Mexican crafts.

Condesa de Pontevel, Londres 104. Highly esteemed by Mexican women for clothing and accessories.

Domus, Hamburgo 40. Custom-made furniture, handwoven materials for curtains, lamps, etc.

La Esmeralda, Madero 51 and Niza 33. Fine china and jewelry.

Gaby, Amberes 58A. Good bags.

Galería La Granja, Bolívar 16. Fine antiques.

India Bonita, Juárez 14. Silver, precious metals.

Jim Tillett, Reforma 124 and Niza 39. **Distinguished** hand-woven fabrics and resort wear.

Lacquered woodwork available at 81 B Genova.

Lena Gordon, Florencia 51, first floor. Beautiful fabrics.

Lila Bath's, Niza 40. Attractive sports and beach wear.

Louvre, Madero 45. Good silver and Swiss watches.

Marisa Ruby, Niza 45. High-style originals in women's clothing and accessories.

Museo Nacional de Artes e Industrias Populares, Juárez 44. Folk arts from the country. Prices often too high.

La Nacional, Juárez 40. Luggage, gloves, and purses.

Oriani, Niza 15. Men's casual clothing and accessories.

Plateria Tane, Amberes 70. Silver flatware and tea services.

Russel Davis, Florencia 32. Gifts, native arts, crafts, etc.

Sanborn, Madero 4 and Reforma 45. Good assortment of folk arts, toys, silver jewelry and tableware.

San Francisco, Niza 46. Good traditional silver.

Taxco Hermoso, Venustiano Carranza 105. Sandals (*huaraches*) for men, women, and children.

Vallina, Córdoba 12A. Good bags and sweaters.

Victor, Filomena Mata 15B. Handicrafts and masks.

Xochipili, Hamburgo 108. Beautiful candles, crafts.

AGENCIES OF INFORMATION AND TRAVEL SERVICES:

The Government assumes responsibility for the safety and happiness of strangers within its borders and regards them not merely as profitable clients of the second largest national industry, the one "without chimney," but as potential ambassadors of amity who, having been shown the country courteously and hospitably, will return to their own with an enlightened understanding of Mexico and Mexicans. No empty policy this, because government agencies exist to help tourists. The chief one, Dirección General de Turismo, the Government Tourist Department, Paseo de la Reforma 35, distributes many informative bulletins, has a large staff to answer tourists' questions and help them solve their problems. Call the Office of Quejas (Complaints), tel. 35-81-20, ext. 14, about overcharging, theft, injustices of any kind, or any emergency such as loss of tourist card or other

The Dirección de Auxilio Turístico, Tourist Aid Department, on the sixth floor (Tel. 35-81-20, ext. 25) maintains a special Radio Patrol Service (Radio Patrullas de Auxilio Turístico) to aid distressed tourists. Its green jeeps cover many main routes; service is being extended. A branch of the Department occupies the street-floor office at Juarez 89 (Tels. 21-13-20, 12-72-08), with the Pemex Travel Club. Here are racks of free publications and personnel to advise regarding trips and interesting art exhibits. On the second floor (stairway at rear) are offices of the Asociación Mexicana de Turismo (Mexican Tourist Association), an organization of private character, cooperating with official agencies to publicize tourist attractions.

The local telephone directory has an easily identifiable green-page tourist section in Spanish and English. Most large hotels have a travel office to dispense information, arrange local sightseeing as well as long trips, make reservations, etc.

MOTORISTS' ASSOCIATIONS:

Asociación Mexicana Automovilística (AMA, Mexican Automobile Association), Club Consejo Nacional, Av. Chapultepec 276 (Tel. 14-93-57).

Asociación Nacional Automovilística (National Automobile Association), Miguel Schultz 136 (Tel. 46-02-67; emergency service 35-08-78).

TOURIST AGENCIES:

A few of many reputable private but government-bonded ones are:

Aguirre, Madrid 69-13

American Express (See Wells Fargo)

Consejeros de Viajes, Génova 30. Tel. 25-75-20

Garza's Travel Service, S. A., Londres 106. Tel. 25-77-05

Gray Line Tours (Linea Gris), Londres 166. For local excursions call 18-64-84; outside city, 11-47-56.

Hopes Travel Agency, Buenavista 3-507

International Holiday Tours, Av. Juárez 30-112

Travel, S. A., Av. Insurgents S. 202

Turismo Pancho Lona, Balderas 32

Wells Fargo, Niza 22. Tel. 18-11-80

Williams, Morris, Av. Juárez 56-504

SHORT TRIPS FROM MEXICO CITY

THE GUADALUPE SANCTUARY—
PYRAMIDS OF TEOTIHUACÁN—
ACOLMAN CHURCH-MONASTERY

Visit the Pyramids in your own or rented car, or join a guided tour (several daily ones) which includes stops at the Guadalupe Sanctuary, the Acolman Monastery, and a roadside demonstration of *maguey* plant handling. There is frequent second-class bus service from Calle Alarcón 19, but the long uncomfortable trip permits no stopovers. Take a picnic lunch or eat at the Grutas, Mirador-Pyramid, or other zone restaurant. Take sun glasses and hat; wear sneakers or comfortable walking shoes. To appreciate the poetic grandeur of Teotihuacán, spend a night or two in luxurious comfort at the Hotel-Restaurant Pyramides in nearby San Juan village.

SHRINE OF THE VIRGIN OF GUADALUPE, in Villa Madero, is a fifteen-minute drive from the center via Calzada de Guadalupe or the broad ancient pilgrim way named for the fifteen Mysteries of the Rosary, Calzada de los Misterios. Of fifteen handsome, sculptured wayside shrines, dedicated August 14, 1696, to these Mysteries, eight still stand in dilapidated melancholy. Or turn right off Insurgentes N. into Calle Montevideo at Cine Linda Vista. Bus and trolley service are available from the corner of San Juan de Letrán and Juárez. This internationally revered shrine, always interesting, is impressively crowded by worshippers on Sundays and Holy Days.

LEGEND OF THE VIRGIN: Ten years after Tenochtitlan fell, the enslaved Indians had lost confidence in the Spanish missionaries' Catholic teachings. New converts were few, earlier ones backsliding. In vain Bishop Zumárraga ordered all pagan shrines demolished. The Indians clung to their own faith, strengthened by the knowledge that a fifty-two-

161

year cycle was closing; the birth of the Sixth Sun was at hand—promise of deliverance from the Spaniards. It was the Aztec Cuauhtlatohuac (Azt., "He Who Talks Like an Eagle"), converted and baptized as Juan Diego, who decided the outcome. Trudging to Mass in Tlaltilolco, December 9, 1531, across the Cerro de Tepeyac (Azt., "First Foothill"), his way was barred by the Spanish *Morena* (Sp., "Dark-complexioned") Virgin of Guadalupe. She showed him where she wished a shrine built for her that she might be near her Indian children, to protect them with her love—the freshly-razed site of the temple of the much loved Aztec Virgin Goddess of Earth and Corn, Tonantzin (Azt., "Our Little Mother").

Juan carried her message to Bishop Zumárraga only to be dismissed as a visionary. He met the Virgin again on the eleventh. The Bishop demanded proof of the apparition. The next day, hurrying for medicine for an uncle dying of smallpox, Juan avoided his usual path—but not the Virgin. Promising him his uncle would recover, she bade him pluck Castillian roses suddenly blooming on the wintry, stony hilltop to carry to the sceptical prelate. But when in the Bishop's presence, Juan opened his *tilma* (native *serape*-like, *maguey*-fiber cloak), in which he had carried the roses, imprinted on its coarse fabric was the bright portrait of the Virgin, painted against a sun-rayed, golden background. The Sixth Sun had risen in unexpected guise! This portrait is said to be the likeness still hanging above the Basilica's High Altar.

The sweet, dark-skinned Virgin consoled the suffering Indians and eventually won the hearts of their conquerors. Converts flocked to her first shrine, built in 1532, and devotion to this miracle-performing portrait burned even more fervently as centuries passed. In 1745 the Pope declared the Virgin of Guadalupe Patroness of New Spain. She smiled from the banners of Mexican Independence fighters in 1810 (The Royal Spanish troops followed the standard of the Virgin of Remedios), and was crowned "Queen of Wisdom and Empress of the Americas" in 1945. Her worshippers multiply; pilgrims flock from far countries. New churches in Mexico and other lands are dedicated to her.

162

THE SANCTUARY: Aloof from streaming traffic lanes and and mundane activities at the rear of a huge fenced atrium, backed against the landscaped rock gardens of Cerro de Tepeyac, the Virgin's severe, gray, earthquake-scarred basilica tilts rakishly westward, its Capuchin chapel and office wing pulling eastward at a sharply alarming angle due to shrinking subsoil. Trim orderliness without and within the basilica denotes a new order—pagan and medieval litter and casualness overcome by modern standards of sanitation and respect for sacred places. Although a multitude gathers to do her honor, the Virgin's chief festival, December 12, the anniversary of her apparition, is a decorous holiday. Street vendors are kept outside the atrium fence, amusement booths well beyond the sanctuary. In assigned parts of the atrium, dignified, brightly costumed dance groups honor the Virgin with dances their ancestors performed for her pagan predecessor.

LA CAPILLA DEL POCITO (Chapel of the Little Well), an exquisite Mudejar tiled and domed shelter for the well dug where a spring opened at the Virgin's feet at Tepeyac's base, is a forlorn wreck, closed now. Up the hill's steep landscaped face a broad tile-decorated stairway winds, decorated with a lone eighteenth-century votive stone sail, "Vela del Marino," the offering of rescued shipwrecked sailors, unbroken survivor of the famous windstorm of May 24, 1916. On the walls of the eighteenth-century chapel, LA CAPILLA DEL CERRITO (Chapel of the Little Hill), built where Juan Diego gathered winter roses, are Fernando Leal's simple, unforgettable murals of Guadalupe's appealing legend.

MOTORIST NOTE: Insurgentes North to Laredo Highway, C.N. 85, now well marked. Keep to inner traffic lane in the city to be able to read signs. At 14 Km. after passing the Indios Verdes statues at City limits, watch for Entronque Morelos (and its toll booth) and turn into the roughly 22-kilometer toll road to the Archeological Zone of San Juan Teotihuacán. Watch for turn right to visit the Museo de Tepexpan, built where a mammoth hunter's body (reproduced here) was found. Open 9 A.M. to 1 P.M., 3 to 6 P.M. Admission two *pesos*. From this museum one can take a road which is a pretty fifteen-minute drive to Texcoco.

SAN AUGUSTIN ACOLMAN is a frowning, buttressed and battlemented, medieval Augustinian church-monastery, right of the road, at the entrance to the village of Acolman, built 1539-1560 and reconstructed in 1785. It was partially submerged in the valley's backed-up lake waters (their mark is still visible) for decades and was rescued and made a national monument in the 1920's. Here is one of Mexico's two finest Gothic churches (the other at Huejotzingo, Puebla). It has a notable vaulted ceiling and distinctive early Renaissance (Plateresque) carved entrance (nude Indians carrying baskets on their heads) and windows. The oddly high chancel has fine column supports. The monastery, a museum, guards old religious books, art, and a few relics of proud pre-Hispanic Alcolhuan, who were made serfs to Conquistado-encomiendista, Pedro de Solis, in 1521. Open 10 A.M. to 1 P.M., 3 to 6 P.M. daily.

THE ARCHEOLOGICAL ZONE OF SAN JUAN TEOTIHUACÁN. Open 8 A.M. to 6 P.M. Admission, 4 *pesos,* Sundays free. Visitors will be restricted in some sections until some 50 or more mounds are excavated and the buildings restored as faithfully as their buried remnants permit—all made easily accessible by a circling road with convenient parking lots. The museum, opened April, 1963, and a restaurant and souvenir shops are located across from the Citadel.

Teotihuacán's place in the historical timetable as the earliest of the three brilliant imperial Meso-American civilizations, will be established only when the findings of the present explorations have been summarized and correlated —probably not before 1967. Already it is demonstrable that Teotihuacán is centuries older than had ever been suspected. Probably the first phase of its Archaic (or Formative) Period began between 300 and 200 B.C. Its first temples and secular edifices were constructed after 100 B.C., inspired by the creative religious upsurge that reached its apogee in the magnificent architecture and art of the Classic period, about 300 A.D., three to four centuries earlier than was ever estimated. From this exalted cultural summit, Teotihuacán slowly and painfully declined, its art and architecture displaying the elaboration, refinement, and embellishment of decadence, not new design or art forms. Hints that its vitality was drained by attacks of hostile migrants or by the absorption of less developed nomad groups (probably Nahuatl-speaking peoples) and by internal dissensions are appearing, but no clear evidence that the city was abruptly abandoned after being overrun and sacked by the semi-nomadic Tolteca about 950 A.D., as had been supposed. It seems more likely that the Tolteca found a dying city, its fanes and palaces decaying, and occupied only its habitable fringe for a brief period. There is still no evidence to contradict the oral tradition that the Nonohualca (literally "deaf and dumb people": *i.e.,* unable to speak or understand the local language), the skilled artisans Ce Acatl Topiltzín brought around 950 A.D. to build Tula (see p. 194) came from Teotihuacán, either persuaded or forced to move by their conquerors. Migrants from Teotihuacán also settled in Azcapotzalco, now part of Mexico City, stimulating its expansion and cultural flowering as a city kingdom.

Designed in conformity with their religio-cosmological concepts by priestly architects to be a religious ceremonial center, every detail of Teotihuacán harmonizes with certain annual movements of the heavenly bodies. Dedicated primarily to the Sun God, the orientation of his pyramid-temple is the key to the city's master plan. The inner metropolis is a series of spacious, temple-bordered plazas; its axis is a fifty-yard-wide corridor, traced recently to the southern foothills, and ill-named the "Calzada de los Muertos" (Highway of the Dead). Civic buildings of palatial dimensions extend the center; less regal residences and oratories frame the known outskirts of the eight-square-mile area. Beyond, the lowly homes of farmers and craftsmen spread out in a wide zone encircling the city proper. That initial design, probably the first instance of city planning, certainly on such a scale, in this hemisphere or beyond, was altered, added to, but never distorted, although buildings were rebuilt or reconstructed for new uses. Only a powerful centralized absolutist government, assuredly theocratic, could have built so grandiosely and reigned for many prosperous centuries, commanding the loyal services of the enormous population needed to build and maintain the city. Dominating, but not by military force, adjacent regions for a hundred miles around, Teotihuacán influenced, at various periods, peoples of such far places as present-day Guanajuato, Guerrero, the southern Mexican states to the Guatemala highlands, and partway to the Gulf Coast. Neither the language its inhabitants spoke nor their name for their city is known. But if not its original name, because of the city's role, Teotihuacán may be the Aztec's literal translation of it.

As the myth of the "Quinta Sol" (The Fifth Sun) relates, Teotihuacán was the terrestrial home of the gods. Despite luxurious surroundings, they wearied of perpetual darkness and tried, unsuccessfully, four times, to create light. For the fifth a huge fire was kindled on the Sun Temple, into which wealthy Tecuciztecatl threw lordly offerings but failed, four times, to cast himself into the blaze. Then lowly Nanahuatzin tossed his humble gifts into the blaze, and leaped unhesitatingly after them. Immediately appeared the sun! The shamed Tecuciztecatl quickly sacrificed himself and the moon appeared. Angered that it was as bright as the sun, a god hurled a rabbit at it so forcibly that the image of the rabbit remained imprinted there, dulling its glitter. Thus Mexicans see a rabbit, not a man, in the moon. Despite this nursery-tale touch, this is a profoundly spiritual myth, understandable only as part of its whole cycle, emphasizing the city's holy character—not merely the God's abode, but the birthplace of the life-sustaining heavenly bodies.

The sober massive grandeur of its ruined buildings reveal their builder's mathematical and scientific genius. Unless the present excavations reveal more painted, ornamented, frescoed buildings and statuary, their poetical, mystical thought and creative powers may never be fully known. For a few centuries the peculiar genius of Teotihuacán lived on in other peoples' borrowings. The best of Aztec culture was fraught with Teotihuacan's noble concepts. Its light was extinguished when the Spaniards came.

*Pyramid of the Sun and Plumed Serpent
on Temple of Quetzalcoatl—San Juan Teotihuacán*

THE PYRAMID OF THE SUN: The stark, fearsome, 215-foot-high, dominant mass of the second largest Meso-American structure (see Cholula, p. 221) is only the ugly, hard-surfaced core, bristling with rows of the projecting supports of its original batter-style stone facing, brilliantly painted and decorated in its heyday, stripped off some sixty years ago by a bumbling seeker of inner chambers—a vandalism that also distorted the pyramid's linear measurements and symmetry. Standing in a temple-bordered court, its east-west axis (17° north of true east-west) coincides exactly—and deliberately—with the horizon point of the setting sun the day it passes its zenith, the primal orientation that dictated the position of the other temples. The western front, which a receding, broad stair flight climbs from one body to another, narrower one, is 715 feet long. On the summit, where peddlers plague visitors to buy "genuine" glass jewels, on a 130-square-foot base, stood the temple sheltering the gold-bedecked monolithic image of the Sun God, Tonatuih.

167

THE PYRAMID OF THE MOON, now being uncovered, has its back to CERRO GORDO (The Fat Hill), the City's chief stone quarry. From its broad forecourt the Highway of the Dead runs southward. Only 136 feet high, its stand on an eminence brings its summit in line with the higher Sun Pyramid's top. The measurement of both the north and south side is 486 feet; the others measure only 390 feet. Centuries ago, on the floor of a newly opened building in this plaza, an idler scratched the design for the ancient game, *patolin*, still played in remote villages, a poignant trace of ordinary humanity in this depersonalized dead city.

PALACE OF THE QUETZALPAPALOTL (Bird-Headed Butterflies), another newly opened building in this plaza, reveals aspects of Teotihuacan at the time of its greatest glory. The inside walls are painted red and decorated with polychromed, geometric designs, not seen here before, and encrusted with mica discs; thick mud-stone roofs, their ceilings painted red, are supported by wood-beam-enforced, adobe-stone posts; and three are elaborately carved pillars, their bas-reliefs once polychromed and their shallow hollows filled with discs and ovals of brilliant black obsidian. Here Teotihuacan's lost beauty begins to glimmer anew. The temple's name is derived from the bird-headed, butterfly-like carvings on several pillars.

HIGHWAY OF THE DEAD: All the unexcavated mounds that line this broad avenue, now coming to be known more accurately and less gruesomely as "El Camino Viejo" (The Old Road), are being opened up, their uncovered building remains being restored rapidly. Of those restored years ago there stands in the first court, south of the Plaza of the Moon Pyramid, the TEMPLE OF AGRICULTURE, named for the stylized murals depicting seed and food being presented to the gods. These faded soon after exposure, fortunately not before they had been copied. Next comes the PLAZA OF COLUMNS. Then, beyond the mounds in the west court of the Sun Pyramid, is the group containing the TEMPLE OF THE MICA FLOOR. Curious the symbolic meaning of mica that two layers, 29 square meters each, should have been laid down, then carefully covered over by an ordinary native cement floor. The next group is LOS SUBTERRANEOS (Vaults) or, more awkwardly, "The Superimposed Buildings," as if one structure upon and over another were not too conventional a practice then to be pointed out. The chambers of the lower original building have buttressed walls, pedestals, wide stairways, and—like every other Teotihuacán building —a drainage and water system. The last cluster restored here to date has a building called, for the numerous clay effigies of the Rain God found within it, the TEMPLE OF TLALOC.

The highway descends on southward between its overgrown mounds, crossing the present motor road and the bridge over the San Juan River, and runs on, passing in front of LA CIUDADELA (The Citadel). Never a fortification, this roughly 400-yard-square ceremonial court, oriented to the Sun's zenith, resembles a walled encampment. But the massive, six-meter-high walls are a continuous broad base for identical two-bodied pyramids; twelve restored ones minus their temples, four to each side; and the rear (east) ones still rough mounds. A rhythmic pattern of identical stairways to the platform, alternating with similar flights to the tops of the pyramids, relieves the starkness of the inner two-stepped walls and the formal severity of the quadrangle. These templed ramparts are, however, subsidiary to the deceptively insignificant, forlorn little pyramid in the middle of the court. A flight of thirteen steps mounts each side, each step symbolizing a year, the total representing the ancients' 52-year time cycle. As each cycle closed, lest the sun not return to begin a new one, and the world perish in cold and darkness, the anguished people and their priests doused every light and lamented and prayed all the fateful night. At the first hint of returning light, the ceremony of the New Fire began. Its climax was the lighting of a new fire, burning promise of another 52 years of existence. The detail that suggests that the little pyramid of 52 steps is the site where the new fire was lit, is its perfect alignment with the exact center of the Sun Pyramid's precinct and the center of a ruined temple on Cerro Gordo. Here, in the Citadel's heart, must the new fire have been kindled; then, on Cerro Gordo, another beacon was lit—visible throughout the valley.

THE TEMPLE OF QUETZACOATL (Azt., "Plumed Serpent") at the rear (east) of the Citadel, dramatizes the custom of building a pyramid over and around an earlier one, usually at the beginning of a 52-year cycle. Four bodies of the six-stepped outer pyramid, its west front interrupted by a broad flight of stairs, still stand—a shield before the uncovered face of the early inner pyramid, the most splendorous, exuberant façade preserved in Central Mexico. The balustrades of the latter's westerly staircase are studded with projecting, fearsome, carved serpent heads. On both sides of this stairway, rows of carven stone masks of the God Tlaloc (or his predecessor) alternate with projecting serpent visages, either zoomorphic embodiments of the aged God, Quetzalcoatl, or the fire serpents who served the sun. The eleven plumes framing each head seem like flower petals. Undulating serpent bodies fill the panels between the masks and carven heads, binding them into artistic unity. Scattered in empty spaces are the Water God's emblems—scallops and other sea shells. Some serpent eyes still gleam with obsidian pupils, and traces of paint are visible.

Temple of Quetzalcoatl

TEPANTITLA: Tlaloc's merry paradise—where the drowned, lightning-struck victims of famine and disfiguring diseases, such as leprosy, disport eternally in a burgeoning, watered garden (dancing, swimming, chasing butterflies, playing ball, eating fruit)—is a startling frescoed concept that can be seen in a cruciform house, on the main street of San Francisco Mazapan, in the Sun Pyramid's shadow; it is the Rain God's shrine in thirsty, cactus-*maguey*-spiked terrain. On another wall a procession of Tlaloc's priests chant as they scatter seeds. Tantalizing mural fragments cling to other walls.

TETITLA (Azt., "Stony Place"), near the zone entrance, is a Tlaloc oratory. Murals present him in varied guises. From the red-painted hands of one portrayal drip exaggerated raindrops. Feral beasts pace some walls. Elegant coyotes are marked as Tlaloc's own by pelts of *petate* weave, a common reed mat design.

YAYAHUALA, just across the road, where the newly uncovered sidewalks—three meters wide and bordered by a drainage ditch—join to form city blocks, has three shrines, many small rooms. Fresco fragments depict the two-sun design and Quetzalcoatl's morning-star device. Its trash pit held a treasure hoard of broken pottery and figurines. Nearby ZACUALA, a larger complex of rectangular rooms around 3 patios (a sanctuary in the largest central one), may have been a monastery. Quetzalcoatl, Tlaloc, and a host of elaborately attired figures occupy murals, painstakingly, almost miraculously, re-assembled from thousands of bits and flakes (the clearly marked fill-ins are modern wizardry). Notable is the man or god bearing a basket of varicolored corn. A jaguar-masked, singing woman or water goddess, wearing a regal plumed headdress and water-symbol-marked jade necklace, carries a similarly decorated shield. In the murals of nearby ATETELA (Presa, "Dam") the God Nanahuatl stands fairly free within an ornate frame, exuberantly bordered by a braided garland of serpent bodies painted with the star of the sea, their masked heads intertwined with heads of Tlaloc and his aquatic animal satellites.

Visit the home workshops in nearby villages, some mere clusters of houses, where skilled potters and carvers turn out beautiful reproductions of old Teotihuacán ceramics and obsidian carvings, even making figurines in the very old clay molds of their grandsires. They are also acute and convincing salesmen. San Juan village has a lively *fiesta* on July 21 or the closest Sunday to that date.

Books to prepare visitors or deepen their memories are *La Población del Valle de Teotihuacán* by the late Dr. Manuel Gamio, who not only restored many structures but also rescued the valley peoples from destitution, stimulating agriculture and crafts; the *Official Guide* to the zone; *The Temple of Quetzalcoatl* by the French archeologist, Laurette Séjourné.

EXCURSIONS TO MEXICO CITY'S SOUTHERN SUBURBS

The exploding metropolis has absorbed many villages of the southern end of the Valley of Anahuac, erasing former boundaries, turning some into indistinguishable *colonias,* granting a few the status of political boroughs—delegations and subdelegations. The personalities of several are withstanding the impact of urbanization. So many rustic delights and Colonial and artistic interests remain, a visitor cannot even peek at them all in one day. Fortunately the many streets and speedways that converge toward the city's southern tip, together with the constant bus and trolley service available, make it easy to visit and revisit any one or more celebrated points during leisure hours instead of dutifully touring from one to another on a grim endurance race to crowd a glimpse of them all into a single outing.

MOTORIST NOTE: Direct arteries south from the heart of the city are the speed lanes of Antonio Abad—Calzada de Tlálpan to Churubusco and Tlálpan, and turn-off to Ixtapalapa and Xochimilco. Avenidas Insurgentes Sur and Revolución cut through Villa Obregón (formerly San Angel) and speed to the University and the archeological zones of Copilco and Cuicuilco, and turn off to Tlálpan. Cross streets connect these avenues with Avenidas Patriotismo and Constitución and the latest speedway Anillo Periférico, others in turn with the Calzada de Tlálpan. Coyoacán is connected with these areas on all sides; the most direct route to its center is south on Avenida Coyoacán.

Insurgentes one-*peso* taxi jitneys go as far as the city limits and enter the University grounds.

DESIERTO DE LEONES, 15 miles along on Camino del Desierto from Insurgentes South (also just off C.N. 15 road to Toluca). A Carmelite convent of great beauty, a fashionable Colonial·retreat of the world-weary rich, built in 1602. Now a national monument, open daily to 6 P.M. Evidence of pentitential self-castigation is ·in sharp contrast to the flowering patios and gardens surrounding the woodland, once the property of the Leones family and now a popular picnic park with playgrounds and rustic restaurants. Or, before proceeding to Desierto de Leones, turn from Insurgentes at the same place into the lane right of the conspicuous marker in the narrow park, Calle de Alta Vista. Park and ramble, or drive at a snail's pace, through these tranquil residential San Angel streets. The Ambassadeur Restaurant has a garden dining room. San Angel Inn, a seventeenth-century Carmelite convent, on Alta Vista, now a beautiful restaurant and shopping center, is across from Diego Rivera's former studio.

VILLA OBREGÓN, sprawling City Delegation, takes in San Angel Inn and other districts and former hamlets. West of Insurgentes and a large area east of it, it occupies and runs beyond the limits of the pre-Conquest city, Chimalistac (Azt., "Place of White Shields"), and others. It was named for Mexico's former president, General Alvaro Obregón, assassinated by a religious fanatic in 1928; the place is marked by a stately memorial with sculpture by Ignacio Asunsolo, in a garden park facing Insurgentes. At the bottom of the central well is the bare cement floor where the General fell dead. In a display case on the main floor is the preserved hand he lost at the battle of Celaya, a pre-Conquest-flavored token of respect.

Turn right from Insurgentes, across from the Obregón Monument and just beyond the gasoline station, into Av. de la Paz (Librería Inglesa, at right, No. 14); ¾ block into Plaza del Carmen, divided into two parts by Av. Revolución. On the right, before crossing the avenue, there is a German restaurant, Jardin del San Angel. Take the street at the extreme right directly into the Plaza of San Jacinto or go up Madero on the left to turn right into San Jacinto. Inexpensive Posada San Angelito, Plaza del Carmen 17, is a pleasant base for rambling and absorbing the neighborhood's delights, or keep left to turn into Calle Dr. Gálvez (Bazar Sábado—is at No. 23), left, back to Av. Revolución near Convento del Carmen.

SAN JACINTO PLAZA, Colonial heart of San Angel (district named for San Angelo Martír, whom Spanish monks persuaded local Indians to accept as their patron saint). Conspicuous on the north side is Casa de Mirador or Casa Risca, art museum and library, given to Mexico by her great international jurist, Isidro Fabela, 1962, along with his library and superb painting collection.

A plaque on the second building from the northwest corner is dedicated to ". . . soldiers of heroic San Patricio Battalion, martyrs who gave their lives for Mexico during the unjust American invasion of 1847"—Irish immigrant deserters from the U.S. Army, who sympathized with fellow Catholics resisting invasion, were tortured and hanged here by U.S. officers. At this corner, go up the cobbled, tree-lined Calle Juárez a few doors, along a tiny *plazuela* (at right is the gracious eighteenth-century house where the Bishop of Madrid lived, at end of Calle Amargura; Centro de Arte y Artesania is at No. 4) to the gate of the large garden atrium of San Jacinto Parish Church, a late sixteenth-century Dominican church-monastery dedicated to this Polish saint by the Dominicans in 1596. Harmonious restoration is under way. The whitewashed cloister pillars wear colored-tile religious mottoes. A monastery gateway opens on the northwest corner of San Jacinto Plaza, beside a handsome old house, Casa Forno.

Convento del Carmen—San Angel, Mexico City

CARMELITE CHURCH AND MONASTERY: Returning via
Calle Dr. Gálvez to Av. Revolución, across the street is the
barefoot Carmelite monks' gay tile-domed church and their
1615 monastery containing a museum. (Open 10 A.M. to 5
P.M.; admission 50 *centavos*. Tip the guard who guides you.)
Sparkling colored tile wainscoting, altars, even wash basins
enliven the cold stone; the crypt passage blazes with tile.

175

In a crypt room is an assemblage of mummies; the clothing of many is well preserved. The guard will permit a peep into an underground grave. Part of the building, sold in 1914, is still a private home. Here, too, is the ceramic studio of Instituto de Antropologia, which reproduces good pre-Conquest statues and ceramics.

The church has fine chapels, Churrigueresque altar-pieces, good paintings. The Feast of Virgen del Carmen is celebrated the Sunday nearest July 16. The Poppy Festival (Fiesta de Amapolas), Thursday after Easter, commemorates Christ's appearance to Mary Magdalene as a gardener. The church is decorated with handsome floral pieces; during the procession women throw poppy petals from laquered bowls. Inspired by this, a secular flower festival and art show around the church and Plaza del Carmen is an annual event.

COPILCO: An archaic cemetery buried about 2,000 years ago by lava flow from Xitle (Azt., "Navel"), 16 kilometers away. Discovered by quarrymen in 1917, under eight meters of lava, the cemetery is now a museum, open 8 A.M. to 5 P.M.—one *peso* admission. The entrance to inconspicuous, but paved, Calle Victoria (avoid the left fork, unpaved Calle Yolanda) off Av. Copilco between Av. Universidad and Insurgentes is simple from Universidad or coming from the Pedregal on San Jeronimo, but requires an awkward swing around coming south on Insurgentes. Best to turn right at the huge "Fuente de Sodas" of Yom Yom chain (don't get stuck for a 40-cent [U.S.] hot dog or 60-cent hamburger here!), into Calle Dr. Gálvez; turn left on Av. Revolución and right soon after into Copilco, right at the arrow saying "Insurgentes" and down across Insurgentes to make a sharp left into Victoria. The pavement ends at the kindergarten which the zone entrance adjoins. It is eerily exciting to go beneath the lava overhang (electrically lit to peer through glass at the earth-colored skeletons of four early American farmers, lying as their relatives placed them centuries before their cemetery was buried, sometime between 900 and 500 B.C., during the middle archaic period. Grave offerings for their eternal personal needs mingle with their bones. Exhibits depict man's development and show the utensils of the area's first agriculturalists.

THE PEDREGAL, a deep layer of Xitle's basaltic lava, is now the most fashionable residential district. Here are spectacular ultramodern homes built of and into the lava rocks, their gardens radiant ornaments among the black stones. The home of President Lopez Mateos is on Av. San Geronimo. A fine Yucatēcan restaurant, El Faisan, is at No. 201.

PYRAMID OF CUICUILCO (Azt., probably "Among the Many Colors"), a short distance beyond the University on Insurgentes S. Go by car, or after visiting Copilco, hop a bus or cab at the gas station on the corner of Av. Jeronimo and Insurgentes. It is the oldest known building in the hemisphere and the shrine where the oldest known Meso-American God Huehueteotl (The Old God) was worshipped. Understandably the deity of fire, he is usually seated, cross-legged, and always a wrinkled, semitoothless old man, a brazier in his hands or on his head. A massive, four-tiered, rounded structure still partly imprisoned in Xitle's lava, an outer ramp and part of a stairway have been cleared. Its inner altar shows superimpositions, indicating long occupancy. Only one of several shrines, most of which are too lava-bound to restore; others are tantalizingly overgrown. (Two across Insurgentes were barred from Tlálpan *ejido* quarrymen in 1960 long enough to rescue artifacts.) Obviously this was the religious center of a large, sedentary population, amazingly cultured 3,000 years ago—and victims of a horrendous natural catastrophe.

TO COYOACÁN: From San Angel and vicinity, at the Obregón Monument, turn west down Av. Taxqueña. (Disregard street signs "Calzado de Miguel Angel de Quevedo," as the post office does, for this broad avenue starting beside the monument.) Turn right into Calle Chimalistac and left into another era, where time loiters in the Plaza de Federico Gamboa. The secretive grilled home of this poet-historian occupies one side of the green triangle, dignified old houses the other; the tiny chapel of San Sebastian broods in its center. Calle Violeta winds back to Taxqueña. Turn right. At Av. Universidad (a few blocks from the University, an alternate afternoon visit) is the convenient, good Restaurant Altillo (Span., "Little Hill"). Continue down Taxqueña to turn left into Calle F. Carrillo-Puerto—the stream of buses and trolleys turning here will be your guide. (Or keep on to Calzado de Tlálpan, following the bright signs that lead to Culhuacan.) It is only a few blocks to Coyoacán's great parklike plaza, the second largest in the metropolis.

There are many good routes to the plaza from the center of the city; most join at Av. Mexico to enter Plaza Hidalgo via Calle Centenario. Fast, direct from Av. Juárez via San Juan de Letrán (the name changes to Niño Perdido), into Av. Universidad to turn left into Calle Francisco Sosa, over old, humped Altillo Bridge, at the corner where the charming Chapel of San Antonio de Panzacola perches on a narrow bank. Sosa becomes one way at the shady oasis of Jardín de Santa Catarina. (The mellowing primitive sixteenth-century Church of Santa Catarina here is undergoing repairs.) Take the right fork at Cine Esperanza, Calle Carranza; go a few blocks to Carrillo-Puerto St., then turn left a block into Jardín Centenario. Another route—take Insurgentes S. to Glorieta Chihuahua, then turn west into Valerio Trujillo (at Pepe's Coca-Cola-sign-dominated Restaurant); into Av. Mexico, meeting Av. Coyoacán, another main route from Insurgentes, to enter the plaza via Calle Centenario.

COYOACÁN (Azt., "Place of Coyote") was the Lake Texcoco city-kingdom of an Aztec vassal-ally, and a Cortés base during the siege of Tenochtitlán. Upon the latter's fall, August 13, 1521, Cortés made the palace of the local ruler, *cacique* Juan Ixtalenque (who became his devoted lackey), on the site of the present Municipal Building in the main Plaza, his home, and until moved to Mexico City in 1524, the seat of the first government council of New Spain. In that expropriated palace, Cortés had vanquished Emperor Cuauhtémoc tortured—in vain—to reveal the hiding places of Aztec wealth. Here his first legal wife, Catarina Suarez, died at night a few hours after a public quarrel with her husband, under circumstances which indicate Cortés murdered her.

The L-shaped Plaza has two sections, Jardin Centenario and Plaza Hidalgo, the whole dominated by the huge parish church of San Juan Bautista, begun as typical Franciscan basilica near these monks' first makeshift chapel. Transferred to the Dominicans in 1528, they changed the style. Renovations have left few traces of the beauty of the early interior, now resplendently tasteless. The monastery cloisters are faithfully restored; their garden patio is crowded with striking pre-Columbian statuary.

Except for a few chapels, no other sixteenth-century building is identified to date. The Palacio Municipal, on the north side of Plaza Hidalgo, was built after Cortés death, by his heirs, as the headquarters of the Marquesado de Valle de Oaxaca and reconstructed as the home of Corregidor de Coyoacán in 1755. It now contains the Delegación and other civic offices. Enter the patio to see the exquisite carved doorway.

The handsome house on the corner of Calle Tres Cruces and Sosa, Casa de Diaz Ordaz, and the present Panamanian ambassador's residence at Sosa 133, Casa de Pedro Alvarado, are splendid seventeenth-century mansions; the first is named after Cortés' favorite companion, and the second was built not by the Conquistador Alvarado, but by a person of that name nearly a century later, as was the first, on sites belong to these Conquistadores.

A few doors from Jardín Centenario, on Francisco Sosa, in the home of that great historian, is Coyote Flaco (The Thin Coyote) Restaurant, where one can eat superb cooking without losing the flavor of old Coyoacán. Unsurpassed lunches.

EL MUSEO FRIEDA KAHLO, Calle Londres 127, a few blocks behind Palacio Municipal (daily except Mondays, 10 A.M. to 5 P.M., Sundays, 10 A.M. to 1 P.M.; admission 1 *peso*).

The former home of Diego Rivera and his painter-wife, whose name it bears, the museum is an extremely warmly personalized national monument, primarily the very Mexican home of this creative couple, enhanced by their unsurpassed collections of Colonial and pre-Columbian art and articles of daily use. Heartbreaking but inspiring are the accouterments of the crippled, pain-tortured woman whose strange poetic paintings hang here in harmony with her husband's and the great diversity around them.

Go along San Juan into Calle Higuera to the garden Plaza of Concepción. In a corner of the green nestles the Church of La Concepción, affectionately "La Conchita"; its time-softened Mudejar façade is a poem of arabesques, scrolls, and tendrils. A simple statue to a gardener stands in a bower beside it.

Diagonally across the park stands the redecorated seventeenth-century house called "La Casa de Malinche" for Cortés' mistress, although built on the site of a house belonging to his first wife, Catalina Suarez, whom, allegedly, he murdered.

Follow the curve of Calle Fernandez Leal out of the plaza to the restaurant in a pleasant old mansion, a restful oasis for lunch during an outing. Return on the same street to Av. Hidalgo, turn right, cross broad Division del Norte (Hidalgo becomes Av. Heroes de 47), into the subdelegation, a former village, of CHURUBUSCO. At Calle Convento turn left for a long block to the cannon-decorated green in front of the CONVENTO DE CHURUBUSCO. The fastest direct route from the center is the express lane of Calzada de Tlálpan to Glorieta de Churubusco; turn right at the gas station into Av. Heroes de 47, then right at Calle Convento. "Churubusco" is mangled Spanish for "Huitzilipochco," the town and shrine dedicated to the Mexican Mars, disarmingly named "Huitzilipochtli" (Left-sided Hummingbird). To extirpate his harsh doctrines of blood sacrifice, the Franciscans started the first church-monastery, dedicated to San Mateos (as is the severe but stately ancient little chapel on Av. Heroes de 47), later destroyed by fire. Transferred in 1590 to the Dieguinos monks, it was entirely rebuilt in 1768 by two pious patrons, Diego del Castillo and Elena de la Cruz. The church, dedicated later (as was the monastery)

Church of La Concepción—Coyoacán

to the Señora de los Angeles, has a glorious, tiled, Churrigueresque baptistry. The present great walled-in, battlemented monastery, with its pine groves, gardens, and tile-decorated patio, was badly damaged by besieging U.S. troops and taken August 20, 1847, when the defenders' ammunition gave out. The museum has magnificent, varied exhibits, from pre-Conquest artifacts to old carriages, plus a hall of U.S. engravings of the 1847 capture of Mexico City. Open 10 A.M. to 7 P.M. daily; Sundays, 10 A.M. to 3 P.M. Admission 2 *pesos.*

TLÁLPAN (Azt., "Place on the Earth") beyond Churubusco via Calzado de Tlalpan. To reach the plaza, turn right into Calle Morelos running right of the garden triangle where the strip of tree-shaded lawn separating the traffic lanes beyond Huipulco Glorieta (marked by the statue of General Zapata) ends; turn right again at Calle Hidalgo. A very ancient Indian community the Spaniards resettled, now a metropolitan delegation, its staid, old-fashioned, rather rural individuality is scarcely touched by modernity. The locality so pleased the Colonial gentry that they built grandiose country homes here, most still well-kept and occupied; the largest are generally religious or educational institutions.

At the southeast corner of Morelos and Hidalgo (you keep on Calzada de Tlálpan to Hidalgo, first turn beyond the triangular park and the rose-colored home behind it) is a museum in one of the country homes—open all day, ring the bell. It is called "Casa Chata" (The Snub-nosed House) because its corner angle was sheared off to a flat surface to provide a wide entrance; the exquisite, carved Baroque rose-stone façade is pierced by a huge doorway. The present massive carved door, rescued from the city's old College of St. Paul, is beautiful. Unusual arches lend majesty to the corridors of the entrance patio. Stately rooms exhibit the appropriate period furniture. A stone-flagged patio-piazza above the rear garden has a stone fountain, decorated wall benches flanked by large masks, and quaint statues in gatepost niches—probably of former owners and chief servants. One man wears an eighteenth-century coat. One wing is a fascinating *museo de charrería,* containing horse's and rider's trappings of several periods. The builder and building date are uncertain, but old Tlálpanites always called it "Commissary of the Inquisition." For a long period it belonged to Don Carlos Rincon Gallardo, Marqués de Guadalupe.

The plaza has its *portales* of shops and stalls, its government buildings, and—set back in a long garden atrium—its handsome parish church of San Augustín de las Cuevas,

1532. Built on this spot to extirpate worship of a pagan cave deity, the church has a splendid Churrigueresque altar and oil paintings by Cabrera. To reach famous Fuentes Brotantes, it is easier to go south on Insurgentes, turn right at the large sign, and go 1 kilometer to the picnic grounds beside the old spring. Very popular, pretty woodland.

Tlálpan may be the last stop of the day on the outings suggested above, or may be seen en route to some of the following ones.

NEARBY VILLAGES SOUTH OF THE CITY

These peripheral villages have good bus and/or trolley service to the city center. Most have 2,000-year-long histories and were settled by pre-Aztec peoples—Tenochtitlan's vassals or allies. Several were magnificent lacustrine cities Cortés admired—but razed.

A very direct route to IXTAPALAPA by car retraces part of Cortés' triumphal way as guest to meet Moctezuma in 1519, down Piño Suarez from the Zócalo to Antonio Abad, to turn into Calzada de Ermita. From Insurgentes S., Av. Popocatepetl becomes Ermita. A swift alternate from the center of town is Calzada de la Viga from Francisco Teresa de Mier, its less crowded lanes separated by a tree-shaded grassy strip over the old Viga Canal, the last in use between Xochimilco and the City. This *calzada* runs through the famous old towns of Santa Ana, Ixtacalco, and Mexicaltzingo, now mere city districts, with old churches no lover of Colonial architecture should miss.

IXTAPALAPA (Azt., "Place of Salt or White Water"), the haughty lakeside capital where, in 1519, Cortés spent the night before Moctezuma's lords came to escort him to Tenochtitlan. He slept in one of the local palaces, which astounded the Spaniards, ". . . vast and well made of cut stone, cedar, and other fragrant woods, with spacious rooms and patios . . . wonderful to see, shaded with cotton awnings . . . ," chronicler Bernal Diaz recalled. Walking through the orchards and watching the boats on the lakes and canals, he stood ". . . thinking that never again in the world would lands like these be discovered. . . ." Now a suburban reservoir of commuting workers for the Capital, the public market and municipal buildings are nondescriptly modern. Behind the barren paved plaza, in a shady weed-choked atrium, old San Francisco Church's stonework and crumbling carved doors are visible through an iron-grilled gate. The tasteless, well-kept parish church of Nuestro Señor de la Cuevita (Our Lord of the Little Cave) on Calzada de Ermita, at rear of the grave-filled atrium sloping up Cerro de Estrella, is built around the entrance to a cave-shrine of the formidable pagan deity it was built to overwhelm. Above the altar, the Saint's brown-habited image, arms flung out protectively, stands before a white curtain, draped like great wings to accentuate the cave's black, jagged, rock-rimmed maw. The local Good Friday Passion Play, though declining in dignity, still merits attendance.

EL CERRO DE LA ESTRELLA (Sp., "Hill of the Star") was the holy place of the Aztec's New Fire Festival, but it is now forlornly littered with old temple blocks. There is a footpath from Ixtapalapa to its top or a fair road almost to it from Culhuacán.

CULHUACÁN (Azt., "Humped Place," from name of Colhua tribe), at the foot of Cerro de la Estrella, was the stronghold of Aztec vassal-allies on Lakes Texcoco and Xochimilco. (It's hard to imagine lacustrine freshness on a day of swirling dust clouds!) Cortés entered Tenochtitlan through here. The Monastery of San Matías, begun with its church in 1562 and completed in 1576, had a *seminario de lenguas* where missionaries could learn several of New Spain's native tongues. Secularized in 1756, it became a school again in the nineteenth century. Abandoned, its cedar beams were sold for firewood and enough stones were taken to build the present parish church on part of the original foundations in 1880. Superbly reconstructed; some early colored frescoes restored. Calvary Chapel, across the road, stands on a partly visible pre-Hispanic temple. The small cave beside it, a former Colhua shrine, is now a chapel.

XOCHIMILCO (Azt., "Flower Gardens"), sometimes called "Chinampas," or "Floating Gardens," was a former lakeside city founded 1265 A.D. by nomadic Nahautl-speaking Xochimilca, led by Huetzatin after subjugating earlier Chichimeca settlers. After 1300 the latter invented the island gardens—originally earth-covered rafts to grow needed food on, some sturdy enough for gardener's huts, which gradually became rooted to the shallow lake bed. The space between became canals—some the pleasure waterways of today. Flower-decked punts, called *canoas,* poled by Aztec Indians and furnished with table and chairs, are for hire. Hourly government-fixed rental price of *canoas*: 15 *pesos* for the yellow-fringed ones, 20 for the green, and 25 for the red-fringed, largest ones; all are moored at the souvenir-stall-lined landing stage.

Stop at the new, large, always animated public market beside the plaza for eye-catching souvenirs. Set back from

Floating Gardens—Xochimilco

the plaza in a spacious atrium is the sixteenth-century Church of San Bernardino, which has good sculptures over the entrance, altars, and images, and dramatic flying buttresses. Its present restoration is being conducted by sixteenth century authority Padre José Reyes.

MILPA ALTA (Sp., "High Cornfield") is a much-studied Nahuatl village on the brink of modernization, on the paved road from Tlahuac (you can continue via Mixquic to Chalco on C.N. 115 and back to the Capital via Los Reyes and Puebla Road, C.N. 190). The market day is Saturday, but the daily morning market is interesting. It is still possible at times to buy sashes woven on pre-Conquest-style looms in the neighborhoods where the natives live. The sixteenth-century Franciscan parish church and monastery, architecturally interesting, is being carefully restored by priest-architect, Padre José Reyes, with sacrificial contributions of townfolk. The annual festival of the church patron, the Virgin de la Asunción, is held on August 15, with dances, flowers, and fireworks.

MOTORIST NOTE: A road from Cuautla, passing through Milpa Alta to connect with the Oaxaca Highway and saving a distance of 60 miles, should be ready soon. Inquire locally.

Allow a full day to enjoy the chief stops on this 65-mile drive over good paved roads, through historically interesting old towns, located in a fertile agricultural part of the Federal District and the State of Mexico. There are large cattle-raising *haciendas* and dairies.

SHRINE OF LOS REMEDIOS—PYRAMIDS OF TENAYUCA—CONVENT OF TEPOTZOTLÁN

Leave Mexico City via San Cosme Avenue. At 71 is the former Jesuit school building, La Casa de los Mascarones, named for the faces carved in the fine Churrigueresque façade. Now a high school, where there is a fresco by Alfredo Zalce. As you enter Calzada Mexico-Tacuba there is the U.S. government cemetery and Colonial chapel, where the soldiers who took part in the War of Intervention of 1847 are buried. Next you pass the Federal Normal School.

At the fork where Calzada Mexico-Tacuba becomes one way south, the Federal Military School is on the left, the remains of the derelict church-monastery of San Jacinto on the right. Keep right, entering the drab, narrow street Mar Mediterráneo. (At Calle Mar Arafuera 8 to the left is the rare book and pre-Columbian art sales gallery of famed antiquarian W. Echanez.) Turn right into Av. Azcapotzalco —it is easy to follow the trolley labeled with that name— to Plaza Hidalgo of this district.

Because of one-way traffic it is necessary to re-enter Calzada Mexico-Tacuba at its terminus and turn back toward the center to see, in POPOTLA (Azt., "Broom Corn"), "Arbol de la Noche Triste," or "Tree of the Sad Night," on a little plaza on the corner of Mar Blanco. It is an old *ahuehuete* tree that derives its name from the legend that Cortés wept under it on the night of July 20, 1520, when the Spaniards had to flee from the Aztec capital. In 1872 a group of natives mutilated the tree in a demonstration against their Spanish-Mexican overlords. The iron fence around it is forged from the instruments of torture of the Spanish Inquisition.

TACUBA (Azt., Tlacopan, "Place of Little Flower Pots") is a district that was once a city inhabited by Aztecs and historically interesting. The parish church of St. Gabriel is on the site of the one first constructed by converts in 1530. On the Sunday following July 4, and every Sunday during the month of October, *fiestas* take place in the Cloisters, with Conchero dancers performing.

ATZCAPOTZALCO (Azt., "Anthill"), so called because it was once a populous native settlement and a brilliant capital. Before the Conquest it was noted for its precious metal refineries, but is now a dingy city district. The old Dominican, now parish, church stands on the site of the ancient slave market; the handsome wall surrounding it was built of material taken from the old Aztec one. The church has three chapels, one containing oils by Cabrera and Rodriguez. On the buttress of the steeple a carved red ant stands in bold relief. Massive portal arches of the Dominican Monastery are still standing.

Keep right around the plaza into the untidy, sprawling

Plaza of Tacuba and turn right in Calzada de San Bartolo Nacualpan (ignore the street signs saying "Av. de 16th de Septiembre") to reach the plaza of this most rapidly growing industrial metropolitan suburb—the most raw, ugly, dusty one just now.

Los Remedios: On the hill just beyond the town of San Bartolo Naucalpan is the shrine. In the vicinity are large *haciendas*. San Bartolo is noted for its expert *charros* and colorful cockfights. It is gay during the Los Remedios festival.

Legend of the Virgin of Los Remedios: The fifteen-inch-high madonna image was one of the first brought to Mexico by one of the Conquerors and the church literature states that she took an important part in the Conquest. Immediately afterwards, however, she disappeared. In 1540, the Virgin of Los Remedios appeared to a native *cacique,* when he was hunting on the hill where the Sanctuary now stands. She told him to search among the *magueys* for the image; but he did not find it until after her third appearance. Then he took the image to his home and built an altar for it and it disappeared three times from the house, the last time after having been locked in a chest with the *cacique* sleeping on the lid. When the chief told the priests at Tacuba about it, they interpreted her actions as an indication that she wanted a more fitting abode and accordingly they constructed the church, 1629. The image was often taken to Mexico City to help in droughts and plagues.

In 1810, during the War for Mexican Independence, the image of this Virgin was on the Royalists' banners competing against that of the Virgin de Guadalupe on the banners of the rebels. The natives pardoned and love her, and have contributed much to the wealth of her crown, gowns, and jewels and her elegant *camarin*.

The imposing shrine and its huge paved atrium cover a broad hilltop, beautifully landscaped on three sides; the fourth side is a bare-earthed marketplace with some stalls on a roofed porch, and beyond are the straggling huts of the miserably poor hamlet of Los Remedios. Good pottery and odd bits of folkcraft are on sale daily. The "day of the plaza" is Sunday. The Virgin's great festival, September 1-8, draws people from far and near, each year losing some of its pagan or medieval secular gaiety as the remodeling of the church and landscaping of the hill inspire more formal conduct. The *Mañanitas,* or "Good Morning" songs to the Virgin, begin at dawn, the most beautiful moment of the *fiesta.*

The views of the *maguey*-covered fields and the ancient towers and ruins of a fine Colonial aqueduct make it an interesting place to visit at any time.

MOTORIST NOTE: Because of road construction, for the quickest passable cross-country routes to Tlalnepantla or Tenayuca, consult the taxi drivers in the Plaza of San Bartolo Nacaulpán.

TLALNEPANTLA (Azt., "Middle Ground"). Almost lost in a welter of great factories (many more being constructed); it is now of interest chiefly to lovers of old churches. Near the Plaza, in an old sixteenth-century monastery, frescoes have recently been uncovered. The church has one of the first images brought to the Americas—a Christ of Mercy.

PYRAMID OF TENAYUCA (Azt., "Where Walls Were Erected"—the glyph of the pre-Hispanic town is a fortified hill.) The pyramid, of simple construction, is one of the best-known examples of Aztec architecture. It is about 50 feet high and is a series of eight superimposed buildings. The proliferation of serpent decorations, many of which are preserved, on the latest and outermost pyramid, begun in 1507, inspired the conquerors to call town the "City of Serpents." Coiled stone serpents, one north, the other south of the pyramid, with squared, almost abstract heads, each having an altar platform beside it, are aligned to the sunrise of spring and winter solstices. Half sunken near the main stairway is a box—painted inside with fading glyphs, skulls, and crossbones, with an exterior frieze of skulls—which the guard will unlock. He will also take you through the tunnels to see the earlier constructions and the small museum nearby.

PYRAMID OF SANTA CECILIA, 1½ miles north on a dirt road, impossible when muddy, but worth hiking to, is the most revealing reconstructed old structure in Central Mexico. In an open-landscaped clearing, behind the mellow village church (which was built centuries ago of stones from the pyramid's companion edifices), the pyramid rises, its combed temple complete—even to an idol installed in its front platform. Whatever original stucco remains is painted with the old rich red earth color. Close by is a small museum.

NATIONAL VICEREGAL MUSEUM in Tepotzotlán (Azt., "On the Hunchback Hill"). A populous pre-Conquest center, now a shrunken hamlet huddled on the outskirts of the vast new terraced plaza, from which village commerce is barred as unsightly. The museum occupies the restored complex of the Jesuits' former San Martin Seminary-Monastery, founded about 1584, and Baroque-Churrigueresque sanctuary of San Francisco Javier. The altars, the Loreto chapel, and the *camerin* of the Virgin are gold-illumined and exuberantly decorated, as are the three-paneled façade and the tower, finished in 1763. In this Sanctuary, within and without, Churrigueresque art reached its pinnacle.

Many of Mexico's most notable Colonial art objects are displayed in the monastery setting they were designed for. Living relics of the great seminario are the 400-year-old orange trees in the novices' cloister patio.

About 25 miles from Mexico City, following Reforma to C.P. 57. The turn left before the first toll booth is clearly marked. Small entrance fee. Closed Mondays. Spend complete day. Lunch in the arcaded patio of the Hostería or in the modest restaurant on the high porch of the plaza's north side.

CHAPINGO—TEXCOCO AND
NEARBY VILLAGES

This region around the old Tezcucan capital, Texcoco, is on the first lap of the trip to Puebla on C.E. 136 or to Cuautla on C.N. 115. There are trains from San Lazaro Station to both Chapingo and Texcoco, and hourly buses from Emiliano Zapata 92-A. This flourishing kingdom, finally outstripped by neighboring Tenochtitlán's imperialistic and commercial expansion, diplomatically maintained a precarious and loyal alliance with its neighbor-rival till Spaniards took the capital, Texcoco. Always more cultured than the Aztecs, one enlightened monarch, Netzahuacoyotl (Azt., "Hungry Coyote") was a philosopher, poet (fragments of his superb poetry exist), and engineer—he planned Tenochtitlán's Chapultepec aqueduct. Cortés built his small armada at Texcoco, then the Spaniards' chief base in the encirclement of Tenochtitlán. After their victory, the Spaniards, keeping the city for their own, began at once to build churches and establish schools—the best known the one Fray Pedro de Gante founded for the Indians. The countryside is dotted with fragmentary pre-Conquest ruins of the vanished Tezcuca and pleasing Colonial churches in picturesque villages.

CHAPINGO was a *hacienda*, converted since 1920 into the Federal Agricultural College. During the Díaz regime it was owned by Gen. Manuel González, who was president for one term and who used the place as a retreat for Bacchanalian festivities. Now it is alive with serious youth from all parts of the country, studying and working in modern laboratories, living in good dormitories, and doing experimental work on its spacious grounds. Thus a visit to Chapingo is interesting for its educational aspect as well as for the magnificent frescoes of Diego Rivera.

The frescoes here, all by Rivera (1923-1925), are in the hall and stairway of the main building and in the chapel next door. They deal with the Revolution in relation to agriculture and the life of the people. Those in the hall

191

depict scenes in the tropics; the division of the land. On one of them is the legend: "Here we teach to exploit the earth not man." They are very fine, but those in the chapel are so superb that no student or lover of art can afford to miss them. The treatment of the ceiling, the beauty and harmony of the whole, but especially of the nudes symbolizing the earth and its elements; the excellent craftsmanship, color, and composition all combine to make this group of frescoes the finest in Mexico.

As you enter the chapel, on each side of the door are two panels of a woman and child—"The Gifts of Agriculture." On the right wall, the agrarian martyrs, Zapata and Montaño, and on the left the "Seed of the Revolution." In the main body of the chapel are eight panels. On the left side are portrayed the various phases of the Revolution and on the right, the forces and elements of the earth, symbolized by nudes. On the central wall, over the archway, is another beautiful nude of "Earth Asleep." In the ceiling are nudes, symbolizing the natural elements. The designs of the carved doors and seats are also by Rivera.

TEXCOCO (Azt., "Stopping Place"), State of Mexico: The most important market for many surrounding villages. The town is pleasant, with fine old churches, the most important being San Francisco (sixteenth century). On the main street not far from the entrance to Texcoco is an old fountain and here and there a good Colonial house, such as the one on Hidalgo No. 23. Reproductions of pre-Hispanic figures and other good ceramic wares are made and sold at Ceramica Artistica de Texcoco, Zaragosa 2.

Opposite the street to the Agricultural School in Chapingo, a road branching off to the right leads to the charming village of Huexotla (Azt., "Place of Willows"). Here is a pre-Conquest wall, 35 feet high by 200 feet long with pyramidal constructions scattered about, which are attributed to the Chichimecas. The church has some interesting architectural details.

TETZCOTINGO (Azt., "Laughing Hill"), five miles from Texcoco. The road leads first to the *hacienda* of the Molino de las Flores, now a public park. The buildings are in ruins but the grounds are beautiful. From there a road to the right takes one to the hill, near the top of which you will find the Baths of Netzahualcoyotl, hewn into the hillside. The villages around the hill are charming and it is a lovely excursion.

CHICONCUAC, about 2½ miles from Texcoco, taking the road to San Andrés and there turning to the left at the church. It is a pleasant village and the weaving center of the Texcoco *serapes*. The weavers are glad to receive visitors and to sell them *serapes* and sweaters. Market day on Tuesday. On September 29, a picturesque *fiesta* takes place in honor of the patron saint, San Miguel. The town is generally called San Miguel de Chiconcuac.

MOTORIST NOTE: Several choices: 1) From Texcoco via Tepexpan to the pyramids of SAN JUAN TEOTIHUACÁN; 2) to NAUTLA on the Gulf Coast via C.E. 136, which becomes 125 after Tezuitlán (turn right just before Apizaco for a side trip to TLAXCALA); 3) cross-country to Veracruz via Puebla-Veracruz Highway, C.N. 140, joining it at either Zacatepec or Perote.

THE TULA ARCHEOLOGICAL ZONE—a most interesting one-day excursion. Take the Queretaro toll road, C.N. 57. Turn about ½ mile beyond the exits to Tepeji del Rio (Good Friday ceremonies here, dramatic pageantry), right on C.E. 126; 9 miles to the zone. Longer alternate (or for circuit trip): Pan-American Highway, C.N. 85, to ACTOPAN. Turn left (west); 35 miles to the zone. Tula is a railroad flagstop, 2 hours from Buenavista Station on Laredo or El Paso lines. No direct bus: Autobuses Anahuac to Tepeji del Rio, taxi to the zone. The conducted tour is advantageous for the non-motorist. There is a soft-drink stand at the zone. Take lunch or eat in town—its hotels are fair. Don't miss the Renaissance-style San Francisco Church and monastery, founded 1550 on the site of an earlier 1529 Franciscan church.

Recent excavations have convinced many archeologists that these ruins are those of the ancient Toltec city Tula. The buildings display the styles and ornamentation the Toltecs reproduced in Chichén Itzá. The five-stepped pyramid, decorated with bands of relief carvings of jaguars, eagles consuming human hearts, and representations of Quetzalcoatl, is now a platform for the gigantic, inscrutable figure columns called Atlantidae, taken from the rubble of another building. An early type of ball court, a court of columns, large Chacmool figures, and a 40-meter wall with a frieze of serpents devouring humans are part of the badly destroyed Burned Palace. Rock carvings and building ruins extend to El Cerro de la Malinche and other hills. The zone museum exhibits stone and ceramic objects found during excavations.

Atlantidae at Tula

CUAUTLA, CUERNAVACA, TAXCO, AND ACAPULCO

This area comprises interesting and colorful sections in the states of Mexico, Morelos, and Guerrero, rich in history, tradition, natural beauty, and noble architecture. The road leads first to Cuautla, past the magnificent snow-covered volcanoes Ixtaccíhuatl and Popocatépetl in the State of Mexico near Amecameca, and all along the way are gorgeous mountains, valleys, waterfalls, rivers, springs, lagoons, tropical flowering and fruit trees, fields of sugar cane and wheat. At the end of the trip are Acapulco and the Pacific, with glorious bathing and stupendous scenery.

Amecameca and the villages beyond, en route to Cuautla, are in a rich agricultural valley of the State of Mexico. There is a gradual drop of several thousand feet into warm, semitropical country, in the State of Morelos, named after the patriot priest and warrior, José Morelos y Pavon. It is an important sugar-raising region. Since the Revolution of 1910, many sugar cane *hacienda* buildings are in ruins.

The State of Guerrero is also named after a hero of the Revolution for Independence, Vicente Guerrero. Less accessible and more primitive than Morelos, its inhabitants have preserved to a greater extent their traditions, dances, and arts. Before the Conquest the natives extracted much gold and silver from its mines but afterwards Borda and other foreigners monopolized their wealth. There are stories still extant of secret veins known to natives, but many adventurers have spent time and money in fruitless searching.

SUGGESTIONS FOR ONE-DAY TRIPS: Amecameca and the road to the volcanoes. Cuautla, returning either via Cuernavaca or Chalco. Cuernavaca and Cacahuamilpa Caves. Cuernavaca and Xochicalco. Cuernavaca and Taxco. A week or longer is not enough to enjoy all the interests of these towns.

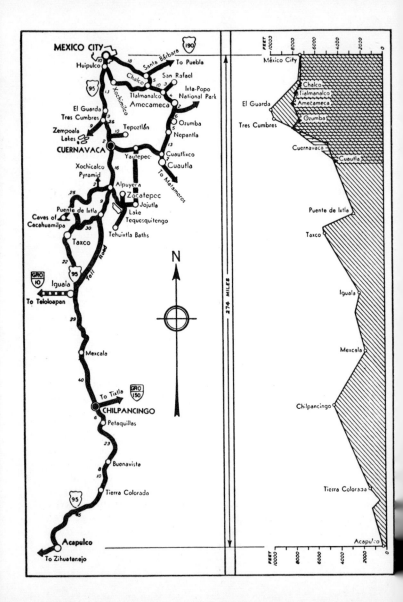

There are excellent hotels along the way. Take summer clothes, bathing suit, walking shoes, sunglasses, and a light-weight wrap for evening.

MEXICO CITY TO CUERNAVACA VIA CUAUTLA

Trains for Cuautla, via Amecameca, leave San Lázaro station; first-class buses start from Calz. de Puebla No. 38.

CUAUTLA AND PLACES ON THE WAY: Turn off Puebla road, C.N. 190, at Hacienda Santa Bábara onto C.N. 115, which passes close to the volcanoes and traverses a pleasant agricultural valley.

CHALCO (Azt., "Many Months"). Former capital of a Na-huatl tribe, the Chalca, Chalco has one of earliest sixteenth-century churches. The road to Xochimilco turns off the highway to the right at Calle Hidalgo, immediately upon entering the town.

TLALMANALCO (Azt., "On a Plain"): To the left of the interesting old Franciscan church and monastery is one of the few remaining sixteenth-century "open chapels," a purely Mexican church architectural innovation to accom-modate congregations of thousands of Indian converts; its arches are elaborately and beautifully carved in Renais-sance Plateresque style with religious motifs, showing native influence.

AMECAMECA (Azt., "Place of Those Wearing *Amate*-bark Fiber Shirts"; Alt. 7,650, Pop. 12,271). A charming Aztec town. Point of ascent to Popocatépetl and Ixtaccí-huatl. A dirt road from the highway, at Avenue Popocatépetl, to the left as you are leaving the town, makes it possible to ride a short distance up the mountainside and then walk through beautiful country.

In the sixteenth-century Dominican church near the plaza is a fine chapel, and the adjoining monastery has some very good unsigned paintings in the corridors.

Above the plaza is Sacromonte, the Holy Mount. The hill rises to a height of 500 feet and dominates the town and valley. There is a paved motor road to the hilltop parking lot, but it is more interesting to walk up the cobbled, terrace-stepped way lined with stately old trees and the Stations of the Cross. Many a pilgrim makes his way (often on his knees) to the former pagan shrine, which has been exorcised and blessed as the hermitage of Fray Martín de Valencia, who was one of the first Franciscan missionaries to come to Mexico and who died here. In a chapel beside his cave hangs the miracle-performing crucifix, El Santo Entierro, one of many holy images miraculously discovered shortly after the Conquest. Clinging to ancestral pagan customs, pilgrims tie rags, hair braids, and other objects to branches of certain revered trees and throw flower offerings into the holy well behind the chapel. A small hilltop chapel above occupies the site of the pagan shrine to Teteoinán. Chief pilgrim festivals: Ash Wednesday; Sept. 8. Market day is Sunday.

PASO DE CORTÉS: Turn left beyond town into the dirt road crossing between the volcanoes, the pass through which Cortés led his army to their first view of Tenochtitlán and other "white" cities in the Valley. There is a hut for climbers at Tlamaca (12,788 feet). Branch roads at the top lead to both volcanoes.

OZUMBA (Azt., "Farther On") is a village with many orchards and a market on Tuesdays. The especially fine Franciscan church has a remarkable sixteenth-century painting of Cortés with some of his men and missionaries meeting Cuauhtémoc. Chimalhuacán (Azt., "Home of Nobles"), a village near Ozumba, has a good Dominican monastery in which is preserved the baptismal font of the great Mexican poetess, Sor Juana Inéz de la Cruz, born in the village of Nepantla in the sixteenth century. YECAPIXTLA (Azt., "Where People Have Sharp Noses"), a left turn from 115 shortly before Cuautla, beside a tropical ravine, has a splendid Augustinian monastery.

CUAUTLA (Azt., "Woods"), State of Morelos: (Alt. 4,217 ft., Pop. 11,847). A languid, semitropical town. There is bathing at Agua Hedionda in warm mineral waters 2 kilometers from town.

The bullet-pocked face of San Diego Church (still in

use, but the adjacent monastery is now a hotel and railroad station) is a reminder of Cuautla's heroic history.

Hotels: San Diego, Posada Lindavista, Quinta Amelia, El Paraiso, all simple, modest to moderate, Amer. Pl. The Vasco has extensive gardens and a large pool; moderate.

During the War of Independence in 1810, the priest José María Morelos y Pavón, for whom the state of Morelos is named, with only 3,000 men, held Cuautla for three months with victorious results against the 20,000 Spanish Royalists besieging the city. Napoleon's comment on this feat was, "With five Morelos, I could conquer the world." A century later, Emiliano Zapata, agrarian leader of the 1910 Revolution, also held Cuautla. Born in nearby Anenecuilco (his semiruined, humble adobe birthplace is now a national shrine) and assassinated in the not-far-distant Hacienda Chinameca, he is buried in the plaza in Colonia Zapata, where a compassionate statue of him stands.

Cuautla to Cuernavaca: The road, C.N. 138, to the state capital, Cuernavaca, 30 miles, runs beneath the aqueduct arches of two old *haciendas*. Outside the town-hacienda Cocoyoc, a road leads right 7 kilometers to Oaxtepec, hidden among trees; rivulets tinkle in channels between many streets. The winter retreat of Aztec monarchs, where Moctezuma created, on the banks of the nearby Yautepec River, the greatest botonical garden in the world at that time, today it is a delightful picnic ground. The town's magnificent Dominican church-monastery stands on the steep rise of its pagan predecessor's ruins, in a parklike atrium. The crumbling ruins of one of America's first hospitals are two blocks from the plaza. In bustling *Yautepec,* the road passes a sixteenth-century church-monastery that has remains of an open chapel and old wooden saints and paintings, and continues through narrow Cañyon de Lobos, former highwaymen's favorite vantage point.

MEXICO CITY TO CUERNAVACA, TAXCO, ACAPULCO

Two roads cover the 46 miles between Mexico City and Cuernavaca, both connecting out from Av. Insurgentes. The old road, C.N. 95, winds over mountains, through Tres Marias and pine woods, reaching an altitude of 10,000 feet at La Cima. On the new one, 95 C.P., a four-lane super-highway to Acapulco (8 *pesos* to Cuernavaca) cuts driving time by one-third, bringing it down to about 6½ hours. Take a different road each way—both offer magnificent views. Near the famous curve La Pera, a toll road branches east to Cuautla, which cuts mileage and time between the capital and Oaxaca.

TRANSPORTATION: One train a day from Buenavista station as far as Balsas via Cuernavaca and Iguala. First-class and air-conditioned luxury buses leave from Fray Servando Teresa de Mier 74. On the same street, at 148, is the departure point for station wagons with reclining seats for night rides to Acapulco. Comfortable limousines (*turismo*) to Cuernavaca share the first-class Mexico-Cuernavaca-Zaca-tepec bus station at Netzahualcóyotl 192 between Ave. 20 de Noviembre and Pino Suárez.

There is daily plane service to Acapulco via Aeronaves de México, S.A.

LAS LAGUNAS DE ZEMPOALA (Azt., "Windy Place"): There is a 7-mile paved road to the first two of seven mountain lakes; foot trails to others. Beautiful spot for picnics, hiking, swimming in the cold mountain lakes, and camping. Rustic lodgings.

TEPOZTLAN ("Place of Broken Rocks"), State of Morelos, 15 miles east of Cuernavaca's outskirts, is a delightful village surrounded by high cliffs. Hilly, cobblestoned streets, a fine Dominican church (1559) and monastery (1580), the Tepoz-teco Pyramid. The inhabitants of whom much has been written, are of Tlahuica descent. The Spaniards relocated their ancestors, who lived in eleven hamlets close to the protective flanks of the hills, in a single village on the present site.

Tepoztlan has seven distinctive lovely old chapels. The oldest, La Santisima, was the private oratory of Martin Cortés, the conqueror's legitimate heir. The house opposite still has some walls of Martin's home; the present owner is named Cortés.

TEMPLE OF TEPOZTECATL: Finished not long before 1502

on a pinnacle of the Hill of The Great Light, 2,000 feet above town (pleasant hour and a half climb), this Aztec-styled three-stepped pyramid was dedicated to Ometochtli (Two Rabbits, one of 400 *pulque* or agricultural gods) and Tepoztecatl (folk-hero deified as the perfecter of *pulque* fermentation; dually endowed with nature of the Wind God, Ecatl). The inner sanctuary bench is still faced with carved glyphs of heavenly bodies, *pulque,* water, and war. Those of the Aztec ruler, Ahuitzotl (The Whip, or Scourge), who reigned 1486-1502, have been removed to museum protection, as well as the date sign, 1503, the year of his funeral —still remembered for pomp and the number of captives sacrificed that day.

Tepoztecatl, depicted as Tlahuica Nimrod, born of a virgin and suffering the trials and tribulations of Moses, Theseus, and Jonah, was, undoubtedly, Ce Acatl Topiltzin, born in 947, son of the Chichimeca chief Mixcoatl and a Tepoztecan princess. He died in 999. Probably he conquered the king of Xochicalco and freed his people from further oppressive tribute-paying. Legend even asserts he met Cortés as he landed, became a Christian and returned to convert neighboring chiefs, a conversion re-enacted in Nahuatl every September 8, the Virgin Mary's chief festival. Details of the lavish costumes of local Chinelo dancers, performing chiefly at the pre Lenten carnival, copy Tepoztecatl's Codex portrait.

Accommodations: Casa Bougainvilla, moderate, charming, friendly. Posada Tepozteco has re-opened.

Local Crafts: Carved *pochote* (kapok tree) spines and tree fungi objects; *maguey* fiber cord; genuine handmade, but not antique, idols. Market days: Wednesday and Sunday. See new archeological museum.

CUERNAVACA (Sp., "Cow's Horn," corruption of Nahuatl *Cuauhnauac,* "Place Near the Woods"), old (1250 A.D.) Tlahuica capital, capital of State of Morelos (Alt. 5,045 ft., Pop. 83,195). Although modernization has disfigured the environs of its Zócalo, this garden-city resort in a beautiful mountain setting merits a long stay for its ideally even climate and its untouched districts, where flaming masses of bougainvillaea, shading from orange to purple, and other flowering vines spill over house walls or where crooked streets lead the explorer to gaily painted or old wrought-iron decorated houses with glimpses through long, grilled windows of flowering patios and ancient fountains. A modernistic suburbia is growing up on the outskirts.

At end of old road, at Km. 71½, just before entering the city, is the pink building of Nuestro Pequeños Hermanos (Our Little Brothers), one of the few children's refuges in Mexico, started by an American priest, Father Wasson. Inspiring to visit.

Hotels: Moderate to expensive is the popular, lively Casino de la Selva, which has rooms and cottages, restaurants, shops, gardens, an outsized pool, and a bowling alley—and offers facilities for all sports. Its theatre presents good movies, Mexican and foreign plays, and concerts. Papagayo, Motilinia 17, near the center, is moderate; has garden and pool.

Modest central hotels: Del Parque on Zócalo; Iberia, Rayón 16; España y Colón, Av. Morelos 150-C; Palacio, Morrow 204; La Casona, Hidalgo 128; and, next door, patioed house called only Hidalgo 26; also Hotel Miraval, Pericón 209, near Casino de la Selva.

Motels: La Joya, on the highway near the entrance, Austrian cuisine; Los Canarios, Av. Obregon through to Av. Morelos 703, central. Several good restaurants; fine Spanish cuisine at El Savoy, near pool.

Apartments and houses: Good furnished apartments at Casa Latino-Americana, Av. Morelos, and Bungalows La Vegas, Calle Nuevo 204. Many private furnished apartments, too. Also bungalows, cottages, houses. Consult local real estate agents—most have English-speaking staff.

Inns: Often converted residences with pools, gardens, all amenities. Few rooms, so make advance reservations. Posada Arcadia, Leyva 200, former Colonial mansion, superb hospitality. Casa de Piedra (Stone House), Blvd. Cuautla 860, international cuisine. New hilltop Arocena Holiday, elegant, expensive, starting well. Villa Galeana, Galeana St., near center. Small Las Manañitas, Linares 22, has no peers; food and service unexcelled; garden haunt of tropical birds. Posada Jacarandas, Av. Cuauhtémoc 805, exclusive, expensive; away from center; gardens; pool; 6-hole golf course; only 16 rooms; no children. Terrazas Majestic, Prado 10, small, restful, away from center, has city's most popular night club-restaurant, La Perla, in rear garden.

Restaurants: Las Mañanitas and most hotels and inns. Casa Cardenas, with an outdoor terrace across from Cortés Palace, has good food, view. India Bonita, Morrow 5, excellent and inexpensive. El Vienés, Lerdo de Tejada 4. Café Viena, Guerrero 104, good coffee, pastries, *à la carte* service. El Savoy, Motel Canarios, Spanish food. Rosita, Blvd. Juárez, very low-priced, fine Spanish and Mexican cooking. Pancho's Place, just before Taxco Rd. in Las Palmas, famed for seafood and steaks. One can eat snacks and buy handicraft from street peddlers at sidewalk cafés around the Zócalo.

Shopping: Shops are all around the Zócalo's three gardens and the streets leading from them. The area is always alive with people selling something or amusing themselves. Best antiques and folk art at Tianguís, opposite Cortés Palace, Jardín Pacheco 2; Trini, Rayón 22C; Galería Trini (antiques), Ruíz de Alarcón 7; Tesoros, Rayón 24A. Lower quality, but not lower prices at Woolworth's, Guerrero 11. Casa Beltran, Guerrero 19, has fine shoes, sandals, will make yours to order punctually; also good line of typical blouses, skirts, shirts, dresses, sportswear. The Bagatelle, near flower market on Galeana, a block from Zócalo, has fine quality, good style clothes, will make your order quickly; also good fabrics. Casa Taxco, Guerrero 5, fabrics, sandals, clothing. Smartest sport clothes at Vera, Comonfort 15, 1½ blocks from Plaza. English books and lending library at English Bookshop, patio of the closed Bella Vista Hotel.

Every day is market day at the enormous new market inconveniently located far from City center, across the Amanalco ravine.

Cortés Palace: Now the State Government Building. On its south side it contains a huge statue of the priest-hero, Morelos. In front is circular Jardín Pacheco, nearly covered by the umbrella of branches of the giant Indian laurel. The Central body of the Palace has the original 1530 walls and balconies with carved pillars. Interior completely renovated. The north and south wings are of a much later date.

The famous frescoes on the rear balcony of the palace were painted by Diego Rivera in 1930, at the behest of the late American ambassador Dwight Morrow, as a gift to the city of Cuernavaca. The motifs are taken from the history of the Spanish Conquest of the region down to the Social Revolution of 1910. From left to right they are—1) The Spaniards attacking an Aztec temple; 2) A battle between the Indians and Spaniards; 3) The Spaniards crossing the ravine just below the palace; 4-5) The taking and occupation of Cuernavaca; 6) The construction of the palace and Cortés receiving tribute from the conquered Indians; 7) The beginning of the sugar industry in the state; 8) Father Motolinía teaching the Indians; 9) Revolution and a portrait of the agrarian leader Emiliano Zapata. In the center panels are portraits of Morelos and Zapata. Under the frescoes is a continuous frieze of excellent *grisailles* with related historical motifs.

The Cathedral and Monastery, 1529, in earliest Franciscan style, is massive and severe in its design and ornamentation. The open chapel of San José connecting it and the Chapel of Dolores to the west, is used for classical concerts and drama. Recently gutted of ancient interior decoration, the cathedral has an ugly modernistic altar and cross. Stripping the walls revealed forgotten colored murals of Mexico's San Felipe's arrival and crucifixion in Japan—the brushwork of the unknown painter and vivid colors lend a playful air to this grim theme. An early, monolithic baptismal font stands near the west door, under the choir. The Chapel of the Third Order (1738), west of Hidalgo Gate, has a riotous Plateresque façade, an unusual, huge, scalloped recess above the south door, and gay domes. Facing it by the east wall of the atrium is the more demure Church of Carmen, with white-trimmed pink steeples.

Across Av. Morelos are the Borda Mansion and its gardens and the adjoining Church of Guadalupe, the latter built by Taxco miner José de la Borda (see Taxco section) for his sole son, Dr. Manuel de la Borda y Verdugo, whose stately portrait hangs in the church behind the pulpit. Mummies of two minor Roman saints, gifts of the Pope to La Borda, Sr., lie in wall coffers on side aisles disregarded by Mexican worshippers. The Borda Mansion (open to the public until 7 P.M.; admission 2 *pesos*) is privately owned, but apt to be national property soon. Many rooms are roofless and sad; and melancholy, too, is the elaborate formal garden designed in 1783 by José Manuel Arrieta for Dr. Borda after his father's death. It was briefly the summer court of Maximilian and Carlota—outlines of the plastered-over door, by which he went to meet the woman he loved, are visible.

Picturesque Pool at Borda Gardens—Cuernavaca

TLALTENANGO, the village to the north, has a parish church on the highway, the shrine of a dainty image of the Virgin, who was famed for miraculous powers—a week-long fair in her honor takes place September 1-8. Cortés heard Mass in the plain south wing of San José, the oldest church in the area. The north chapel has an amazing collection of votive paintings. A block west of the highway, the early Chapel of San Geronimo, with exquisitely carved façade and bell-tower, stands on a pyramid base.

Saltillo de San Antón is a dramatic waterfall in San Antón suburb, near the cemetery; San Antón has been a pottery-making village since long before the Conquest. Methods of firing simple hand-molded home vessels has scarcely changed. Painted pots and grotesque Indian figures in violent colors are sad novelties.

The first sugar mill (1535) was built in Tlaltenango by Cortés, another in ATLACOMULCO (2 miles from Zócalo by bus) by his son Martin, where it and other *hacienda* buildings stand in broken splendor in this tropic village where cane fields flourished. Giant tunnels still carry water here and beyond, from springs above Chapultepec Park at Cuernavaca's western exit to Cuautla. Nearby the Park at Calle de San Juan 5, on the lawn of Textiles Morelos factory, is mounted the huge stone carved with an eagle, the Aztec *quaxtl*. In the suburb of old San Miguel Acapantzingo, on city bus lines, is the primitive chapel of the patron saint, the partly restored Hacienda of San Miguel, now a folkloric museum of few, but unusual, exhibits. Behind this building, in a parklike tract, is the roofless Casa del Olvido, where Concepción Sedano, Maximilian's sweetheart and mother of his only son, lived—and died of a broken heart a year after his execution. Their son was shot as a spy by the French in 1917.

PYRAMID OF TEOPANZOLCO, Aztec, sole survivor of the many pyramids here, is 1 miles from the center on the city bus line. It has a double stairway showing two epochs of construction and a few sculptural heads on the ruins of two summit temples. Current excavation reveals many platforms and tombs.

MOTORIST NOTE: For the following trips, take the Cuernavaca-Acapulco old road, C.N. 95, to Km. 100 at Alpuyeca. For the first two goals, take the right fork, which connects above the Grutas with the Toluca-Ixtapan road and returns to C.N. 95 at Km. 138.

XOCHICALCO (Azt., "House of Flowers"). Ruins of holy citadel spread over three hilltops, and name also of the first restored pyramid, banded with friezes of elaborately garbed Mayan personages framed within borders of coiling plumed serpents; other carvings contain Zapotec glyphs. The paved road goes almost to the hilltop. *No* bus service direct to the zone. The most startling find of current investigations consists of three imposing stelae, carved with the face of some personage and glyphs, painted red, and carefully buried under the floor of the most recently restored pyramid—hundreds more await uncovering. Newly discovered objects and architectural details confirm the role of this city as a melting pot of many cultures and blendings of major faiths, including Teotihuacán, Olmec, Toltec, Mixtec, and Maya. Besides the pyramids, ball courts, residences, a calendar disc walk, sacred caves, a network of tunnels, and beautiful vistas will interest visitors. For a full day's outing continue to:

CAVES OF CACAHUAMILPA (Azt., "Cacao Fields"), about 40 miles southwest of Cuernavaca, beyond XOCHICALCO through villages built around former *haciendas,* some now sugar mills. These magnificent grottos are open to the public daily; guided tours at intervals after 10 A.M. through chambers showing gigantic stalactite and stalagmite formations, most named after the forms they resemble—Organ, Fountain, Palms, King's Throne. Above the steps leading down to the cave entrance is a parking lot next to rustic restaurants, one with a swimming pool.

MOTORIST NOTE: From Km. 100 on C.N. 95 take left turn to the following towns:

ZACATEPEC, a modern sugar refinery financed by the Government, a co-operative enterprise serving nearby cane-growing *ejidos,* farm co-operatives. Visitors welcome.

TEQUESQUITENGO, a charming artificial lake—signs indicate side roads to its shores. Bathing, rowing, and fishing. Many resort homes have been built on its banks.

Accommodations: Hotel Tequesquitengo—de luxe—offers good food and facilities for water sports.

Hotel Proa, on the lake—pleasant and inexpensive.

Hotel Hacienda Vista Hermosa, in the village of San José Vista Hermosa on one branch road to lake; quickest route is via toll 95. A Cortés *hacienda* converted into a comfortable hotel without being spoiled. Unique swimming pool, lovely surroundings. Expensive.

TEHUIXTLA. Beyond this tropical village is La Fundición, with warm outdoor mineral water swimming pools and a lovely river. Restaurants at baths. In the village is an inexpensive hotel.

LAS ESTACAS, via Jojutla. Lovely spot for picnics and swimming in a tropical river with a warm, blue, mineral pool. Rustic restaurants; bungalows.

MOTORIST NOTE: From Cuernavaca take the old free road 95 through Alpuyeca to TAXCO or ACAPULCO—or toll 95 C.P. to Amacuzac, turn just beyond into old 95 for the winding climb to Taxco, meeting Ixtapan de la Sal-Toluca Highway at Km. 138.

TAXCO DE ALARCÓN (simply called Taxco. "Ball Game" in Aztec. Alarcón, the famous Spanish dramatist, was born there in the seventeenth century) in the State of Guerrero. (Alt. 5,740 ft., Pop. 16,604.) Taxco has a delightful year-round climate and is the most picturesque Colonial town in the Republic. 7 miles from an old Indian mining town (Tlachco); moved to the present site in 1528. Suburb, CANTARRANAS (Where Frogs Sing), was founded by new Spanish settlers (1539), many of them Jewish refugees overtaken and executed later during the Inquisition. It remained a crude mine town until, after 1742, José de la Borda used part of the wealth he was extracting from the local mines to transform it. He built bridges, aqueducts, and fountains, still in use. He cobbled streets; erected new and rebuilt old homes, including his own five-story one; and gave his miners decent, healthy living conditions. In 1751 he began the great parish church of Santa Prisca and San Sebastian, lavishly decorated in late Baroque and Churrigueresque styles. Finished in seven years, costing over 8 million *pesos,* it towers over the main plaza of today's Taxco, dominating the town and countryside. The ornately carved towers and façade and richly gilded altars, excellently preserved, are fine examples of Mexican Churrigueresque. In the Sacristy are splendid oils by Miguel Cabrera, among them a portrait of Borda and one of Santa Prisca, to whom the church is dedicated, showing her in the act of saving it from destruction by catching with her bare hands the lightning and thunderbolts which threatened it. There are several other smaller churches scattered about the town. The biggest *fiesta* takes place on the fourth Friday of Lent at Santa Veracruz, other *fiestas* taking place throughout the year. Holy Week is also very picturesque in Taxco.

Church of Santa Prisca and San Sebastian—Taxco

Hotels: First-class hotels, generally Am. Pl., moderate to expensive, include Borda, the largest on the hill opposite the center.

Los Arcos, attractive Colonial house, former convent. Popular bar.

Posada de la Misión, pleasant. Pool; dancing.

Street in Taxco

Rancho Taxco, terraced gardens, pool. Good food; dancing.

Taxqueño, oldest.

Victoria, long popular for hospitality and good food.

Santa Prisca, pleasantly situated, well managed.

Meléndez, old Mexican hostelry on plaza, remodeled, modest.

Humboldt House (German), historic building, Villanueva mansion, friendly, modest.

Guest Ranch Hotels:

El Chorillo, at entrance to town, in an ideal spot in the hills. Only 20 guests. Home atmosphere and food. Good taste in rooms. Swimming pool. Horseback riding.

San Francisco Cuadra, 20 minutes from Taxco, in a handsome old smelter *hacienda*. A comfortable hotel, in a quiet, lovely valley. Swimming pool, sports.

The small central plaza shaded by giant laurels is always gay with people. There are several concerts a week. On *fiesta* nights boys and men play at bullfighting with fireworks-bulls and there is outdoor dancing. The popular drinking places on the plaza are Paco's Bar and Berta's. Also dancing at Paco's Bar.

Shopping: Taxco's chief sport, so easy and pleasant with attractive shops, compactly situated. The market, too, is picturesque, especially on Sundays, when the Indians come from the hill towns, or at *fiestas,* as on Wednesday before Holy Week, when they bring in unusual pottery and clay toys. In plaza shops are tin work, *serapes,* sandals, and pottery.

For sport and peasant dresses, Adriana's, the Borda Shop, Margarita Figueroa, Tachi's, and Elizabeth Anderson. The Susi Shop has looms and nice materials.

Silver: Taxco is the silver capital of Mexico. Here William Spratling started the industry decades ago. Now a street is named after him and Silver Day is celebrated during the last week of June with prizes and gay social events. Among the shops outstanding for good designs are the Borda, also handling Spratling silver. Spratling's Ranch,

Km. 171½ (15 km. from Taxco) workshops and salesroom of his silver.

Castillos have a most attractive shop. One of their latest features is the "marriage of metals," original objects made from a mixture of silver, bronze and copper.

Casa Dominguez, Palma 8, offers pleasing jewelry. Almost every house has a silver shop, so look around.

Art: Palma 8, painting by Jeannette Dominguez and jewelry by Rafael Dominguez and Fidel Figueroa, Figueroa house.

Bernice I. Goodspeed Galleries, Arco 9. Paintings by Carl Pappe and others, silver, and dresses. Publications by Bernice Goodspeed.

Taxco Art School, Fidel Figueroa, director. Classes in all the fine arts.

There are various interesting reconstructed houses, among them the handsome Casa Humboldt, once owned by Borda but named after the Baron Alexander von Humboldt, who stayed there when he visited Mexico.

Casa Figueroa, overlooking the plaza, just above the Borda fountain, is a restored palace, now the studio and home of Fidel Figueroa, a native Taxco artist. The palace was constructed in fine Colonial style about the middle of the eighteenth century, by a Spanish count. For a long time it was known as "La Casa de Lágrimas," or "The House of Tears," because the man who built it was a judge who cruelly imposed unjust fines on the natives and forced them to work on the house in order to pay them. Fidel Figueroa, who bought and renovated the house, has not changed the exterior; but the interior is a sort of past-and-present combination with Colonial and modern Mexican furniture and a patio and fountain of Puebla tiles. The house still has a reputation of being haunted and of having hidden treasures. Several secret chambers have been discovered. Visiting hours 10 A.M. to 1 P.M. Small fee.

Around Taxco are many hills to climb and picturesque and interesting places to visit on foot and horseback. For mines see El Pedregal, near the Borda Hotel, or the larger ones in the mountains, at Tenería, reached either by car over a dirt road or on horseback—your hotel will help you secure horses.

To Acapulco: 278 miles from Mexico City. The trip can be made easily in one day, but one usually visits Cuernavaca and Taxco on the way. By leaving Taxco fairly early in the morning, you can spend a little while around the charming Plaza of Iguala. Then plan to stop at Chilpancingo. The road passes through the magnificent mountains around Cuernavaca, Taxco, and Iguala. On every side is luxuriously temperate and tropical vegetation. Beyond Iguala is Zopilote Canyon with its interesting rock formation and splendid mountain views.

Chilpancingo (Azt., "Wasp's Nest"), also known as Ciudad Bravo, is the capital of the State of Guerrero. It is a pleasant break in the trip to wander about the place and to have lunch there. The town is partly old, partly too new, constructed in the usual Mexican manner—streets raying out from a pleasant plaza, with low, one-story gaily painted houses. In the old church are some interesting paintings. The festival to the patron saint lasts for about two weeks, beginning December 16, with dances, fireworks, and much interesting popular art. Unexplored ruins nearby.

Approach to Acapulco: Beyond Chilpancingo are more canyons and towns, with coniferous trees, cactus predominating. Nearer to Acapulco the country becomes more tropical, with palms, banana and flowering trees.

The Bay and town of Acapulco as seen from the highway atop a high hill, form one of the most dramatically beautiful vistas in the world. It is a thrilling experience, like the sudden lifting of the curtain on a fantastic stage-setting —the brilliant blue waters of lovely Acapulco Bay, surrounded by green mountains, the tiled roofs of the exotic town nestling at their feet; beyond, the majestic Pacific in all its tropical glory!

Acapulco (Azt., "Place of Reeds"), State of Guerrero. The first port at which Spanish brigantines landed in the sixteenth century, now the most popular resort in Mexico because of its many magnificent beaches, dramatic views, and fun-loving atmosphere.

213

Winter is the ideal time of the year to visit Acapulco, but it is always enjoyable even during the hotter seasons, when the rains help to enrich the vegetation. The swimming and fishing are good the year round. There is always color and beauty—a rhythm that beats into the very blood.

The popularity of Acapulco makes so many hotels necessary that it is impossible to list them all. Those listed are attractive, with fine views, tropical gardens, and swimming pools. Some offer entertainment.

View of Acapulco

Large De Luxe Hotels: Expensive in season.

Caleta, on hill over Caleta Beach. Very agreeable.

Club de Pesca. Pleasant and popular. Has fishing dock.

El Mirador. Cottages on Quebrada cliffs. Long popular for good food and service. Some air-conditioned rooms.

El Presidente. Air-conditioned, de luxe.

Las Brisas-Hilton. Small bungalows on terraced hill; many small fresh-water pools above a private beach.

Majestic, wonderfully situated and very good.

Palacio Tropical, dominating the entire scene. Lovely gardens. Dancing on Starlight Roof.

Prado-Americas. Romantically situated cottages. Dinner dancing and floor shows.

Acapulco-Hilton Hotel is new. The de luxe **Pierre Marquez** is actually part of an elegant American resort built away from the rest of Acapulco on Puerto Marques. It is entirely air-conditioned, has its own purification and power plants and luxurious furnishings.

First Class, Smaller, More Intimate: Moderate.

La Riviera. Very pleasant. Breakfast only.

Los Flamingos. Pleasant cottages on cliffs. Popular.

Del Monte. Very good. Dancing. Popular Hi-Ho Bar.

Pozo del Rey. Small, cozy, and good American food.

La Bahia, a short walk from Caleta Beach. Pleasant.

El Faro. Very popular.

Las Anclas, on Hornos Beach.

Quintas Maria, on Los Hornos Beach, is well liked.

Hotel Aloha, near Caleta Beach.

Monte Carlo, near Caleta, is small and fairly expensive, but the French cuisine is worth it.

Hotel Paris. Furnished rooms; meals furnished.

Motels:

Acapulco, Imapala, El Morro, Ritz, Toro, Anclas.

Dancing: At the hotels or barefoot on the beach at the Copacabana and Armando's; clubs.

La Perla at El Mirador, on a cliff overlooking the ocean. Romantically lighted. Good food. Night with flares is part of the floor show; cover charge.

There are night clubs in many hotels and new places of entertainment springing up. It is best to consult hotel and tourist bureau personnel and other visitors about currently popular night spots.

Swimming: In the pleasantly warm ocean water in and

around Acapulco, free from sharks and other dangers, sea bathing can be delightful. Caleta, a lovely sheltered bay where the waters are never rough, is the favorite morning beach; in the afternoon, it is Los Hornos, where the breakers come in and later one goes to view Acapulco's glorious sunsets at Pie de la Cuesta. Among other lovely beaches are La Roqueta (on an island across from La Caleta), La Condensa, Revolcadero, and Puerto Màrquez. Since the undertow is strong in some of them, it is best to ask whether a given beach meets your swimming capacities.

Easily accessible, also, are water skiing, skin-diving, occasional bullfights, jai alai, and pleasurable beachcombing.

Shopping: Around the plaza, the central streets, and in the hotels are good shops, some of them specializing in sports clothes and shoes for men and women; also stands selling shell trinkets. Some blocks away from the waterfront is the city market where one finds pottery and other crafts —and the people of the region who are often obscured by the masses of tourists.

The best shops for attractive and unusual sports clothing are: Lila Bath's, Jim Tillet's, Peggy Peña's, Tachi Castillo, Chilpas, Suzanne, La Sirena, La Siesta, the Vagabundo Shop; for men, Jaime and Casa del Sol. For Mexican arts try Mex-Art; books, magazines, and records can be found in Hudson's Book Shop.

Fishing and Hunting: (Hotels make arrangements for these sports.) Acapulco's deep-sea fishing is world famous. One hires a launch by the hour, and the men who run it help take in the catch. Special fishing permits may be obtained for each trip. The swordfish, the long graceful sailfish, and all other tropical fish are abundant. In the surrounding mountains are deer and all sorts of wild game.

Delightful drives around the beaches and the hills and to the old Spanish fort or to Pie de la Cuesta and to Puerto Marquez, which has a good beach. There you can get fish lunches served by the natives, many of them with Negro blood, handsome looks, and musical voices. Your hotel will also announce excursions through tropical lagoons and on rivers in coconut, palm, and banana groves with rich vege-

216

tation and brilliantly plumed birds, including parakeets and flamingos.

Seasonal Diversions: Every year from November to March there are special sporting and cultural events: fishing tournaments; swimming meets; yacht, sailboat, and motorboat races; fairs; an international movie festival in November; concerts. Ask your travel agent to get the year's program or write Asociación Mexicana de Hoteles en Acapulco, A.C., Apartado Postal 334, Acapulco, Guerrero, Mexico.

ZIHUATANEJO is a scenic, though difficult, drive along the ocean or an hour by plane from Acapulco. It has a lovely bay, good beaches and fishing, and is very quiet. As soon as the road from Acapulco is sufficiently improved, it probably will be rapidly developed. Hotels Belmar and Catalina are modest and inexpensive.

STATES OF PUEBLA, TLAXCALA, VERACRUZ, AND OAXACA

These states, all accessible from Mexico City, offer a greater variety of scenery, climate, peoples, architecture, and popular arts than any other region in the Republic and should on no account be omitted from your itinerary.

PUEBLA AND TLAXCALA

PUEBLA has beautiful valleys and mountains and its capital is the most important Colonial city near the federal capital. It has natural mineral springs and many lovely villages and towns accessible over good roads. The natives of the State are Aztec, Otomí, and Totonac. Those of the

Sierras speak their own languages and preserve many pre-Conquest customs. Their dress, folk dances, music, and popular arts are very interesting.

The best way to make the trip to Puebla is by car, in order to be able to stop along the way or make detours at will. First-class buses leave from Buenavista 9, making the trip in about two hours. Train trip longer.

There are two roads to Puebla. Older, narrow, free C.N. 190 has nerve-racking curving mountain stretches; is more than a two-hour trip from the Capital; passes through charming towns. Trip via C.N. 150—well-graded, easy (only sixty curves), new direct toll Highway Cinco de Mayo—takes about an hour and a quarter. Branch roads to C.N. 190 towns.

Río Frío is just beyond the highest point on the old road. Centuries ago it was noted for its bandits—and now for its excellent *tacos,* or Mexican sandwiches.

San Martín Texmelucan (Azt., "Place of Stone Cutters") is on C.N. 190, road link with C.N. 150. The Tuesday market is quite colorful. The town boasts a fairly good provincial hotel and two sixteenth-century convents, Franciscan and Carmelite. Take C.N. 188 from here, 14 miles to Tlaxcala.

Tlaxcala (Azt.-Tlaxcallan, "Land of Bread") (Alt. 7,100 ft., Pop. 15,307), capital of the State of Tlaxcala. 14 miles from San Martín Texmelucan over a paved road, Tlaxcala is a restful and well-kept town, in a small valley surrounded by wooded hills. Hotel Tlaxcala is inexpensive and pleasantly situated.

San Francisco, on a terraced hill near the plaza, dates from 1521 and is noted as the church in which the Christian Gospel was first preached on the American continent and where the first baptisms of four Tlaxcallan chiefs took place. These same chiefs, governing the independent kingdom of Tlaxcala at the time, provided the Spaniards with the help which made the Conquest possible.

The Sanctuary of Ocotlán (Azt., "Place of the Pines"), one of the most dramatic spots in Tlaxcala, stands on a hill and commands a sweeping view of the valley and

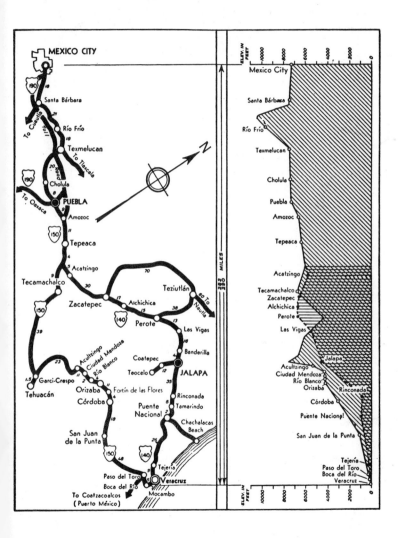

Sanctuary of Ocotlán—Tlaxcala

snow-capped volcanoes. It is said to occupy the site of the palace of a Tlaxcallan prince. The ornately carved white façade and towers contrast strkingly with the red hexagonal tiles used on the exterior wall. Most splendid, however, is its richly carved "Camarín of the Virgin" by the native sculptor Francisco Miguel, who required twenty-five years to complete the work. The church was constructed to commemorate the apparition of the Virgin in 1541. A well near the hill is said to have sprung forth from beneath the feet of the Virgin. Water from the Ocotlán well supposedly cured the entire populace of a smallpox plague at one time.

RUINS OF SAN ESTEBAN DE TIZATLÁN, a short distance by auto from Tlaxcala. The people of this village are engaged in agriculture, simple weaving, and pottery making. Its tiny houses cluster around a church constructed over another palace of a Tlaxcallan prince. Nearby are ruins with very interesting symbolic, well-preserved frescoes. To date only a portion of the monument has been uncovered and most of that was excavated in a single night by the natives who were convinced, through a vision experienced by one of them, that great riches were to be found there.

SANTA ANA, near Tlaxcala, is noted for wool homespuns and *serapes*. APIZACO (pop. 15,622), just after the junction with C.E. 136, makes painted, carved canes. Sunday market.

HUEJOTZINGO (Azt., "In the Little Willow Grove") is back on C.N. 190, not linked with C.N. 150. The pleasantly shaded plaza is the scene of an attractive Thursday market in front of the stately domed, sixteenth-century Franciscan church and convent (now a museum) with huge, handsomely carved doors. In the corridors are black and white murals of the first Franciscan friars who came to Mexico.

In Colonial days Huejotzingo, a main stagecoach stop between Mexico City and Veracruz, in the heart of the bandit country, was a favorite hold-up stop. The annual carnival, on the Tuesday before Ash Wednesday, portrays the history of Augustín Lorenzo, one of the most famous of these bandits. Hundreds of natives masquerading in fantastic Spanish, French, and Mexican military uniforms give chase to the "bandit" and his men, who not only steal silver but also kidnap the beautiful daughter of a rich *hacendada*. Capture of the bandit is made just after a mock marriage ceremony has been performed. This carnival, blazing with wild color, wild music, and exploding gunpowder, is the most spectacular in Mexico.

CHOLULA (Azt., "Place of Springs") is about 9 miles from Puebla. Frequent local bus service. Formerly center of the kingdom of the Toltecs. A church in which is venerated a small image of the Virgin of Los Remedios surmounts the top of an ancient pyramid dedicate to Quetzalcoatl, now overgrown with shrubs and trees. Excavations revealed many passages and stairways of early civilizations from the Archaic to the Cholulan, each superimposed upon the other. The caretaker will show visitors the remains of a Cholula burial with the skeletons of the dead in their original positions.

A small museum at the foot of the pyramid contains interesting exhibits of the Cholulan cultures.

It is claimed there are 365 churches, one for each day of the year, within a close radius of Cholula. The Capilla Real (Royal Chapel), with its many naves and domes, was intended for the natives, but never completed. It contains many large canvases, the scene of the apparition of the Virgin of Guadalupe being the most outstanding. San Francisco nearby has notable doors.

SANTA MARIA TONANTZINTLA, a village a few miles away from Cholula, has a church worth visiting. The inhabitants have repainted the interior and the ornate altars in vivid colors and gold leaf, and the effect is amazingly gay and heathen. Here also is the Observatorio Astro-Físico Nacional, one of the finest in the Latin Americas.

SAN FRANCISCO ECATEPEC: From Santa María one can continue 7 miles to the Atlixco road, where stands the church famous for its tile façade and towers with majolica serpents. Its ornate interior has been destroyed by fire.

PUEBLA (Puebla de Los Angeles, or City of the Angels) (Alt. 5,052 ft., Pop. 287,952) is the fourth largest city in the Republic and is situated on a plain with a sweeping view of four volcanoes—Popocatépetl and Ixtaccíhuatl to the west, Malintzín to the north, and Orizaba to the east. It is one of the most beautiful Spanish Colonial cities in Mexico, founded in 1531 on the Eve of St. Michael. Popular fancy, however, attributes its name to the legend relating that the natives were unable to lift the heavy bells into the Cathedral towers and that the angels did the work for them during the night.

Hotels: The Lastra, on the outskirts, is the best. Comfortable central ones are Colonial, Palace, Royalty, others, and almost central Pan-American Courts. Agua Azul, on the edge of town, is semi-resort, with a thermal swimming pool and golf course. All moderate.

Shopping: Mexican-Talavera pottery and tiles are made here and the potteries are open to visitors. The potteries Uriarte, 4 Poniente No. 911, and La Concepción on the same street, No. 723, have good variety. Objects of Puebla onyx, such as inkwells, paperweights, and beads, are sold

Church of Santa María Tonantzintla

in shops, especially at the center called the Parrian. The large and interesting market, open daily, has many handicrafts. Immediately behind the cathedral, Av. 2 Sur, No. 304, is the folk art store of Samaniego, where peasant blouses and other textiles may be found.

The Cathedral (facing the main plaza). This seventeenth-century building is second in importance only to the cathedral of Mexico City. The paintings of the fourteen stations of the Cross are attributed to the Zapotecan Indian artist Miguel Cabrera. Each altar has its individual beauty, especially one of colored Puebla onyx. The exquisite carving found in the choir loft is by Pedra Muñoz. Flemish tapestries, designed by Rubens and given to the Cathedral by Charles V, are said to be in the church.

Municipal Palace, across the plaza, opposite the cathedral. A modern building of Spanish Renaissance design.

Capilla del Rosario (Chapel of the Rosary) in the church of Santo Domingo, near the market, on Cinco de Mayo. Probably the most ornately beautiful individual chapel to be found in the Republic. Tiles of the best Puebla period, polychrome sculptures and Churrigueresque altars of gold leaf characterized by native craftsmanship, show exquisite detail, beautifully combined. The church itself dates from the seventeenth century. It is massively constructed.

Church of San Francisco: The present edifice dates from 1667 and is noteworthy for the rich and unusual Churrigueresque stone carving of the façade and delicate towers. The small figure of Nuestra Señora de los Remedios, one of the first holy images brought into Mexico by Cortés, is enshrined here.

Nuestra Señora de la Luz: A lovely little tile-domed church just beyond San Francisco.

Hidden Convent of Santa Mónica: On 18 Poniente, No. 103. This convent and two others were discovered in 1935 by government officials. Entrances to all three were by secret doors through private residences. The nuns who had been living there secretly since 1857 were forced to vacate. Santa Mónica being the largest and most important, the effects of the other two were concentrated there and the place opened as a museum. Santa Mónica contains 39 rooms. Formerly these were entered by intricate passages, trap-doors, and other means of assuring secrecy. Some of the rooms have been left almost exactly as found and are a revelation of the austerity of the former life in the convent. In other rooms are splendid old paintings, handsome vestments, and beautiful embroideries and laces. Open daily from 11 to 1 and from 4 to 6. An authorized guide is on hand to take you through.

State University and Church of La Compañía. Resting place of the China Poblana. This old Jesuit convent is now a University building. The books and manuscripts in the library are of great historical value. In the church, at the entrance to the sacristy, is a plaque in Latin, which marks the remains of the China Poblana, a mythical Chinese princess deeply loved by those who knew her generosity, beauty, and gentleness. She is said to have been stolen by pirates and sold to a Puebla merchant when the ship arrived at Acapulco. She embraced Christianity and took the name of Catarina de San Juan, putting aside her silks and finery for a simple red flannel skirt and embroidered white cotton blouse. In reverence to her memory, her simple dress became quite widely adopted and is the basis of the present China Poblana costume.

State Museum, Calle 6 Norte No. 16, at corner of Av. 4 Oriente, in seventeenth-century seignorial mansion, Case del Alfeñique (named for the almond-paste candy-like scrollwork of the tiled façade). Has notable regional, historical, and archeological exhibits, old paintings, authentic Colonial rooms reproduced on the second floor.

Arts and Crafts Permanent Exhibit (La Exposición Permanente de la Artesanía Poblana), set up by the State Toursit Commission, Av. Maximino Avila Camacho 1401 to 1426. Visit before buying as guide to kind, quality, and prices of local wares.

Museo José Luis Bello y González, Av. 3 Poniente No. 302. Old residence. Fine exhibit of Puebla Talavera pottery, old Saltillo *serapes,* ironwork.

Santa Rosa Convent, noted for its all-tile Colonial

kitchen, is now the Museo del Estado de Ceramica, or the State Museum of Ceramics, 3 Norte and 12 Poniente Streets.

Forts of Guadalupe and Loreto, near where C.N. 150 enters, where Mexicans defeated the French, May 5, 1862. The latter is the historical Museum of No-Intervención. Casa de don Aquiles Serdan is Museo de la Revolución.

PUEBLA TO VERACRUZ VIA TEHUACÁN

Take C.N. 150, Veracruz Highway. AMOZOC produces clay toys, silver horse gear, guns, knives. TEPEACA, one of the earliest Spanish settlements, a late stagecoach stop, has an immense Franciscan monastery (1530) and a finely constructed Colonial plaza on which stands a Moorish tower with carved heads. In front of the parish church nearby are some interesting sculptured Toltec dogs.

TEHUACÁN (Azt., "Place of Those Who Have Stones") (Alt. 5,509 ft., Pop. 31,724). Railway junction for Oaxaca and Veracruz. The highway to Orizaba and Cordoba branches off here. A charming town with a pleasant plaza,

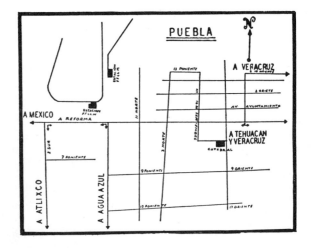

Tehuacán is the earliest known farm site in the hemisphere; corn and squash were cultivated about 7,000 B.C. near this popular modern spa city, which has a Saturday market. One usually finds local embroideries and onyx, straw, and horn articles.

The countryside is hilly, with much interesting cacti, and is suitable for hiking and horseback riding. There is also hunting. It is a delightful vacation spot and its waters are health-restoring.

Hotels: The Spa-Peñafiel, the largest, has its own springs and pools in lovely gardens. The Riego, less comfortable, also has springs and pools. There are less expensive hotels in the town—the Ibero and the Mexico are recommended.

Churches: The sixteenth-century Franciscan monastery has fine frescoes; the Convento del Carmen, an underground frescoed passage. Also ruins of Calvario and Guadalupe Chapel.

VERACRUZ

VERACRUZ: This state is rich in agriculture and oil and has one of the most important seaports in the country. It lies in a tropical region and its highways lead into some of its most beautiful parts, where fruit and flowers and trees grow in great profusion. Its people are gay and colorful in dress and customs. The folk-dances of Veracruz, called *huapangos* and *sones,* are fascinating. Socially, the state is very advanced.

One of the most dramatic roads in Mexico is C.N. 150 from Tehuacán into the state. After about twenty miles of dry cactus country and pine woods, there is a sheer drop of some 2,000 feet in five miles of hairpin turns and magnificent views. The experience is breathtaking. Then you find yourself in a fertile valley, rich in natural semitropical beauty where you can stop at altitudes of eternal spring without suffering the jungle heat at sea level.

ORIZABA is a Spanish corruption of the Aztec Ahuaia-lizapan ("Rejoicing of the Waters") (Pop. 69,672). It was an old town before the arrival of the Spaniards in 1533. At an altitude of 4,028 feet, it is above the sea-level heat of Vera-cruz, yet not too high to lack tropical beauty. It stands near hills, and in the distance are the mountains dominated by the Pico de Orizaba. The city has quiet streets, blue-walled, tile-roofed houses with long grilled windows close to the sidewalks, and lovely gardens and patios.

This part of the country, because of its fertility and beauty, was chosen by Hernán Cortés for the establishment of his first *haciendas* in Mexico. Sugar cane was first planted at the *hacienda* called El Ingenio, and the first flour mills in America were built here—forerunners of today's many industries, cotton mills, breweries, and others. The first *camino real* was constructed through Orizaba, parts of which are still used.

There are many churches in the town, the most im-portant being the San Miguel, a stone building completed in 1720, resembling an oriental temple. It has many large oils by the Barrancos, father and son, and in the Sacristy is a handsome ebony inlaid chest of drawers for church vest-ments. There are various interesting federal schools in Orizaba and the one on Avenida Colón has a fine fresco by José Clemente Orozco.

The countryside around Orizaba is indescribably beau-tiful with its tropical fruit and flowering trees, rarest of flowers—orchids, gardenias, night-blooming cereus, and others—coffee and banana plantations, orange groves, riv-ers, waterfalls, hills, and mountains. Tuxpango, a few miles distant, has a large hydroelectric plant, and there are other lovely nearby villages.

Hotels: Grand Hotel de France. Modest to moderate.

FORTÍN, a beautiful village on the 15-mile paved road to Córdoba, from Orizaba, is a veritable flower garden and famous for its gardenias. Here is the Ruiz Galindo Hotel, with lovely gardens and flower-strewn swimming pool. Ex-pensive. It is a fine place for a vacation with delightful outdoor sports. The Posada Loma auto courts nearby are less expensive.

228

CÓRDOBA, Veracruz, founded in 1618 and named after the Spanish viceroy. A small city of gardens, with a lovely plaza. Easy to visit from Orizaba. There are fair hotels in the center.

Near Córdoba are picturesque villages. In Amatlán, within walking distance, Aztec women still use beautifully embroidered *huipils* during festivals like the colorful one May 3.

From Córdoba C.N. 150 continues to Veracruz.

PUEBLA TO VERACRUZ VIA JALAPA

C.N. 140 turns off C.N. 150 at Km. 176, just beyond San Hipólito (connects with C.E. 136 at Zacatepec), continues via Jalapa to Veracruz—a 202-mile trip. Several roads connect these two routes. C.E. 139 links Jalapa via Coatepec to Fortín.

ACATZINGO, the first village on 140 has a fine sixteenth-century convent. Farther on, one passes through other villages and interesting haciendas. Límon and Perote are small railroad towns, and from the latter a road leads to Teziutlán, a charming Colonial town in the Sierra of Puebla. After crossing the mountains, the villages near Jalapa become more tropical and the vegetation more profuse. At Banderilla are fine gardens, those of the Lecuona family the most noted.

JALAPA (Azt., "Sandy River") (Alt. 4,541 ft., Pop. 66,317), capital of the State of Veracruz. Situated on the site of a native village, Jalapa is hilly and picturesque with its cobbled streets, tropical rains, trees, and flowers. Has many attractive houses, old churches, and modern schools. The modern university has its own theater, press, art gallery, and good symphony orchestra. Its Anthropology Institute is the custodian of the magnificent Archeological Museum on Puebla Highway.

Hotels: Salmanes, excellent; Mexico, best restaurant—Asturian cooking; Del Pardo, new, no meals. All moderate. Principal and Continental, modest.

Excursions: to coffee-growing *hacienda* Pasquel; garden village, Coatepec; village and waterfalls near power plant at Teocelo; train trip to Apasapam, then on horseback to Jacomulco.

JALAPA TO VERACRUZ: The road continues through quaint villages, and the leisurely traveler may make several interesting detours. From San Carlos, a road leads to Barra de Chachalacas, where there is both salt and fresh water bathing. On banks of a beautiful river at Puente Nacional is a *balneario* of same name, a spot to loaf and swim.

RUINS OF CEMPOALA: May be reached by train from Mexico City or Jalapa to Cardel, thence by bus to Angostadero; or by car—13-mile trip from Puente Nacional on good dirt road. The white stuccoed buildings of this Totonac capital (30,000 inhabitants), ruled by a "fat chieftain" when Cortés arrived in 1519, shone so in the sun that the Spaniards thought the walls were silver. Huge archeological zone. Restored buildings reveal a blend of Totonac "niche" and grim Aztec styles. The best preserved, Templo de las Caritas (Temple of the Little Faces) has clay faces in its niches.

VERACRUZ, so called because Cortés landed there on Good Friday, 1519, and called it La Villa Rica de la Veracruz. (Pop. 144,232.) An important seaport on the Gulf of Mexico. Connected with Mexico City by the Pan American Airways, two railroad lines, the two highways, and by boat with Tampico, Progreso, Cuba, and the United States.

Hotels: Mocambo, a few miles from the city, is a pleasant resort hotel with a good beach. Moderate to expensive. Two other hotels on the beach in the city are Villa Del Mar and the Castelan. On the central plaza the Diligencias and Prendes are the most popular, and on the wharf, the Victoria; all moderate. A large de luxe hotel, the Emporio, is on the plaza near the wharf.

A charming city, with a strange mingling of the old and the new in its architecture and life. The sidewalk cafés of the last-named hotels are always alive with people—all sorts of foreign and Mexican types, including hoboes, vendors, and itinerant musicians. As there are many Negroes in this port, the sensuous Cuban music and dances are very popular. It is fun to wander around the docks, take streetcar rides, and visit the markets, to mingle with the people. The girls are pretty and have high, pleasing voices. The outdoor life is always gay and colorful.

The city is constantly under improvement, with modern buildings and plazas appearing. See the grandiose Bank of Mexico Building on the wharf.

There is good fishing. Launches and guides can be hired for this purpose, as well as for cruises around the harbor and visits to the rocky fortress of San Juan de Ulúa, constructed in 1528, now a federal prison, and La Isla de los Sacrificios, or the Isle of Sacrifices. Boca del Río, a few miles out on the beach, is a pleasant excursion either by car or bus. The fish dinners are good and the swimming pleasant.

VERACRUZ TO COATZACOALCOS

You can travel by first-class buses either from Prim and Doblado. The same bus line runs direct buses from Mexico City, leaving Buenavista 9, without passing through Veracruz.

At ALVARADO (Pop. 12,424), a lively fishing town, vehicles cross the Papaloapan River on a ferry. Car ferries run up the river to pastel-hued TLACOTALPAN—even its churches painted pink and blue—the summer retreat for coastal dwellers.

Beyond Alvarado, C.N. 180 runs through SANTIAGO TUXTLA. (In its plaza are Olmec sculptures from TRES ZAPOTES in the hills, on a poor dirt road.) The road continues on through SAN ANDRES TUXTLA (two fair hotels—Colonial and Figueroa), to the LAGUNA DE CATEMACO and its cottage hotel, Playa Azul. There is good fishing, swimming, boating, and exploring of ruins on the Lake's many islands. The next big town is foul-smelling, industrially drab, oil- and sulphur-refining MINATITLAN, the nearest plane stop for COATZACOALCOS.

COATZACOALCOS (Pop. 36,989), on the Gulf and turbulent river of the same name spanned by a great new bridge, includes free Puerto Mexico in its dock space; is the terminus of the Trans-Isthmus Railway, and junction of C.N. 180 with C.N. 185, road across Isthmus between here and Salina Cruz. Has a magnificent Gulf-side beach, contrasting with the town's raw frontier atmosphere. Many hotels—only fair. Trains from here plunge across Tabasco's swamplands to Campeche and Merida in Yucatán, a long, pleasantly adventurous trip through whistle-stop hamlets. Pullman and diner service and a very low fare.

Motorists cross the new bridge or ferry outside the town to reach the highway to Yucatán—a quick level run to Villahermosa (see TABASCO) where the road swerves to the Gulf coast, to the old port of FRONTERA, and on to ISLA DE CARMEN (long waits may occur at one of the many ferries as the route crosses rivers and passes to and from islands), a good place to spend the night. On to Champotón and then to CIUDAD CAMPECHE. The 125-mile drive to Merida may be conveniently broken to visit KABÁH or at least pause to see the mask-façade of the building nearest the highway.

NORTH OF VERACRUZ

TECOLUTLA and NAUTLA, are both situated on the Gulf. Take C.N. 150 to these fine beach resorts with palms, good fishing, and all sports. Hotel Balneario at Tecolutla is the most comfortable in the area. Moderate to expensive.

PAPANTLA at junction of C.N. 150 and C.N. 130, highway via Pachuca, Hidalgo, to Pan-American C.N. 85 and Mexico City. An attractive town in vanilla-growing district. The Totonac natives resemble the Mayas in stature and appearance. Their *fiestas* are among the most beautiful in the Republic, especially the one to celebrate Corpus Christi, on a movable date in June, but the famous pre-Conquest *volador,* or flying pole dance, has become a professional routine performed for a fee. The dancers climb a hundred-foot pole, dance on a tiny platform, and with ropes around their waist, fastened to the pole, fly down like birds. They resent photographers and ask high prices to pose for snapshots.

THE PYRAMID EL TAJÍN (Huasteco, "Place of Smoke") is an archeological zone nearby on a bad road. Take the paved road from POZA RICA, oil refining town on C.N. 130, 12 miles from PAPANTLA. The most dramatic of the many edifices uncovered to date in this enormous ancient Totonac holy city is the seven-tiered Pyramid of Los Nichos, faced

Flying Pole Dance in front of Pyramid of El Tajín

with 366 framed recesses—a handsome uniquely Totonac decoration. Other buildings are decorated with carvings of hieroglyphics and animal and human figures.

Direct bus service from Mexico City to Papantla—Soledad 65—via ZACAPOAXTLA, ZARAGOZA, and TEZIUTLÁN. From ZARAGOZA a newly paved road leads to the exotic coffee town QUETZALÁN—its Sunday market is thronged with statuesque women with exotic hair-dos and costumes.

TUXPAN. Take C.N. 131 from POZA RICA, visiting CASTILLO DE TEAYO ruins near the road. Better seafood than at Veracruz. Magnificent beach. Visit bird-thronged LAGUNA and fishing village of TAMIAHUA—sportsmen's mecca. Continue to TAMPICO via PÁNUCO on paved road 122. First-class bus for this trip leaves Canal del Norte 23, Mexico City. Returning to the latter from Poza Rica via PACHUCA, C.N. 130 passes through fascinating towns yet unscathed by modernity, with old-fashioned, hospitable, inexpensive lodgings.

Hotels: Club de Yates, on beach. Los Mangos and Hotel Florida in town. All moderate.

VILLA JUÁREZ has a truly native market, Thursday and Sunday. Stay at Hotel Mi Ranchito—excellent food, moderate. Try regional fruit liqueurs. C.N. 130 runs on along Nexaca Lake and dam.

HUAUCHINANGO, 63 miles before Pachuca, warrants a special visit to the great Saturday market, crowded with Huastecan Indians from the Sierra villages, selling gay embroideries and unusual native wares. At the Flower Fair, the third Friday in Lent, regional dances like the *Huapango* are still spontaneous, natural. It is a good starting point for horseback trips into the Sierra of Puebla.

TULANCINGO, former Toltec city, industrialized with modern woolen and other mills, has points of interest. Last big town before Pachuca.

VERACRUZ TO MEXICO CITY BY TRAIN

Nonmotorists may alternate bus trips to or from Veracruz by a 12-hour, day-or-night comfortable train ride—a choice of two routes, via Jalapa or Orizaba.

VIA ORIZABA BY TRAIN: Scenic day trip, climbing 7,500 feet—first the lush tropics, then over mountains with many *maguey* fields and views of snow-peaked volcanoes. The train stops at Córdoba, Fortín, Orizaba, and many villages, where the natives come to stations to sell gardenias, fruit, and food—a fascinating panorama of scenery and peoples.

THE VOLCANO PICO DE ORIZABA, in the State of Veracruz, lords it over the region. It is 18,225 feet high and the most difficult to climb. (Its train station is Esperanza.) The natives call it Citlaltepetl (Azt., "Mountain of the Star") because one of the legends accounting for the mysterious disappearance of the Toltec god Quetzalcoatl from Cholula relates that, after his death, his body was taken to the Pico de Orizaba, consumed by divine fire, and his spirit, transformed into the Morning Star, flew to heaven.

VIA JALAPA BY TRAIN: New first-class trains both night and day, and this trip too offers fine scenery.

STATE OF HIDALGO

First-class buses of Lineas Unidas leave Canal del Norte 23, Mexico City, for Pachuca.

PACHUCA (Alt. 8,209 ft., Pop. 64,564), capital of the State of Hidalgo, is 5 miles off the Mexico-Laredo Highway. One of the oldest and still the largest silver mining center in the Republic, its mines date from pre-Conquest times and have been operating continuously ever since. Like most mining cities, it is built on hills and has some picturesque spots. See eighteenth-century Casas Coloradas, now government offices, and La Caja, former Royal Treasury. Only fair modest hotels. Starting point for many interesting excursions.

EL CHICO, a picturesque mining town 15 miles away with picnic spot en route at Penas Cargadas. The town, surrounded by wooded hills, has some deep old mines.

EPAZOYUCAN, on Rancho el Ocote Road to Santa Mónica, is 9 miles from Pachuca. (Just off C.N. 130, on branch road to Apam, chief *pulque* center surrounded by great *maguey* plantations.) Has a splendid Augustinian convent with four well-preserved religious frescoes and an unusually fine open chapel.

REAL DEL MONTE, in the mountains 6 miles from Pachuca on a paved road, is a large, active mining town, where one may visit the mines. Nearby is a lovely drive through woods called "El Hiloche."

SAN MIGUEL REGLA, 25 miles northeast of Pachuca Valley, is the over-200-year-old ore refinery *hacienda*-home of El Conde de Regla, the founder of Monte Piedad. Now a hotel, in wooded country, with lakes and rivers, fishing and swimming.

STATE OF OAXACA

OAXACA is one of the most interesting states in the Republic. In and near the capital, Oaxaca City, are some magnificent examples of Colonial architecture and pre-Conquest ruins. It has a great variety of native peoples, some of them quite primitive and others very progressive. Two of Mexico's great presidents, Juárez and Díaz, were Zapotecs, and the state has given the country other leaders. It has every kind of scenery and climate and the people are very industrious and skillful in their handicrafts. Their folk dress, costumes, and dances are varied and outstanding.

MEXICO CITY TO THE CITY OF OAXACA

BY TRAIN: Nightly express trains with Pullman service from Mexico City. Day-time trains changing at Puebla—a long, dusty ride, but interesting, through the Temollin Canyon.

236

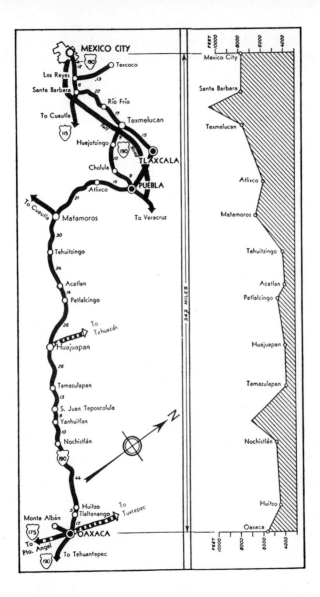

By Plane: One daily A.M. flight of Mexicana de Aviación. Aerolineas Vega has daily flight from Puebla to Acapulco and vice versa via Oaxaca.

By Car: Pan-American, C.N. 90, about 344 miles, via Puebla. Shorter trip via Cuautla on good road. First-class buses from Mexico City via either city.

See Puebla either on the way to Oaxaca or when returning. If the latter, save time by turning off from Cholula to Santa María Tonanztintla; stop to see the church and Observatory, and from there proceed to the Puebla-Atlixco Highway. This town lies in a fertile valley and is an important textile manufacturing center and has some good churches. The one on the hill is worthwhile climbing to for the view. Refreshment is available on the plaza.

The remainder of the distance to Oaxaca should be made at least once in daylight, for at Yanhuitlán is one of the finest of Mexican Colonial monuments—a sixteenth-century Dominican monastery. It is simply yet majestically constructed and is said to have been planned by the same architects who designed the Escorial, under Philip II. On the massive walls of the church are frescoes, recently uncovered, and the vaulted ceiling rises 75 feet in height. The parish church at Nochistlán is also Dominican and has some good oils.

If you have time to wander off the highway, the Saturday market at Tlaxiaco, about five hours away, is interesting with Mixtec costumes, arts and crafts. The open chapel at Tepozcolula on the way is also worthy of a visit.

Oaxaca City (Azt., Huaxayacan, or "Protruding from Calabashes") (Alt. 5,071 ft., Pop. 72,313) is the capital of the state of the same name. Has an agreeable climate practically the year round and is a delightful city, situated in a beautiful mountain valley. The city and surrounding places offer one of the most interesting trips in Mexico.

Hotels: Hotel Victoria, de luxe, a short distance outside the city; pool and good food. Moderate to expensive. The Monte Alban, Marques del Valle, and the new Hotel Plaz in the center of the city are all moderate. Hotel Frances, Ruíz, modest.

Motels: Motel Margarita on road into Oaxaca, new, no pool, moderate. Oaxaca Courts, on highway, cottages, pool, American food, moderate. Rancho San Felipe, a few miles out of town, is a *hacienda* which houses a few guests.

Life in this city centers around its two lovely plazas. Flanking the larger one are *portales,* or arcades, with stores and out-of-doors drinking places, where it is delightful to sit and watch the people. Here the natives and bootblacks gather and amuse themselves and each other. A good band and a marimba group give frequent concerts in the main plaza.

Oaxaca has a symphony orchestra and a university and its streets are very pleasant to wander through. El Fortin, the hill where the statue of Juárez stands, offers an attractive view. Juárez is pointing away from the city; the *oaxaqueños* interpret his gesture as meaning, "If you don't like it, leave." But most visitors to Oaxaca leave it regretfully.

The *City Market* is one of the most interesting and picturesque in the Republic. It is open daily, but on Saturdays the natives come from the surrounding villages, so it is livelier and larger. One finds there the *serapes* from Teotitlán del Valle, the lovely black unglazed pottery and toys from Coyotepec, and the green glazed ware and toys from Ozumpa. There is also the pottery which is made in the city, as well as attractive homespun cotton goods. Establishments in which these textiles are made, such as Casa Brena and Casa Bellón, may be visited. Fine steel *machetes,* or knives, are also local specialties.

Casa Cervantes, Porfirio Diaz 5, occupies one of the old houses surrounding a patio and has a variety of archeological, Colonial, and objects of folk art. Other good places for handicrafts are Arte Popular, M. Bravo 12, and Casa Audiffred, Hidalgo 59C. Arthur Train has unusual crafts and will ship for you, no matter where an item was purchased. Los Castillo, of the famous family, offers well-designed dresses, homespun men's shirts, and silver. El Granate, Hidalgo 44, sells copies of the Monte Albán jewels.

The Cathedral, constructed on the general plan of the

cathedral in Mexico City, was begun in 1563, completed in 1750. The Altar of the Monarchs and the Altar of the Señor of Pardon are interesting; the most ornate is the chapel of the Virgin of Guadalupe. The façade, with its bas-relief carvings, is still lovely despite the many revolutions and earthquakes which have damaged the church as a whole.

Santo Domingo. Started by the Dominican friars in 1572, and completed a century later. This massive fortress-like edifice has withstood earthquakes better than any other

Main Altar, Church of Santo Domingo—Oaxaca

building in Oaxaca. It is Baroque in style, and the interior is one of the most ornate in Mexico. The walls and ceiling are covered with gilt ornamentation of intricate design and polychrome sculptures in high relief. In the Capilla de la Virgen del Rosario, where the richest decoration is to be found, the background for the figures is in the form of a branching tree representing the Dominican genealogy. The chapel has its own choir and sacristy. The adjacent convent is now used as a military prison. Between the pillars around the patio are paintings of some of the early church dignitaries.

La Soledad: Splendid example of Colonial Baroque, carved in black stone. Shrine of the Virgen de la Soledad (The Lonely), patroness of the State of Oaxaca and of the sailors, who have brought her marvelous pearls as gifts. Festival on December 18 to celebrate her miraculous appearance; attended by people from all parts of the state. This *fiesta* runs into Christmas week and is very gay, with food stands, fireworks, and religious parades. Usually, on the afternoon of the 18th the plume dance is performed in the village of Teotitlán del Valle in honor of the Virgin. It is advisable to inquire about it, however, before making the trip, although the village is interesting to visit.

Church of San Felipe Neri, constructed of green stone, with highly gilded Churrigueresque altars.

San Juan de Dios, a favorite church of the natives, has some interesting paintings of the Conquest by Indian artists.

Christmas Week in Oaxaca City begins with the *fiesta* to the Virgen de la Soledad, on the 18th. Evenings there are *calendas,* or religious parades, to announce the *fiesta,* with music, costumes, and flowers; on the night of the 18th, splendid fireworks—a magnificent castle and other pieces. The night of the 23rd is the *fiesta de los rabanos,* or radishes. There are fantastic figures cut out of radishes, dry fish, birds made of seeds, and other objects for sale. The people eat *buñuelos*—thin pancakes fried in lard and covered with syrup—after which it is the custom to break the plates on which they are served. The outdoor life is very gay and *posadas*, or Christmas celebrations, take place indoors.

241

Monte Albán Ruins

There are many *fiestas* during the year in the city, a particularly colorful one being that at which regional dances are performed outside the city. Check dates in July.

MONTE ALBÁN: 4 miles from Oaxaca City. The road leads to the top of the hill where the ruins are dramatically situated, and the view of the valley and distant mountains is magnificent. The archeological zone covers a considerable area, including many uncovered mounds. There are remains of elaborate buildings, foundations, terraces, and patios belonging to several civilizations—from the Archaic to the Zapotecan and Mixtec—dating from about 500 B.C. to about 1,000 A.D., when building ceased and only the free spaces were used for tombs of eminent persons until the arrival of the Spaniards.

The Great Plaza is symmetrically enclosed by four large platforms. The most outstanding is the Patio Hundido (Sunken Patio) approached by a monumental stairway. Another of the platforms, inscribed with hieroglyphs on the upper part, is believed to have been used as an astronomical observatory.

A very striking landmark is the Edificio de los Danzantes (Edifice of the Dancers). On stones at its entrance are deformed figures transfixed in dance poses, dated by glyphs to 500 B.C., distantly related to the Olmec culture of La Venta.

Dr. Alfonso Caso, Mexico's leading archaeologist, who has directed several excavations at Monte Albán since 1931, has discovered numerous tombs. Some of these, decorated with bright-colored frescoes, are interesting to visit. The most important, Tomb 7, that of a Mixtec nobleman, had been surrounded by funerary urns, precious jewels, and goblets and bowls carved of quartz. Most of this amazing collection, known as the "Jewels of Monte Albán," is now in the city museum.

CUILAPAN (Azt., "Painted River," for ancient *cochineal* dye industry) is a Mixtec hamlet south of the city; its massive abandoned Dominican monastery is most poignant. Here the Zapotec Princess Donaji was held as hostage by the Mixtecs, who killed her for warning her kinsmen of the Mixtec-Spanish alliance against them. She is supposedly buried with her Mixtec husband in the local churchyard.

ZAACHILA, Zapotec capital founded by Zapotec king, Zaachila, about 1390, is now a country village on a bad dirt road. Take the early train on the local rail spur to enjoy a morning exploring the village; visit the market (Monday the chief day) and the newly opened and restored pyramid by the church. You can return to Oaxaca by train before lunch.

MITLA (Zap., "Place of the Dead") is about 28 miles away on a paved road (see route below). The Zapotec holy city Lyobaa (tomb) lies half a mile beyond this village of cactus-fenced houses.

The zone has five building complexes; the most important is beyond recovery, as the local church was built of its stones and standing walls.

Architecturally, Mitla is a geometric symphony of cyclopean stones and small delicate blocks arranged in four-

243

teen different Greek-style fretwork designs. Astounding geniuses handled weighty stone lintels, arranged foundation blocks to swing freely during earthquakes, and raised these walls of precisely patterned, small blocks, fitted together with little or no cement. Once painted red, the stones are time-bleached. There was never other decoration or sculpture beyond the unique fretwork patterns. Outstanding restorations: Hall of Monoliths—columnar pillars, block lintels; Patio of the Crosses with tomb chambers. Embrace La Columna de la Muerte (Column of Death) with both arms. The guide will measure the space between your fingertips and calculate the time of your demise. The remarkable skill and artistry exhibited in the construction of these palaces are even more remarkable when one remembers that the builders had no metal tools.

Museo de Art Zapoteca, founded by E. R. Frissell, now Mexico City College's Center of Regional Studies, is on the village plaza, the pleasant Posada de la Sorpresa attached to it.

EL FUERTE, a fortified hill surmounted by ancient ruins, is about 2 miles from Mitla. A trip by horseback or on foot provides splendid views of the surrounding country, and the remains of the one-time fort are of interest. You can hike to an old *hacienda,* now in a state of decay, with curious subterranean passages, and to the quarry where Mitla's stones were cut. Semipagan New Year festivals occur at Cruz de los Pedimentos (Cross of Petitions) and Cruz de Matatlán in a neighboring hamlet.

VILLAGES BETWEEN OAXACA AND MITLA

TLACOCHAHUAYA (Azt., "Damp Place") has a most interesting seventeenth-century church, decorated with the apparitions of the Virgin of Guadalupe, flower motifs, and gay-looking angels. The Municipal Palace has unusual carvings.

SANTA MARIA DEL TULE is where the giant *ahuehuete* —El Arbol del Tule—stands in the churchyard. It is 165 feet high by 160 feet in circumference. Nearby another tree

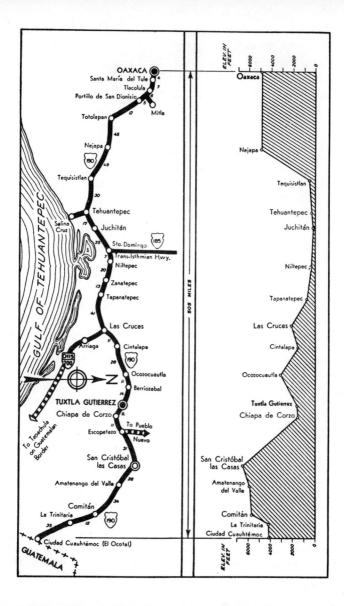

Tule Tree—Santa María del Tule

of the same kind, 75 feet high, is referred to as "The Son of the Giant."

YAGUL, 19 miles south, just off C.N. 190, is a newly opened zone. You may visit the digs.

TLACOLULA (Azt., "Place of Twisted Things") has a chapel decorated in the Santo Domingo manner. The little village church of San Teitepac nearby has two famous anonymous paintings of the Apostles and Purgatory.

TEOTITLÁN DEL VALLE (Azt., "Among the Gods of the Valley"), off C.N. 190, is a famous *serape* center. The ancient village church is of simple architecture, showing primitive Zapotec carvings where the stucco has fallen off from the exterior walls.

Excursions: Picturesque days of the plaza: Friday at pottery-making OCOTLAN—specialties are unglazed primitive bowls and toys; Wednesday at ETLA—cheese center; Sunday at TLACOLULA—all regional wares. COYOTEPEC makes black pottery; SANTA TOMÁS is a weaver's town. Rare experiences are visits to HUATLA DE JIMENEZ, center of a holy mushroom cult, and to a mountain town, YALALAG, in the Sierra. Here the appearance of the people and the houses is almost Greek. Everything is white and clean and the setting is magnificent.

The road to SAN PABLO GUELATAO, Benito Juárez' birthplace, is being paved; this and many other secluded villages in the Mixtec Sierra and on the Pacific coast are accessible by bus or jeep over new dirt roads or by plane from Oaxaca City. Second-class buses get to PUERTO ÁNGEL's fine beach; only planes or jeep to more exotic PUERTO ESCONDIDO.

THE ISTHMUS OF TEHUANTEPEC

This picturesque, tropical narrow neck of Mexico is crisscrossed by paved highways—north and south by the Pan-American Highway (C.N. 190) in the west and the Gulf Coast Route C.N. 180 on the east. Trans-Isthmus C.N. 185 starts at Salina Cruz on the Pacific, ends at Coatzacoalcos on the Gulf. Motorists can make a fabulously exciting circuit from Mexico City via Puebla, Oaxaca, Tehuantepec, Coatsacoalcos, Veracruz, and back to the Capital. The same trip by bus or train is longer, requiring stopovers.

FROM OAXACA CITY TO THE ISTHMUS OF TEHUANTEPEC on C.N. 190, about 160 miles south, takes about a half day of easy driving. Scenic points are the drops to Totolopa and Rio Hondo. If you wish to explore a little, a short detour to the charming village of Nejapa, near the Rio Camaron Bridge, would be rewarding.

IXTEPEC, JUCHITÁN, AND TEHUANTEPEC, the three important towns of the Isthmus, are within a short distance of each other. Buses run between the towns and one can hire a car.

IXTEPEC, the most commercial, is the railroad junction and plane stop for the Isthmus. Hotel Panamericano, moderate but filthy.

JUCHITÁN, the most primitive of the trio, is the century-old rival of more publicized Tehuantepec, and cleaner; people more kempt and cordial; *fiestas* more spontaneous and lively—the May one is the gayest. Accommodations poor. Best at Posada San Vicente or Hotel Gonzales.

TEHUANTEPEC, near the Pacific, in a beautiful tropical region, where fruit and flowers grow in profusion, is noted for its beautiful women, the famous Tehuanas. Proud and arrogant, they dominate the men, whom they outnumber, as well as the market trade. Their dresses, consisting of a short embroidered cotton *huipil*, or blouse, and a long skirt with a white, sweeping flounce, are among the most picturesque in the Republic. For holidays their dresses are of better materials, and for church they wear a lace *huipil* which frames the face; their adornments are intricate gold earrings and heavy gold chains, hung with ten, twenty, and even fifty U.S. gold pieces. Their markets are alive with color. The native language, Zapotec, is still spoken and many traditional customs are preserved. Dances and *fiestas* take place often.

Tehuana Girl

Hotel Tehuantepec, the best on the Isthmus. Gardens, swimming pool, good food, modest to moderate.

SALINA CRUZ, a reactivated seaport, 17 miles southwest of Tehuantepec, is the terminus of C.N. 185. Good bathing and fishing. Hotel Guasti serves fine seafood; also Restaurant Pinguiños. LA VENTOSA (Sp., "The Windy Woman"), a tiny fishing hamlet 2½ miles from here, accessible by several sandy roads from C.N. 185, has superb beaches, good seafood, hammock lodgings in thatched huts or outside.

STATE OF CHIAPAS

This state, bordering on Guatemala, lies in the tropics. It has mountains and jungle, ocean and rivers, and a great variety of fauna and flora. It is exceedingly fertile and can grow almost anything—coffee, rice, wheat, cotton, rubber, and quinine. Its ruins and native tribes, especially the Lacandón and Chamula, are among the most interesting in Mexico.

This section of the Pan-American Highway, Carratera Cristóbal Colón, C.N. 190, continues from Tehuantepec through Chiapas to the frontier town of CIUDAD CUAUH-TÉMOC (former El Ocotal). Its last winding stretch is improved. At LAS CRUCES, turn right on C.E. 195 to the railroad junction, Arriaga, where autos can be put on trains to Guatamala. Or from TONOLÁ, a prettier town, near PUERTO ARISTA's good beaches. At ARRIAGA, the end of the railroad line from the Isthmus, one can stay at the simple Pan American Hotel or continue on to the state capital.

TUXTLA GUTIÉRREZ (Alt. 1,805 ft., Pop. 41,532) is the capital of Chiapas. Can be reached from Mexico City by Cía. Mexicana planes via Oaxaca, the plane continuing as far as Tapachula; by train with Pullman via Veracruz to Arriaga, from where there are buses to Tuxtla over a good auto road, through picturesque country, taking 4 to 5 hours.

Hotels: The Bonampak, on the highway; the Rex, in the center, and the San Francisco motel, at the airport, are all good. Modest to moderate.

Tuxtla is a pleasant modern city with its streets all paved and many new public buildings—a government palace, hospital, penitentiary, clinic, market, stadium, schools, and a Museo Regional with some fine archeological pieces.

The botanical gardens and zoo, with the tropical flora and fauna of the state, and the State National History Museum, on the outskirts, are most interesting.

It is always hot in Tuxtla, but the river offers refreshing swims. Night life around the plazas is pleasant. On one is a curious relief map.

Excursions: BERRIOZABAL, a few miles from Tuxtla, has large nurseries of orchids for which the state is famous; and EL SUMIDERO, about 12 miles southeast of Tuxtla, is a 6,000 foot-deep gorge of Rio Grijalva, where Chiapanecos—warriors and their families—committed mass suicide, rather than surrender to the Spaniards. First explored in 1960 by army-supported daredevils, You can visit other scenic spots on this river, but better start out from CHIAPA DE CORZO.

Zoque families, living around the edge of the city, weave and embroider and celebrate interesting *fiestas* with dances on August 4 and 23-25, September 29, and during carnival time and Corpus.

CHIAPA DE CORZO, founded 1528 on an Indian town site, is 9 miles from TUXTLA on C.N. 190. Buses run frequently. The town overlooks the Grijalva River, has a good church, a unique brick fountain in the form of the Spanish royal crown, and picturesque cobbled streets and houses. The popular arts are the painted gourd bowls, called *xicapexlis*, leather bags, and the embroidered blouses worn by Zoque women. A good museum is especially devoted to lacquer. The big *fiesta* takes place on January 22. Near the cemetery the U.S. New World Archaeological Foundation is exploring and restoring pre-Hispanic edifices, chiefly Mayan in origin.

LAS CASAS: San Cristóbal, former capital and still the religious center, is a charming old Colonial city founded in 1528 (Alt. 7,464 ft., Pop. 23,355). It is a scenic drive, climbing four hours from Tuxtla through woods and villages, and buses run regularly.

Hotel Español and Posada Maya offer modest comforts and a restaurant. Inexpensive.

LAS CASAS, situated in a fertile valley of ever-green mountains and meadows, has fine Colonial houses, the handsomest the residence of founder Diego de Mazariegos, and churches—the Cathedral in the plaza, with Baroque *retablos* and gold-decorated pulpit; the church and dilapidated monastery of Santo Domingo, begun 1547; Iglesia del Carmen, its tower arching over a narrow street. Exciting to visit is the training school of Instituto Nacional Indigenista, to observe its dedicated service to the area's native peoples. For those who are interested in Indians the place has an additional fascination. One can spend many delightful hours around the plaza and in the tiny shops on Victoria Guadalupe Street, where they come daily to buy and sell their handicrafts—wool and cotton textiles, a pleasing unglazed primitive pottery, and a great variety of unique *sombreros*. The races are the Tzeltal and Tzoltzil, each village with its own style of dress and hat, the Chamula women wearing heavy black hand-woven wool skirts and *huipiles,* the men plain white or striped wool *jorongos* reaching to the knees and belted in at the waist. Much weaving is done in Las Casas on upright looms and in the villages on the horizontal or the pre-Conquest type.

Best place to shop is museum-like La Segoviana, G. Victoria 2. Owner Don Joaquin Hernanz, an encyclopedia of local lore, is a helpful substitute for an official tourist information office.

The cultural center is a private archeological museum, folk arts museum, and library in the old *hacienda,* now Na-Balom (At the Sign of the Jaguar) founded by the distinguished matrimonial team of Drs. Franz and Gertrude Blom and maintained by them until Dr. Franz Blom's recent death. Dr. Gertrude Blom remains in charge.

Excursions: Car trips to SAN JUAN CHAMULA—market in its community center, Sundays; AMATENGO, where charming, unglazed pottery is made by hand and baked in a bonfire; ZINANCANTAN, a Tzoltzil village, whose natives are most attractive and whose men sit or walk about the roads weaving their hats; TENAJAPA, the most picturesquely situated, where the regional dress is very colorful; and many others nearby and in the mountains, such as MOXIQUIL, a Maya ruin. Horses and guides are inexpensive—about three dollars a day each.

COMITÁN (Alt. 3,682 ft., Pop. 15,378) is a picturesque Colonial hilly city between Las Casas and the Guatamala border—six hours by car or bus from the former. Noted for its beautiful women, also for a sugar-cane beverage called *comiteco,* cotton textiles, and leather work. Nearby are several small archeological ruins. Comitán is the starting point from which to visit the varicolored Lagos de Campobello in the nearby National Park. The largest of these lakes has a beach, but all are fine for swimming. Arrange at Hotel de los Lagos for guides, camping gear, and food. This hotel is the newest and best. Montebello Hotel in center. The shop of Raul Aguilar is the best for suede skins.

TAPACHULA, 7 miles away by paved road, is situated in the fertile tropical Soconusco region at the foot of the Taconah Volcano near the Guatemala border and is important because of the products of the surrounding country. (Pop. 41,701.) The city itself has nothing of interest but is the landing place for all planes going south and is connected with Tuxtla by those that leave Mexico City via Oaxaca, as well as by the Isthmus train. It is also the point from which the station-wagon buses leave for Guatemala.

Hotels: Gran Internacional, Fenix, and Colombia; moderate.

PALENQUE (Sp., "Barricade") is the famous Chiapas archeological zone and the most exotically beautiful in the Republic, located at about midway between Coatzacoalcos and Campeche, on the Ferrocarril del Sureste, about 15 hours from either city. At present there is only a landing strip for private planes from Villahermosa, Tabasco. Fare very low.

Hotel de la Cruz de Palenque, for all its elaborate name, is small and uncomfortable, with primitive sanitation facilities. The same is true of the rooms of Domingo Lacrois. However, despite its discomforts, Palenque is a marvelous experience. When the new hotel, now planned, is completed, it will also be a delightful vacation spot because of the beauty of its tropical forests, vegetation, and rivers.

The station wagon of the hotel and the jeep of Domingo Lacrois meet trains and take tourists up to the ruins. Barbachano Tours operates tours to Palenque out of Merida.

The ruins, consisting of a palace and several temples on pyramids, are dramatically situated in the foothills of the Sierra—white edifices against the green of the tropical woods. In the zone are flowering trees and wild flowers, strange bushes with huge green leaves; song of birds and the music of the stream, known as the "Baths of the Queen." The whole region is indescribably beautiful.

The temples at Palenque, while not so extensive as those of Yucatán, show the greatest delicacy and beauty of detail of all the Mayan ruins so far discovered. The exquisite artisanship, beauty of design, and sensitive handling of architectural masses as reflected in these temples have never been surpassed by any ancient peoples. Their achievements at Palenque, as in other Mayan cities, are all the more remarkable in that their superb architecture evolved entirely from their own culture without benefit of contact with or ideas from the outside world.

Palenque Archeological Zone

The Palace (El Palacio) is the largest and most imposing structure in the group. It stands on a large artificial terrace 40 feet high, originally ascended by spacious stairways on all four sides. The main building is 228 feet by 180 feet, and houses a large court, in which are other buildings and courts and the remains of a high tower. The exterior stone walls are stucco-covered, and the well-preserved portions which remain show the whole palace was decorated in brilliant colors both inside and out. The building contains a wealth of figures, bas-relief, idols, and hieroglyphs, executed in stucco and beautifully wrought. The inner courts, which appear to be later additions, contain exquisite decorations and are among the finest examples of Mayan architecture. The most prominent object of the Palace is the ruins of the tower in the second court, originally four stories in height, and a most unusual feature in Mayan architecture.

There are five exquisite temples in the Palenque group, each superimposed upon a high terrace or pyramid. The basic plan of all five is almost identical, the differences being principally in decorative treatment. Each contains an open portico leading to three inner chambers, the central one housing the elaborate altar and sanctuary. The most unusual feature of each temple is its double-sloping roof rising above a beautiful cornice, closely resembling the mansard-style roof of France, but surmounted by a high central roof comb. These vertical roof combs are stone, pierced by many openings, and richly decorated with sculptured designs. The faces of the roofs are also exquisitely carved.

The Temple of the Sun (Templo del Sol) has in its interior an elaborate altar in the rear of which are three huge stone slabs, joined together and elaborately carved. In the center is an allegorical representation of the sun, flanked on each side by costumed human figures. On the

Maya High Relief—Palenque

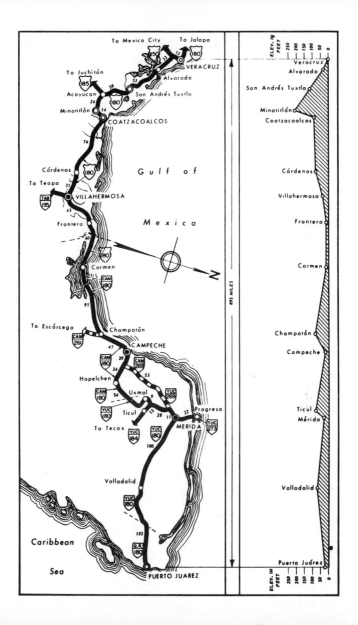

sides are almost 200 carved hieroglyphs, which probably hold the key to the meaning of the carvings. Weapons of war and other allegorical designs are also inscribed. The front panels and lintel of the altar are beautifully sculptured.

Temple of the Laws (El Templo de las Leyes), the largest of the group, has a large altar on the panels of which are hundreds of finely carved hieroglyphs which probably explain much of the history of the people and their economic organization. The roof crest of this temple is much smaller than the others, and the handsome carvings on the sloping roof are treated differently. This edifice is also known as the Temple of the Inscriptions.

In 1952 the archeologist Alberto Ruiz discovered in the Temple of Inscriptions the first tomb ever found in a pyramid of Central America. This will greatly influence archeological conclusions. The descent to the tomb is by a magnificent inner stone stairway, almost a hundred feet high, and the chamber is practically filled by the sarcophagus, covered with a handsomely carved stone weighing tons. The body buried there, that of a great Mayan personage, was literally covered with precious jewels, now on exhibition in Mexico City, together with masks and other objects. Excavation is continuing and more revelations are expected.

The Temple of the Cross of Palenque (El Templo de la Cruz de Palenque) originally contained an altar of elaborately carved limestone slabs, portraying a large cross symbolizing a tree, surrounded by allegorical figures, hieroglyphs, and decorations. These slabs have been removed intact to the National Museum in Mexico City, where they are set up in the Hall of the Monoliths in their original form. The temple is distinguished by beautiful, restrained carving, almost Chinese in its feeling.

Temple of the Foliated Cross (El Templo de la Cruz Foliada). Contains bas-relief altar panels similar to those which came from the Temple of the Cross. The panels are exquisitely carved, and at their outer edges are a series of about 150 hieroglyphs.

Temple of the Bas-Relief. Most distant of the central-Palenque group. On the rear wall of the temple are the badly mutilated remains of what was once an exquisite bas-relief carving, depicting a nearly life-size human figure seated upon a throne terminated on either side by tiger heads. This temple is the smallest of the five and differs somewhat from the others in its general plan.

There are other pyramids and mounds in the same neighborhood, but the temples which they once supported have been entirely destroyed. Another interesting ruin near-by is a very ancient and remarkably well-preserved bridge.

There are other minor archeological ruins in Chiapas, some near Comitán, already mentioned, and others near Ocosingo, but the following two are comparable to Palenque and belong to the same culture and epoch. Both are situated in the jungles along the Usumacinta River. The nearest approach to them is from Tenosique, Tabasco, a trip of several days on muleback.

JACHILAN, a magnificent stone city, is in good condition. But although known to outsiders for a long time, it is seldom visited except by the Lacandones of the region, who consider it a shrine.

BONAMPAK AND ITS FRESCOES. The existence of these ruins—temples on platforms, altars, and stelas—was first reported to the Instituto Nacional de Antropología e Historia, Mexico City, in 1946. The murals in one of the temples are the most important yet discovered, both from an archeological and artistic point of view. They contain priests, nobles, servants, slaves, musicians, and dancers in processions and ceremonial acts, brilliantly painted in their varied costumes, masks, adornments, symbols, and other paraphernalia.

Augustín Villagra Caleti, artist of the National Museum of Anthropology, a member of an expedition that visited Bonampak in 1947, has copied and reproduced these frescoes in color. The reproductions are in the National Museum of Anthropology in Mexico City. In January, 1962, the work of protecting these murals, keeping the jungle open and the air strip usable, began.

STATE OF TABASCO

TABASCO, the State between Chiapas and Campeche, on the Gulf of Mexico, has two important navigable rivers—the Grijalva and Usumacinta—and many minor ones, lakes, and lagoons. From the air it seems mostly water. The state is rich in fine woods and all the tropical products.

VILLAHERMOSA, the capital, is on the Grijalva River. With a population of 51,611, it has the air of a busy town rather than a city.

Connected with Mexico City and Mérida by car or bus via Gulf Coast Highway, C.N. 180, and by air via Mexicana de Aviación. Train connection at Teapa, 30 miles away by bus.

To avoid the sultry, tropical drizzle, visit in winter and enjoy river jaunts, fishing, hunting.

Hotels: Rafael, with riverside balcony; good. Manzur and San Diego passable. Restaurant Portales, fairly good.

World-famous for two incomparable museums. One, Museo de Tabasco, on the plaza, houses an unsurpassable archeology collection. Its companion, Museo de la Venta in Parque Tabasco, beside the Laguna de Ilusiones (Lake of Dreams) and zoological garden, re-creates the old Olmec religious center, La Venta. Both are poetic monuments of Mexico's Catholic poet-scholar, Carlos Pellicer.

STATE OF CAMPECHE

CAMPECHE, also on the Gulf, is the State that lies between Tabasco and Yucatán, has many rivers, islands, and forests, rich in tropical fauna and flora and game for hunters and fishermen.

CIUDAD DEL CARMEN (Pop. 20,901), a plane stop on C.M.A. daily Mexico-Mérida flight, is the only stopover on its island for travelers on the Gulf Coast Highway, C.N. 180. Fair hotels: Fernandez, Roma. For a long stay, rent an apartment. Many superb seafood eating places. A quaint island town, hidden under coconut palms, its wharf is lined with shrimp and other fishing boats, and it has a lively plaza, a few movies, a small archeological museum, and good swimming at Laguna Azul. The fishing is extraordinary. The boisterous *fiesta* of Carmen, July 15-31, also celebrates the final expulsion of pirates, July 16, 1717.

CAMPECHE, the capital, is connected with Mexico City by plane and with Mérida by railroad, a paved highway, and buses. Campeche (Pop. 44,426) is a C.M.A. air stop on Mexico-Mérida daily flight; stop on Ferrocarril de Sureste; on Gulf Coast Highway C.N. 180, served by A.D.O. buses from Mexico City. Its houses, old pirate forts, and sea wall mellowed by the sea and sun make it a charming place, but the modern breakwater spoils the waterfront. There is a fine archeological collection in the State Museum, in an old church, and the Museo de Armas (arms) in the San Carlos Fort is interesting. There is hunting, fishing, and swimming nearby.

Castle Part of the Pirate Wall at Campeche

Hotels: Lopez is air-conditioned. Has good dining room. The older Castlemar, across from waterfront, is simpler. Other hotels: Colonial and Baluartes. Mirador Restaurant is best for seafood.

ITZNAB, an archeological zone nearby, has pyramids and temples of the Uxmal epoch (about tenth century) their façades showing decorations of processions and reliefs, some in vivid colors.

Other interesting places may be visited from Campeche, especially on ocean and river boats. Various archeological tombs have recently been excavated on the island of Jaina, with offerings in them of exquisitely-carved sculptures and fine pottery, exhibited in the Museum of Campeche and Mexico City. Arenas Island, an hour further by launch, is a trip into a tropical paradise, with red flamingos and other colorful birds.

CHAMPOTON, a scenic drive a few hours from Campeche along the sea. Here Cortés met Malinche, the Indian maid who became his mistress and was a great help to him in the conquest of Mexico. Now it is the fishing port of Campeche, a charming village on the sea and a tropical lagoon, with a famous seafood restaurant.

A highway is in preparation from Champoton south-westward to Coatzacoalcos and north-eastward to Puerto Juárez, where there will be ferry service to Cuba. Completion of this project is still several years away, although some sections may be usable sooner.

STATE OF YUCATÁN

YUCATÁN (Azt., "Land of the Yucca") is the State on the peninsula of the same name. The bulk of the population is Mayan, descendants of the remarkable race who built the marvelous pre-Conquest cities in that state. The country is flat, and is covered with dense brush, the climate hot and humid. The peculiarities of the soil, coupled with a relative scarcity of water, afford an ideal situation for the raising of *henequén* or *sisal* plants which provide fiber for rope-making. Before the 1910 revolution large fortunes were made on these *henequén* plantations. Later the industry declined but World War II revived it again.

The Mayans have a high tradition of culture and Yucatán is the only Mexican state in which all social classes speak the Maya language. The natives, who call themselves *mestizos,* are small of stature and fine-featured. The women wear long embroidered cotton *huipiles;* on holiday occasions they are of silk, trimmed with fine laces. Their hair is worn in braids coiled on top of the head and tied with colored ribbons. They adorn themselves with gold jewelry, principally earrings and long gold filigree rosaries. Both men and women always dress in white and are very clean.

From an archeological standpoint Yucatán is one of the world's most interesting places. The two ancient Mayan cities of Chichén Itzá and Uxmal, both easily reached from Mérida, are magnificent and in themselves offer sufficient inducement for a trip to Mexico.

PROGRESO: The most important seaport of the Yucatán Peninsula and one of Mérida's two marine playgrounds. Connected with Mérida, the capital, by a 23-mile railroad and a paved highway, Progreso dates from comparatively recent times, has modern buildings and a concrete wharf two kilometers long.

CHICXULUB, farther east, is the other resort. Has better swimming, deep-sea fishing facilities, and resort hotel, the Cocotero, serving fine seafood.

MÉRIDA (Pop. 170,513) is the capital. Founded in 1542 by Francisco Montejo, Jr., on the site of the old Mayan city of Tiho and named after a Spanish city. Practically at sea level, it is always hot. Connected by Pan American planes with Mexico City, Miami, Fla., and Cuba; by boat with Veracruz. Daily A.D.O. bus service from Mexico City—a 36-hour trip on C.N. 180.

The Southeastern Railroad runs direct from Coatzalcoalcos via Campeche to Mérida.

Barbachano Travel Service owns a network of hotels, one at each major point of interest; tours are rigid, expensive, hotels expensive, services variable.

Yucatán Trails Travel Agency, friendlier services; its "Economy Tours" are excellently managed.

Hotels: The Mérida, the largest and best, has pleasant patios and a swimming pool; the Colon, smaller, offers luxurious Turkish baths. Also: the Gran Hotel, the Montejo, and Casa Camara on Paseo Montejo (once an elegant home, has gilded French furniture in the *sala* and one or two palatial bathrooms—all moderate. Flamingo and Posada Toledo—modest.

Food: Yucatán cuisine is gourmet fare—recipes of native antiquity blended with Spanish and French ones, the ubiquitous Mexican chile used sparingly, if at all—*but* hard to meet at its best outside of private homes. Venison, wild boar, duck, and seafood are plentiful. Among the specialties are the famous *cochinito* (suckling pig) and *pollo* (chicken) *pibil,* barbecued in banana leaves. *Pavo relleno negro,* turkey stuffed with chopped pork and served with a rich, black sauce. *Escabeche Oriental,* roast turkey with an onion and chili sauce, and *chocolomo,* a spicy stew, for a hangover.

Some of the popular dishes, numerous and savory, are *panuchos,* corn and bean flour cakes, covered with pieces of chicken or meat and seasoning; *salbutes,* tortillas filled with minced meat, fried and served with a sauce of onions, herbs and bitter orange juice; *cozitos, tacos* filled with chopped pork and covered with tomato sauce sprinkled with Holland cheese; *papazul, tacos* of ground squash seeds, egg and a sauce of the seeds with tomatoes; fried beans and a variety of delicious *tamales.*

Places to Eat: The hotel restaurants serve good food, but the favorites of the Yucatécans are the Itzá and Tulipanes. Evenings the Tulipanes restaurant serves good regional dishes outdoors (dancing). Café Express and other small restaurants around the plaza are good and inexpensive. Popular dishes are served from stalls on the neighborhood plazas. One of the best and most pleasant is El Chato Xpil, near the old San Sebastian church. La Prosperidad is an agreeable sort of beer garden, patronized by intellectuals. For ice cream, the Colon on the large plaza is the most popular.

Diversions: Golf and dancing at the Country Club, swimming and fishing at Progreso, and hunting in the country. The Tulipanes is delightful for outdoor dancing, also for a swim in their specially-lighted *cenote*. The Farolito has good dance music Thursday, Saturday, and Sunday nights and there is dancing in various other clubs.

The Yucatecos are a gay, pleasure-loving, friendly people. Among them are good composers, whose songs are popular everywhere in the Republic, with those of the late Guty Cardenas internationally known. And in Mérida are many good singers. The regional folk dance is the *jarana,* a sort of *zapateada,* danced gaily by many couples at all their affairs. Carnival time is celebrated with street parades and dances in all the social clubs and there are many other *fiestas* throughout the year.

Shopping: *Mestiza fiesta*-dresses, hand-embroidered and trimmed with fine lace; gold filigree earrings and rosaries with coral; finely-woven *henequén* hats, purses, fans, bags and the hand-made hammock-beds, simple pottery—all regional—and the handicrafts from outside. The Hotel Mérida shop carries a very fine selection, also Barbachano's across the way. The Hollywood and other shops around the plazas and the large city market.

The separate Museums of Archeology and State History are now consolidated in the former Governor's residence on Paseo de Montejo. It has a good collection of Mayan sculptures, ceramics, and jewels. Flanking the Parque Cepeda Peraza on 60th St. is Jesuit Iglesia de Jesús (founded 1618) not far from the University (corner of 60th and 57th streets), a descendant of the school founded by the Jesuits in 1618, but in a fairly modern building.

The church of San Juan de Dios, in the next street, has an unusual belfry composed of a high wall punctuated by openings in which the bells are hung. In the cemetery and elsewhere in the city are monuments to the Revolutionary governor, Felipe Carillo Puerto, who with three of his brothers was assassinated during the 1923 De la Huerta revolt. During his term of governorship he instituted many improvements in the city and state, and consistently endeavored to improve the standard of living.

The city is picturesque and gay, with windmills rising above the tree tops, new spacious boulevards bordered by villas in gardens and parks, old gates, plazas, and streets, the corners of some preserving the ancient names of animals and birds represented in sculpture so that Mayas and Spaniards could understand them. The old-fashioned carriages are still popular.

In the Plaza de la Independencia, landscaped with laurels, palms, and flowers, is the stately, severe, sixteenth-century Cathedral, built 1561-1589 on the site of the Templo Mayor of old Tiho. In the present very ugly interior hangs a historical painting of the Maya submission to Montejo. A door carving depicts conqueror resting feet on heads of defeated Mayans. The scarred crucifix of the Christ of Blisters (*Cristo de las Ampollas*) has hung in its own chapel here since its rescue from the burned church of Ichmul. *Fiesta* of this miracle-performing image occurs September 28 to October 13.

On the plaza, too, are the deteriorated Archbishop's Palace, occupied by government offices; the municipal and federal government palaces; and the handsome Plateresque Montejo mansion (1549).

Other places of interest are the University, new modern schools and hospitals, the peasants' Casa del Pueblo, and the buildings of the Sindicato de Camioneros (Union of Busmen), whose social and educational organization is notable. The Parque de las Americas has gardens, fountains, an open-air theater and library, and the Parque del Centenario has a fine zoological garden and aviary of colorful tropical birds, among them pheasants and wild turkeys.

At the end of the handsome Paseo Montejo rises the Monumento a la Patria. It is semicircular, about 130 feet in circumference by 30 feet high, encircled by a sculptured frieze depicting the history of Mexico with life-size figures of people, and in the center the tree of life with the arts, a colossal undertaking, on which by 1954 the sculptor Romulo Rozo had worked eight years and expected to take two more for completion.

264

ARCHEOLOGICAL ZONES

CHICHÉN ITZÁ (Chee-chen EE-tzáh) the most famous and largest of the zones, is 75 miles east of Mérida on C.N. 180 to Puerto Juárez. En route are attractive villages and towns, with oval white huts, where you can see the life of the *mestizos*. One may stop to visit a *sisal* mill at the picturesque *hacienda* of San Pedro, the sixteenth-century convent at Hocton, and the lovely old rose-colored church at Xocchel, with its charming plaza. Also there are hidden *cenotes* along the way. A short detour leads to the quaint historical town of Izamal, with an immense, fine old convent and unexplored archeological mounds, in which, according to legend, is buried a part of the body of a Maya savant.

Castillo—Chichén Itzá, Yucatán

Pisté, the picturesque little village nearest to Chichén Itzá, has the Restaurant Cuchanchen and rooms to rent.

It takes a long time to see and enjoy Chichén Itzá and the Hotel Mayaland is one of the loveliest in Mexico. It has hut-style cottages, also rooms in the main building, all charmingly furnished, and set in a lovely tropical garden with swimming pool. Good food and entertainment by the attractive young *mestizo* personnel, who sing and dance the *jarana* and make you feel at home. Expensive.

There are many puzzling gaps in the history of Chichén Itzá, but evidence points to its founding in the 4th or 5th century, its abandonment in the year 698, and reoccupation in A.D. 964 when it grew large and powerful. It was permanently abandoned in 1448. The remarkable development of the Mayan culture in all the arts and sciences, and the magnificent edifices they left for posterity as proof of their high civilization, constitute what is probably the most vivid and remarkable phase in the early history of the Western Hemisphere. Apart from their great beauty, all of the Mayan buildings reveal superb artisanship and splendid engineering skill. It is a curious fact, however, that with all their ingenuity, the Mayans never discovered the principle of the segmental keyed arch; hence a dominant feature of Mayan interiors is the flat-sided vaulted ceiling.

Many of the large buildings in this zone, however, show Toltec influence and are said to have been constructed by the Toltecs expelled from the Central Plateau, and not by the Mayas. Among them are the Castle, Ball Court, and Temple of the Warriors.

NOTE: It is dangerous to wear high-heeled shoes climbing the steep, narrow stone steps of the edifices, especially those inside the Castle. Take along a big hat and sun-glasses and avoid going out during the midday hours. Wonderful to visit the ruins by moonlight.

The highway passes through the zone and divides it in two. The side dominated by the Castillo is cleaned of all vegetation and almost looks like a modern civic center, while the buildings on the opposite side are still in the woods and convey a deeper sense of age and mystery.

The Castle (El Castillo), or Great Temple of Kukul-Kan, one of the largest and most striking of the monuments, is a huge pyramid almost 100 feet high, surmounted by a beautiful temple ornamented with sculptured stones. Wide central staircases, one on each side of the pyramid, lead to the temple. The staircases are flanked by low balustrades decorated with writhing winged serpents, but only two are restored. Inside El Castillo is an older pyramid, with a high, steep stone stairway of narrow steps, leading to a small dark chamber. The entrance is guarded by a huge well-preserved Chacmool, a human figure reclining on its back, with knees drawn up and head turned up sharply to one side. There you are confronted by a stone jaguar, his attitude expressing surprise and anger. He is painted bright red, with eyes of shining green jade, white teeth, his body spotted with green jade discs and on his back a plaque set with turquoise. This fascinating, lifelike jaguar is believed to have served as a throne. Over the portal of the chamber are some fine carvings.

EL CENOTE SAGRADO AND THE STORY OF THE BRIDE: An ancient causeway of less than a quarter of a mile leads from El Castillo to the Sacred Well, an immense pool, its dark green opaque waters far below the surface, set in white-to-gray sculptured walls, the rim surrounded by green shrubbery, gray stones, and a small platform, a part of a small temple no longer there. In the old days, when the Mayas of the region suffered or feared some disaster, such as plague, famine, war, or drought, they appeased the anger of the gods by precious gifts, prayers, and human sacrifice. In this case the victim would be the most beautiful and most pure of the young virgins, who was offered as a bride to the god of the well. On the day of the sacrifice, she would be dressed in a bridal *huipil,* adorned with jewels and flowers, and led in procession from El Castillo to the sacred *cenote,* accompanied by masked priests and musicians playing flutes and drums. At the *cenote* the music became more intense, the priests threw in their precious jewels and ornaments and chanted prayers. The bride, promised everlasting happiness for saving her people, and her senses drugged for the occasion with *balche,* the ritual Maya liquor, was still unwilling to die and shrieked with horror as she was flung into the deep well.

Spectators would wait anxiously to see if the bride would reappear. When such a miracle came to pass, it represented an immediate answer from the gods that the prayers of the people had been heard. But it is said that this happened only once or twice.

Verification of this legend came from Edward T. Thompson, U. S. Consul in Yucatán for forty years. Intrigued by the mystery of the Sacred Well, he bought the property. At the turn of the century he dredged it and found the bones of the young girls, also the treasure thrown into it by the priests. Most of the latter, kept for decades in the Peabody Museum in Cambridge, Mass., were recently returned to Mexico. Present explorations with modern diving and dredging equipment will continue until the *cenote* yields its last mud-hidden offering and the great blocks of the old temple are raised and set in place.

Temple of the Warriors—Chichén Itzá

Temple of the Warriors (El Templo de los Guererros). An immense and spectacular pyramidal construction in a spendid state of preservation, surmounted by a temple containing many elaborately carved pillars, on some of which the original painting is still visible. Expressive bas-relief sculptures adorn the exterior walls. The temple is reached by a wide and steep staircase. An older construction was discovered inside of the pyramid, known as the Temple of

Temple of the Warriors—Upper Platform

269

the Chac-mool, or rain god. Because of protection from the elements, its colored decorations are still lovely. At the base of the temple lies the Court of a Thousand Carved Columns, originally roofed over, and apparently used as a market place or public square.

Ball Court. Two parallel walls and small temples at each end remain of this huge court which was used in playing the ancient ball game called *tlachtli*. The small temples are a long distance apart, yet the acoustics are so extraordinary that two persons, one at the north end and one at the south, can carry on a conversation in an ordinary tone of voice. Projecting from the center of each side wall about 20 feet above the ground is a huge stone ring 4 feet in diameter. The point of the game was to throw the ball through these rings without touching it with hands or feet—only with elbow, knee, or thigh—a very difficult feat. Rewards for the winners were generous, but the captain of the losing team sometimes paid with his life.

The Temple of the Tigers (El Templo de los Tigres), adjoining the Ball Court, is one of the finest of the ruins. The name derives from a frieze running around the exterior walls in which a procession of tigers is sculptured in bas-relief. The immense columns of the portico are beautifully carved with serpent motifs and the pillars along the side walls contain sculptured human figures and allegorical designs. The inside walls are decorated with hieroglyphs and mural paintings, portraying human figures and probably representing historical and religious festivals.

The only other structures on this side of the zone are three small platforms, each sculptured and marked with its title. The Tzompantli Parapet is surrounded by a frieze carved with human skulls impaled on poles, undoubtedly victims sacrificed to the gods, showing Aztec influence. The other two are eagles and Venus, the latter probably a dance platform.

The zone across the highway also has remarkable edifices. Near the entrance through a wooded path stands the Tomb of the High Priest and next, on a high terrace, Chican Chob, with an ornamental roof crest, believed to have been a dwelling of priests.

270

El Caracol, or The Snail, deriving its name from the interior circular stairs in a round tower, is a striking edifice, its beauty resulting from harmonious lines rather than from decoration. It is believed to have been used by the Maya astronomers as an observatory and may also have served as a watch tower. The tower rests upon a double-terraced base, approached by wide stairways. In the five-member cornice encircling the upper part of the building are some strikingly narrow slits used for astronomical observations and so placed that they are hit by the sun on the four days of the solstice. The Mayas developed a year count as perfect as ours and their calendar served as a base for the calendars of all other pre-Conquest tribes.

The Nunnery (Casa de las Monjas) is the most richly sculptured of the entire zone. The main structure is of three stories with ten rooms and the annexes of one story. Some historians believe it was a home for vestal virgins, hence the name; others incline to the belief that because of its size and grandeur it served as a residence for rulers.

Near Las Monjas is the elaborately carved temple called the *foloc,* or "church," and the Temple of the Wall Panels.

Akat-Tzib, House of Dark Writing, also near Las Monjas, consists of a series of rooms with impressions of red hands on the interior walls. The House of the Deer, close by, it sometimes called the Red House, because of the wide red band encircling the antechamber walls. It is one of the best preserved of the zone.

At a short distance from the zones are some excavated columns that were a part of the extensive slave market and a cemetery.

RUINS OF OLD CHICHÉN ITZÁ: A mile from the major ruins, reached by a path which leads through the jungle. These ruins, more purely Mayan, are the oldest in the Chichén Itza and still mostly unexcavated. While they lack the awe-inspiring immensity and magnificence of the major ruins, many are very beautiful. Noteworthy are the Temple of the Two Lintels, the Phallic Temple, with the date carved on a linten corresponding to A.D. 619, the Temple of the Four Lintels, the Temple of the Little Heads, and the oldest temple of all, generally known as the Paul Martin Temple (because he directed the excavating and restoring of it) which dates from the fifth century. The surrounding jungle is full of monoliths, idols, statues, and other fragmentary remains.

VALLADOLID, the second city of Yucatán, is a short drive from Chichén Itzá, on the same highway. It has charming old Colonial homes and church, a picturesque *cenote,* and a lively market, as it is the metropolis of that region.

NOTE: The highway continues on to Puerto Juárez.

COLONIA YUCATÁN, on a branch road beyond Valladolid, is an amazing experience. After bumping along in a truck for five hours through a magnificent forest, you arrive at a model village. It has modern bungalows with all conveniences, schools, radios, a movie, facilities for games and outdoor sports for some two thousand employees of the company mills and factory for the sawing and finishing of a variety of fine regional woods. Except for its setting, its appearance and social organization are similar to a U.S. model village, but the inhabitants are Maya Indians, who are quickly becoming accustomed to modern life. There is no hotel, so it is necessary to make arrangements for a visit at the company office, in Mérida.

UXMAL (Oosh-máhl) 50 miles south on the Yucatán-Campeche highway, is an interesting drive through *henequén* country with red *sisal* mills, old *haciendas,* various towns, and low hills. Uman has an unfinished, sixteenth-century church that was intended to rival the Mérida Cathedral and a large lively market where the natives barter and bargain in Mayan as they did centuries ago. Muna is a quiet old Colonial town with a charming church on a laurel-shaded plaza. And agricultural Ticul has lovely gardens.

The new hotel Hacienda Uxmal, managed by the owners of the Mayaland Lodge, is exceedingly attractive, with gardens and a swimming pool. The rates range from 150 *pesos* single to 350 double. Amer. Pl.

MAYAN RUINS: The Maya ruins at Uxmal are among the finest, although unlike Chichén Itzá, the major temples seem not to have been laid out in a pattern corresponding to a civic center. In richness of detail, imagination, and heroic conception, the constructions known as the Nunnery and the Governor's Palace stand among the finest of the pre-Columbian ruins on the American Continent. Of the history of Uxmal little is known except that around A.D. 1000, several centuries after its founding, it joined the federation of Mayan states, whence followed two centuries of great prosperity. It was later abandoned for unknown reasons, and a new capital was established at Mani, 30 miles distant. The discoveries to date at Uxmal indicate that it was a very large city, probably equalling Chichén Itzá in size and grandeur.

House of the Prophet (La Casa del Adivino), the first temple visible upon arrival at Uxmal, is composed of a huge steep pyramid surmounted by two temples, one higher than the other. The exterior walls of both temples are magnificently sculptured. The lower temple seems to have been erected at a later date. A feature unique in Mayan design is the elliptical shape of the pyramid. From the upper temple, the panoramic view of the surrounding ruins is breathtaking.

The Nunnery (La Casa de las Monjas), which lies to the west of the pyramid, is an immense quadrangle composed of four large rectangular buildings which enclose a huge court. The buildings are elaborately ornamented and sculptured, each with a different style of design, but harmonizing with the whole. A huge arched gateway on the south side gives entrance to the court. Some 88 rooms in the adjacent buildings open out upon this court, with no windows or other openings on the outside walls. The eastern façade is exquisitely ornamented with intricate designs and human figures and heads. Two immense serpents whose intertwining bodies enclose many sculptured motifs ornament the western side. The north side, entirely different from the rest, reveals a marvelous array of delicately carved designs. On all sides the ground or field design is composed of beautifully carved stone lattice. Strange hooks resembling elephant trunks are found at all corners. The typical Mayan arch is used in the construction of all the chambers or rooms. The design of this monumental building group would indicate that the court was used for great pageants and religious ceremonies.

The Ball Court, similar to the one at Chichén Itzá, is near the south side of Las Monjas. Close by are a group of smaller ruins, one of the most important of which is called The Turtle, deriving its name from sculptures of turtles on the upper cornice. This temple is in ruins, but the original chaste beauty of the building is still evident.

House of the Governor (La Casa del Gobernador). This magnificent palace is considered the finest single Mayan edifice in existence. It is the most elaborately sculptured of all ruins in Yucatán and the decorative designs adhere to the pure classic Mayan forms. Some 20,000 sculptured stones are estimated to have been used in its construction, each one fitting perfectly and carved with superb artisanship. This Second Empire Building, erected about A.D. 1200, is 325 feet in length and rests upon a huge three-tiered terrace originally faced with stone. The large interior rooms are without carving, all with the typical Mayan vaulted ceiling.

The Pigeons (Las Palomas), lying to the east of the House of the Governor, is a ruined building which derives its fanciful name from the pierced openings in its gabled walls, somewhat resembling the pigeon lofts common in European rural houses. The building is 240 feet in length and was composed of a double range of rooms. The style is severe and impressive, lacking the elaborate ornamentation seen in neighboring buildings.

The cemetery has its own court and temple. Note the many stones carved with the conventional skull and cross-bones as well as the kneeling idol; the House of the Old Woman (La Casa de la Vieja), named after a statue of an old woman discovered there; the House of the Dwarf; and many fragmentary ruins scattered about the neighborhood.

IZAMAL, 15 miles east of Mérida on C.N. 180, has Colonial and pre-Hispanic ruins.

KABAH is 14 miles south of Uxmal on C.N. 180 between

The Nunnery—Uxmal

Uxmal and Campeche. The most interesting of its reconstructed buildings is the Palace of Masks, the entire façade covered with long-nosed serpent masks, probably of the Rain God, Chac.

Tours in Model-T Ford to LABNÁ, LAMNÁ, and SAYIL over woodland roads leaving highway at Santa Elena, 3 miles beyond Kabah, are arranged by Barbachano or Yucatán Trailways. A less expensive tour can be arranged directly with the Model-T owners, Sr. Hector Arana or Sr. Crescencio Castillo, who live near Mérida in Muna. It will be necessary to take camping equipment and food to spend the night in the ruins. Labná is noted for its unique façades of columns in pipe-organ formation and Sayil for its three-story palace.

Closer to Mérida, a half-hour drive, is exciting DZIBIL CHALTUN, still being excavated.

Flights by plane from Mérida or boat trip from Cozumel are the only means to reach white-walled TULUM, atop cliffs overlooking the Caribbean Sea. Lodgings at Tancah Ranch, but take own hammock and supplies.

Lodgings and transportation improve in this area—permits for new hotels were issued in 1962 and authorization given to start a shipping line from Puerto Juárez and Progreso to Miami, Florida.

Motorists can safely leave the car in Puerto Juárez with the Aduana and take one of two daily ferries to a wondrous vacation spot, ISLA DE MUJERES. Simple hotels and high prices; cottages for moderate rent skimpily furnished.

Daily flights (Tamsa and Aero Safari) and irregular boat service from Mérida to COZUMEL ISLAND, Quintana Roo. Aero Safari connects back jungle lands and archeological sites of Quintana Roo with major cities and leading airlines. Offices in Mexico City, Mérida, and on the island of Cozumel. Motorists can drive to Puerto Morales (not wholly paved after leaving C.N. 180) for the daily boat, or Puerto Juárez for the weekly one. Several de luxe, expensive hotels: La Playa, El Caribe (bungalows and pool), and Mayaluum, with cabañas, dining room, and art gallery. Cabaños Cozumel, modest, as are lodgings in private homes. Beach vacation spiced by visiting Mayan ruins on island, hunting

Cozumel Beach Scene

sunken treasures in the many ships lost here since discovered by Spaniards in 1518.

CHETUMAL, capital of Territory of Quintana Roo, and free port, now accessible by car and second-class bus from Mérida on gravel highway or by Aero Safari or one of triweekly flights from Mérida. Can go on by bus to Belize, British Honduras.

Hotels: Nuevo Hotel Los Cocos and Hotel Jacarandas —moderate, comfortable. Jungle-hidden city ruins such as CHUNYAXCHE are being explored.

BAJA CALIFORNIA

BAJA CALIFORNIA (Lower California) is the 760-mile-long peninsula at the opposite end of Mexico from Yucatán, but, unlike Yucatán, it has no great cultural tradition nor archeological monuments. However, it is richer in natural beauty, wonderful gulfs and bays, mountains, desert, and oases to satisfy the most exacting lovers of nature, fishing, and hunting and has the highest per capita income of any part of Mexico, offset somewhat by higher living costs.

The Indians who inhabited the peninsula upon the arrival of the Spaniards have disappeared, and the missions built for their conversion are now chiefly ruins. Foreigners and foreign influences are apparent near the northern border. The interior and the south are mostly Mexican, but it is a different Mexico from the mainland—no Indians, no folk arts and music, no colorful religious festivals.

In spite of this, it is interesting; yet until recently it was one of those far-flung, neglected territories, better known and more extensively exploited by foreigners. But this state of affairs has been changing. Now northern Baja California is a state and communications with the Mexican mainland are improving, along with tourist facilities for exploring the beauties of the interior. The southern, less populated section, still a Federal Territory, faces a brighter future when C.N. 1 is paved to Cabo San Lucas.

U.S. citizens can enter border cities without immigration documents, stay as long as they please, fish without license, take back their catch and all their purchases up to $100 worth each trip. Baja California is a free zone, without tariffs or duty.

BY PLANE: The Trans-Mar de Cortés runs Douglas DC-3 planes from Tijuana to many points of interest, especially to those with tourist accommodations, also from Guaymas to La Paz; and Aeronaves de Mexico flies to La Paz from Los Angeles, Tijuana, and Mexicali and connects with many Mexican cities. Schedules are seasonal. Countless resort hotels fly in their clients from the nearest large town.

BY BOAT: A water trip is the most ideal, but present services to any B.C. port are uncomfortable, irregularly scheduled freight boats. The trip does offer adventure, however. A daily ferry service for autos and passengers connects Mazatlán and La Paz.

BY CAR: Paved roads connect with all border towns from California. The Trans-Peninsular Highway, C.N. 1, from the border at Tijuana to the Peninsula tip is paved for less than 150 miles to ARROYO SECO; a good gravel road-bed continues to SAN QUINTIN, 60 miles south. There is a 130-mile paved section before La Paz, starting at VILLA CONSTITUCIÓN, but paving continues south only a short way after leaving La Paz. Then C.N. 1 goes perilously on through SAN JOSÉ DEL CABO to southernmost CABO SAN LUCAS. A rough Pacific coastal road heads north from here to TODOS SANTOS and an equally rugged crossroad returns to LA PAZ. This trip is an exciting adventure in scenery, places, and friendly people. A jeep or light truck, camping equipment, facilities for carrying gasoline and water and food, and a willingness to rough it are required. Much of the way is uninhabited and the road runs through sand or narrow dangerous mountain passes. Sometimes a day's progress will be 15 or 20 miles; a good average is between 50 and 75. The entire route has been carefully explored and marked with road signs by the Automobile Club of Southern California, 2601 S. Figueroa St., Los Angeles 54. They print and keep revising an amazingly accurate, up-to-date, informative log and publish the best road map of the whole peninsula, which also indicates best game and fishing areas.

TRAIN SERVICE: The only railroad lines in Baja California are two short local spurs that connect TIJUANA with TECATE and MEXICALI with ALGODONES; and Ferrocarril Sonora-Baja California to BENJAMIN HILL, Sonora, to connect with Ferrocarrilo del Pacifico to GUADALAJARA and all Mexico.

PLACES NEAR THE BORDER

MEXICALI, state capital of Baja California del Norte. Across from Calexico, Calif., it suffers from the same extremes of climate. However, the valley is good for the cultivation of cotton and grains. Consequently Mexicali has changed from a town of adobe huts to a city of over 172,554 with good modern buildings and residences. The city retains its tourist border attractions, but is no longer dependent upon them for its economy. It is connected with Mexico City and the U.S. by plane and highway and with all of Mexico by train and road.

Good paved C.N. 2, roughly 435 miles long, begins at Tijuana, passes through TECATE (a minor border entry port and famous for its beer of the same name), 30 miles farther east, continues through MEXICALI (125 miles from start) to SANTA ANA, Sonora, to join West Coast C.N. 15. At SONOYTA, 150 miles before the finish, a paved road, C.E. 5, branches south 87 miles to PUERTO PEÑASCO.

SAN FELIPE, on C.N. 5, 122 paved miles from Mexicali, is an unspoiled fishing village on the lovely gulf of the same name, where climate and fishing are good most of the time. A fine beach with camping and parking facilities and good accommodations at Augie's Riviera Hotel.

MUD VOLCANOES are near Cerro Prieto (Black Hill) 10 miles off the San Felipe road, along Cerro Prieto Canal to the tiny village of Pascual. The cones cover a vast area in an abandoned channel of the Colorado River, and they growl and grumble as they belch forth their underground volcanic gases, which, like the Solfatara near Naples, reproduce a bit of Dante's *Inferno*.

TIJUANA (Aunt Jane) has been and still is the "pleasure" capital of Baja California, patronized chiefly by Americans, the majority, perhaps, Marines from nearby San Diego. Tijuana has developed into a well-built city (Pop. 151,939). It still trades in pleasure, though in a more dignified way, and is establishing many industries. On weekends dog and horse races, *jai-alai* games, and occasional bullfights take place.

Accommodations: Hotel Caesar, Foreign Club, and Nelson's are quite satisfactory. Motels—De luxe Agua Caliente, near the race track of Hipódromo de Tijuana. La Sierra, Tropicana, Rancho de Gloria (all have air-conditioned units) are strung southward on Enseñada Highway, C.N. 1.

Away from the gay streets, it is pleasant to drive up the hill to the television studios, to the Dam, Presa Rodríguez, Tecate, or the once-famous gambling Casino Agua Caliente, converted into a school after ex-President Cardenas prohibited gambling in 1935.

Tijuana is a junction point for planes to all parts of Baja California, the mainland of Mexico, and California via the Trans-mar de Cortés and Aeronaves de Mexico (Douglas DC-3 planes), and the largest and best planes of the Compañia Mexicana de Aviación (CMA). For reservations, apply to the Ata Travel Bureau, Nelson Hotel, Tijuana, B.C., or to your own travel agent.

Bus service from here to ENSENADA (68 miles) on C.N. 1, skirting the ocean between rugged hills and white beaches. After passing inviting places for food, drinks, camping, and swimming, you arrive at the interesting village of EL SAUZAL. Here ex-President Abelardo Rodriguez established fishing cooperatives with canneries, and also built houses and a school. He has a home there himself and is experimenting in olive-growing. Just before Ensenada (about 16 miles), a road branches off to the Colonia Guadalupe, founded by White Russian pacifists in 1940. Since then many have intermarried with Mexicans, and not much remains of their picturesque customs. But some of them still speak Russian, drink tea from samovars, and the men wear red blouses on festive occasions.

ENSENADA is a delightful, friendly resort city, its beaches circling around lovely blue Todos Santos Bay. Here Robert Louis Stevenson wrote his *Treasure Island,* inspired by the locality's colorful history of pirates, treasure-laden ships from the Orient, and mysterious Santos Island. Around the turn of the century Ensenada was the prosperous little capital of northern Baja California, the center of the Alamo gold rush and a busy seaport. In 1914 the capital was transferred to Mexicali, the gold rush ended, ships stopped coming to the port, and the town went dead. Recently it has come to life again, its population shooting up from 4,000 to 42,770. It is now a thriving fishing and agricultural center, with canneries, the Santo Tomas winery, and has good Mexican handicraft shops and accommodations.

Hotels: The Riviera Pacifico, a former gambling casino, has stately salons, restaurants, and cabarets, set in lovely gardens on its own beach. Of the smaller cottage hotels on the beach, the Villa Marina is outstanding for its comforts and good restaurant. The Villa Carioca, Del Paseo, and other motels are good, but likely to be expensive. Hotels Isobel, Plaza, Monte Mar, and Del Mar offer special rates to U.S. citizens wanting to experiment before complying with Mexico's easy resident terms for retired people.

Islands: About 200 miles south-southeast of Ensenada are the striking rock-bastion Islands of Guadalupe, the home of the sea elephants. These are huge, ugly, aquatic mammals, resembling seals with the males about fifty times as large, some of them reaching a weight of several tons. The female is much smaller and less ugly but both are torpid and emit cries that can be heard over a mile away. Sea lions live on the San Benito Islands, farther south. There is no regular boat service to the islands, but one can go in a private boat. Inquire at Ensenada.

Rancho Hamilton, a hunting lodge 104 miles from Ensenada, is a favorite with sportsmen for its comfort, hospitality, and good food. Ruins of Santo Domingo Mission are nearby. It has an air-strip but the drive is pleasant along the sea, and the vineyards and village of Santo Tomas. It is less expensive to stay at the motel in the nearby village of Colonia Guerrero, where fishing boats and horses and guides for hunting are available.

VARIETY IN THE WILDERNESS

The road, C.N. 2, continues good for about 20 miles beyond Colonia Guerrero. For the rest of the 1,000 miles it alternates between sand and rocks, *arroyos* and precipices, with small ranches and villages far apart in time, if not in space, some of them offering supplies and opportunities for fishing and hunting of big game in the mountains and small prey in the air. Here and there roads branch off to ruined missions, built by the Jesuits and Franciscans centuries ago. The date-palms they planted are still good. In the desert are interesting varieties of cacti and strange trees, like the silvery-barked *cirio* with short green branches and brilliant blossoms shooting 150 feet straight into the air, or the *ocotillo* bristling with thorns ending in red tassels.

EL ROSARIO, 231 miles from Tijuana and 52 miles from Colonia Guerrero, is an attractive and large fishing and agricultural village, where the road turns inland. No passenger car should go beyond here.

EL MARMOL (The Marble), not far away, is said to have the largest onyx deposits in the world. When they were nearer the surface, at the turn of the century, a U.S. company extracted one block large enough for a bathtub, which they sold to an American millionairess at a fabulous price. Of the 200 inhabitants all the men work in the quarries.

SAN IGNACIO (535 miles) is the first real oasis and large village in the Vizcaino Desert. It lies in a declivity, hidden amidst date palms, laurels, fruit and flowering trees, and is pervaded by the typical *mañana* spirit, its people friendly and gay. The San Ignacio Mission, built by the Jesuits in 1728, is perfectly preserved and has a handsomely carved and gilded wooden altar. It is still used as a church.

SANTA ROSALIA (584 miles), a copper mining town practically owned by the French Boleo Company, has a small hotel, telegraph, telephone, airmail, and all other services. Freight boats taking passengers reach it irregularly from

Guaymas and passing tourists should report to the customs to show their papers. The town, with its rows of company frame houses and imported metal church looks most un-Mexican, but the Mexican workers are typical.

MULEGÉ (Moo-leh-héy) is another beauty spot in the wilderness, with the Club Mulegé offering comfort and light-cabin cruisers for sport fishing on beautiful Concepción Bay, Playa de Mulegé has primitive camps to rent. It is situated on a narrow strip of land along an inlet, amidst date palms, citrus fruit orchards, and sugar plantations, and has an old mission. A few hours in a jeep or on horseback brings you to the recently-discovered, painted cave of San Borjito in the mountains, also for the hunting of big game. The Club has a landing strip for private planes or meets guests at Santa Rosalia.

Driving along Concepción Bay on a side road, after leaving Mulegé, you come to the rocky shelf called La Punta de la Pintura de la Muerte (The Point of the Picture of Death), a skull and crossbones painted on a rock, described by Erle Stanley Gardner in his *Land of Shorter Shadows*. The road has been improved since Mr. Gardner made his trip in 1947, but it still requires careful driving.

LORETO, founded by the Spaniards in 1698, "on direct orders from the Virgin," legend says, became a proud and prosperous little city, the capital of both Alta and Baja California and the chief center of pearl fishing. In 1829 it lost both titles to La Paz. Now it is a delightful village for a vacation. Its houses are set in gardens with palms, fruit trees, and many flowers, and the waters of the gulf teem with numerous varieties of fish. Loreto is not on the *camino real* but connected with it via Comondú, also with Tijuana and Guaymas by plane. Delightful excursions are possible by boat to the nearby islands and the lovely Puerto Escondido (Hidden Port) and by horseback into the La Gigante mountains rising nearby to a height of 6,000 feet for hunting. The well-preserved Mission of San Javier, one of the most interesting built by the Jesuits, may also be visited in the same Sierra.

Hotel: Flying Sportsmen's Lodge offers comfort, all

sports facilities, and American food for about 15 dollars a day.

LA PAZ (Peace) (pop. 23,324, capital of Federal Territory of Baja California and a free port) is true to the name conferred upon it by its patron saint, Nuestra Señora de la Paz (her great fair-festival begins January 24). A peaceful little white city, its wide straight streets end at the handsome Ocean Boulevard, lined with palms and laurels. On and around the central plaza are some well-constructed buildings and houses; the rest are white-plastered adobe huts with a faded pink or blue border, and tall metal windmills rise from gardens amidst palms and fruit trees. Planes come in regularly from many places and La Paz is becoming popular with tourists for its mild winter climate and water sports. (A fishing tournament is held there in the fall, with marlin and sailfish always plentiful.)

La Paz was visited by Cortés in 1537, settled by Spaniards as the Mission of Nuestra Señora del Pilar de la Paz in 1721, became a town in 1810, and made the capital in 1829. Since pirate days much romance has been connected with its pearls, considered among the best in the world, especially the dark ones. Fortunes have been made on them but not by the poor divers. During World War II, the pearl oysters began to die off, poisoned, some said, by the Japanese. Since then agriculture has been developed, and now the pearl oysters are gradually coming back. (A reliable place for the purchase of pearls is the Rufo Department Store.) Various shops sell Mexican handicrafts from the mainland.

Amusements: A few movie and drinking places (the Mirador Bar on the hill, with "lady" hostesses but not for ladies), deep-sea fishing, swimming, and skin-diving on Coromuel Beach, named after Cromwell, a mythical English pirate. El Coromuel is also the local name for a cooling summer wind. It is pleasant to drive about the town to the handsome government guest house, in landscaped gardens on the beach (permission to go through it may be obtained from the military authorities in town), and to watch the rich changing coloring of the bay and hills and the glorious

284

sunsets; to watch the morning fishing at the wharf, where freight boats are often anchored, as well as white yachts on the bay and the long graceful canoes. Concerts and *paseos* along the boulevard several nights a week to music. Dancing and good food at the rustic tavern in the palms a short distance from the center.

Hotels on the boulevard: La Perla, the largest, well managed by Spaniards, Spanish and Mexican food. The smaller La Mision de la Paz, without restaurant, its patio bar the meeting place of English-speaking residents. And Los Arcos, a charming patio hotel, a bit away from the others. Moderate. Amer. Pl. The other two are a little lower in cost. Beyond town Los Cocos and Guaycura—make reservation.

South of La Paz the lonely wilderness coast is starred by some incredibly sumptuous modern hotels and exclusive clubs (each with its own air strip)—at Las Cruces (the former hotel is now a club), Los Barriles, Buena Vista Lodge, Bahia de Palmas, San José del Cabo, and Cabo San Lucas—the farthest south, with a new million-dollar, sixty-suite hotel of the same name. Each is near teeming primeval fishing grounds, which attract the world's keenest anglers. Write Sr. C. Riva Palacio, Tourist Department, La Paz, Baja California, for information.

Cars are available at La Paz for trips to Las Cruces or to picturesque San Antonio, 38 miles away, an agricultural village on the gulf, with an old mission. Scenic, but dusty, shaky drives.

THE FOLK ARTS

Mexico was a completely handicraft country for centuries before and after the Conquest and outstanding for the variety and beauty of its folk arts. About the middle of the nineteenth century machine-made goods began to be imported and the demand for handmade objects began to decline. However, some craftsmen continued to weave *sera-*

pes and cloth and to make pottery, masks, lacquers, toys, and other objects for their own use, though many crafts villages disappeared, as the people poured into the cities or went to work in local factories. The rural, as well as the urban Mexican, developed a liking for the (to him) exotic objects manufactured in Mexico and the United States, and in many cases he can now afford to buy a plastic basket rather than weave his own.

The influx of tourists into Mexico has again created a big demand for handmade objects. But with it has come a more rapid deterioration in both craftsmanship and good taste. The craftsmen, the majority of them artists, have to work at greater speed than ever in order to fill orders, so cannot make their products with the same *cariño* (loving care) as previously, and the shopkeepers impose either their own or the patrons' tastes upon them. They are often asked to make many objects that are foreign to them, such as dinner and tea sets. But in spite of all this, there are still beautiful handmade things to be found.

The old centers of production have not changed too drastically. Those that have most to offer are the following:

STATE OF MEXICO, in which the Federal District is situated. Villages around Toluca, capital of the state, make *serapes,* generally of undyed wool and loosely woven, cloth, utility pottery, clay toys, *petates* (the ancient type of reed mats) and *petate* toys; baskets of all shapes and sizes, decorated with colored designs of animals and figures; small embroidered tablecloths and napkins. Many of the Otomí women of the region wear *chinquetes,* or skirts, which they lay in deep pleats either in front or back and tie with a wide sash. The cloth, which is of dark wool homespun with a fine white crosswise stripe, and the sashes with inwoven designs, may occasionally be bought in the Toluca market. All the other objects are for sale there, as well as in the Mexico City markets.

Tenancingo, one of the villages of that region, is a *rebozo*-weaving (*rebozos* are the women's shawls) center, which supplies markets and stores in the entire state, as well as in others nearby.

286

Texcoco is another handicraft center of the state, noted for *serapes* and common pottery. From the village of San Miguel Chicumcuac come the well-known Texcoco *serapes*. The typical style is with a blue background, heavy and tightly woven, with a diamond in the center and an opening for the head, called a *bocamanga*. Dark colors are also used and they are good for rugs.

STATE OF GUERRERO: Silver jewelry is the chief industry in Taxco, where the best designs are made. The Spratling silver, and that of other silversmiths, are now internationally famous. Tin frames for mirrors, pictures, and candlesticks, as well as objects of copper, are also made there.

The village of Olinalá, in the interior and difficult to reach, is one of the most ancient lacquer centers in Mexico. The handsome old chests come from there, and now the lacquer workers make large trays and boxes in two colors, one forming a background over which the designs are cut out with a sharp point. They also form birds and tropical fruit of gourds, painting them in their natural colors, and paint gourds for drinking cups.

From other interior villages come simple unglazed clay jars, light in background with stylized designs in dark colors; also both glazed and unglazed toys. The unglazed ware is too breakable to ship far, so has to be bought in regional markets. One of the largest and most accessible is that of Iguala, a few miles farther than Taxco. Here one may find also silver jewelry, made in the town, as well as masks, and many other interesting folk arts and foods.

STATE OF PUEBLAS The city of Puebla, capital of the state, is a famous pottery center. For centuries it has been making the Puebla Talavera, much of it now turned into dinner and tea sets, vases, and flower pots. Tiles are still being made, but they are no longer of as good quality nor are the decorations as original as they used to be. A very good type of common pottery is also made here, which is less spoiled than the better class.

Fine palm-leaf *petates* and toys come from the mountain villages. Amozoc, on the highway from Puebla to Tehuacan, is noted for clay toys and harness. From Santa

Ana, near Tlaxcala, on the railroad line, Mexico City-Puebla, come those very fine *serapes,* some with diamond centers and *greques* in the borders; other with bright roses on a white background; others ugly with shrieking colors, which some tourists like very much. These are sold in all the markets on the highway from Mexico City to Puebla, in Puebla, Mexico City, and in many other places.

In the mountain villages women wear a pre-Conquest type of garment, called a *quexquematl* (kesh-keh-mehtl). It is sleeveless and hangs over the shoulders like a short cape, one point falling in front, the other in back. These are either of wool or cotton and beautifully embroidered and so are their long full cotton or wool skirts. Occasionally one may purchase a lovely *quexquematl* in some market, as for example in Huachinango.

STATE OF OAXACA: Oaxaca City, capital of the state, has potteries where simple glazed dishes are made, and also has many weavers of cotton tablecloths and napkins. These are sold in the market, open daily, as are all the other folk arts of the Valley. From Coyotepec come the black unglazed jars and charming animal toys with whistles in their tails; from Ozumpa, green-glazed dishes and toys; and from Teotitlán del Valle, the well-known Oaxaca *serapes*. These are generally of natural wool colors, lightweight, adorned with a red center or with stylized deer; some are blue and white and others have the calendar stone or idols inwoven in bizarre colors, a type apparently made for tourists. The women of Mitla weave handsome coarse scarves and sashes.

Not all the things from other towns come to Oaxaca City. For example, the unglazed brownish bowls and toys, with surrealistic designs in black or brown, are only sold in Ocotlán, where they are made; market day is Friday.

Women from many mountain villages wear different style regional costumes, consisting of a homespun cotton or wool *huipil* (wee-péel), also a pre-Conquest-style garment; loose with short sleeves and varying in length from the waistline to the ankles. This is usually worn over a long skirt with an embroidered band or ruffle at the bottom, or plain. Occasionally one finds one of these costumes, new, but more often already worn, for sale.

Oaxaca *serapes,* table linen, and pottery are sold in Mexico City and elsewhere in stores and markets.

STATE OF MICHOACÁN: There are many pottery villages in this state, some of them along the Mexico City-Guadalajara highway, in which simple but handsome water jars and deep cooking bowls are made. In Petamba are made the lovely green-glazed pottery dishes; in Santa Ana they make black-glazed pottery, adorned with gay roses; in Pátzcuaro, simple dishes and in Tzintzuntzan, plates, cups and saucers with cream background, adorned with stylized designs in brown and several other charming styles and colors. The primitive Santa Clara copper is now formed into ash trays and other objects for the use of city people, as well as into pots for the natives.

Uruapan is the chief lacquer-producing center, ancient as the lacquer itself, which is about as old as the Conquest. Here, too, it has found new forms to please the new purchasers—small boxes, pin-trays, little bowls, and many-sized trays. The surface is lacquered in black and the floral designs are cut out with a sharp point; then each color is rubbed in with the palm of the hand, the succeeding one being put on after the first is dry.

A combination of lacquered and painted trays is also made in Quiroga; most of it is ugly. But the lacquered trays being copied from the old models in Pátzcuaro are usually handsome.

Paracho, a village near Uruapan, specializes in musical instruments, some in toy-sizes for children, which reach every market. The Michoacan *rebozos,* dark blue with white lengthwise stripes, are also made there.

Most all of the handicraft objects of the state are sold in the Pátzcuaro market, Fridays, but very few ever reach other cities, except lacquer. Of the shops, Casa Cerda has the very best selection.

The regional costume, which women of the Lake villages and others wear, consists of a dark or red homespun wool skirt, laid in deep pleats at the waist in back to form a fan and held on with several narrow handwoven sashes of different colors with floral or animal designs. The waist or *camisa* is of white cotton, with short sleeves, and is embroidered around the neck. Blouses and sashes may sometimes be purchased in the Pátzcuaro market, but never the material for the skirt, which each woman weaves for her own use only.

THE STATE OF JALISCO has always produced good pottery. The village of Tonalá is noted for its unglazed pieces, decorated with stylized designs of animals, flowers, and palms, or soft gray or brown backgrounds. In Tlaquepaque, a short distance from Guadalajara, the potteries, which have adjoining salesrooms, make glazed dinner and tea sets; water bottles, mugs, painted pigs and other animal toys; figurines of people, and fruit, as well as some large vases and jars. Designs tend to increasing vulgarity. The glassware of Tlaquepaque retains good style and color.

The city of Guadalajara has some silversmiths, and the Avalos glass factory, producing dinner and tea sets in various colors and all kinds of glasses, which are also shipped everywhere.

In the Guadalajara shops one may sometimes find one of the nice heavy *serapes* from Coyotepec. They have centers and borders of bright roses inwoven on a dark background and are seldom found anywhere else.

The Huichol Indians living in the Sierra often come down to the Guadalajara markets to sell some of their textiles—a few of their smaller bags or a long girdle of dark brown wool with primitive inwoven designs or bright-colored mats and little flags; their designs were once sacred symbols. The Huichols who live in the Sierra of Nayarit come down to the market in Tepic.

This is but a brief summary of the things that tourists can purchase and see in the making, as they travel their usual routes. To describe all the folk arts takes a book. The simpler, better things rarely reach markets except for such government-sponsored shops as the Museo de Artes e Industrias Populares in Mexico City (see p. 160).

Every region has its own styles of pottery, textiles, and folk arts in general, but the techniques are similar and equally primitive. Both men and women weave and make pottery, the children assisting. For weaving, the pre-Conquest type of horizontal loom and the upright one introduced by the Spaniards are used everywhere; women operate the former and men the latter. Pottery is fashioned by hand, on molds, or with the Spanish wheel, men working with the latter. Spinning is done on beautifully carved pre-Conquest spinning wheels and the European-style wheels. Primitive methods are still mostly employed even in the large Puebla potteries and everything is hand-painted.

RITUAL ARTS

Certain objects are made for ritual and can be found in the markets only during the *fiestas* for which they are intended. These arts have maintained their purity to a greater extent than others, because they have not yet become commercialized and are for the saints.

During the Christmas celebrations, for example, the predominating objects are the clay figurines of the Biblical characters, of types and animals with which to make the

Papier-mâché Figures for the Day of the Dead

mangers; also the *papier-maché* figures to cover *piñatas,* the clay jars filled with sweets and toys, for the *posadas,* or celebrations of the nine nights of the journey to Bethlehem of Mary and Joseph. For the Day of the Dead there are special censers and candlesticks, black-glazed in the more catholicized places and unglazed gaily painted ones in the pagan; skeleton masks and toys of *papier maché* dealing with death themes; candy skulls; bread formed into human figures and animals, and special sweets of seeds and fruits. Candles, some of yellow wax and man-sized, are also specially adorned for this *fiesta.* And the adornment of the churches for every *fiesta* is an art in itself. The elements used are flowers, seeds, China paper, branches, pine needles, tinsel, all harmoniously combined.

NATIONAL HOLIDAYS, RELIGIOUS FESTIVALS AND DANCES

Mexican patriotic holidays are similar to those in the U.S.; some are celebrated nationally and others only by schools and banks. In addition Mexico has innumerable religious festivals, which are held in honor of the patron saint of each village and town, and to the saints to whom the various churches are dedicated. Each day of the year sees a festival being held somewhere and frequently several take place simultaneously in different towns.

Since the 1910-20 Social Revolution, religious festivals have lost much of their former glamour and importance. During the ten years of internal strife, it was not always possible to hold celebrations, and since 1920 the rural schools have brought entertainment to the villages that have in a measure competed with the church. The church festivals, however, are still popular and important because they gather people scattered over wide areas, who come to pray, to barter their wares, and to enjoy themselves socially. A festival to a very miraculous saint often lasts a week, generally resulting in a large market or fair to which dealers in the popular arts, wearing apparel, etc., bring their wares.

For that reason the important festivals take place on scheduled dates but with less emphasis on the indigenous dances than formerly. Smaller festivals that last but one day cannot be counted on to happen on the day of the saint to whom they are given, for if they fall on a week-day, they are often celebrated on the nearest Sunday before or after the actual date.

A religious festival usually begins at dawn, with *maña-nitas,* or the "Good Morning" song to the saint. Rockets and church bells announce the first mass, which may be at five in the morning. The dancers in groups attend mass and generally stay after the service to dance in the church for the saint. Afterwards they continue their dancing in the churchyard throughout the day. In the evening there are fireworks, sometimes fashioned into fantastic castles that take a long time to burn. Frequently there are daylight fireworks castles, on which are amusing *papier-maché* doll figures and animals, which dance and cut capers as they are being shot off. In some villages it is customary to announce festivals by playing a drum and *chirimía,* the pre-Conquest type of flute.

A great variety of dances are performed by the natives at religious festivals. Most of them have Spanish-religious themes, as they were introduced by the early missionaries to substitute for the heathen ones. The following are most generally performed—*Los Moros y Cristianos,* portraying the battles between Moors and Christians—a dance drama with text and duels; *Los Santiagos,* with St. James on his white horse, leading his men against the infidels; *La Conquista,* or *La Danza de la Conquista,* also with texts, duels and dances related to the Conquest, the dancers in highly picturesque costumes; *Los Apaches,* or *Concheros,* no texts but many intricate steps to simple rhythms, which the dancers play on stringed *armadilla* instruments. The two outstanding pre-Conquest dances are the *pascola,* or Yaqui Deer Dance of Sonora, to rich primitive melodies with fine choreography; the *Volador,* or flying pole dance, in which the dancers climb a 100-foot pole, and after dancing on a tiny platform at the top, fly down from unwinding ropes— a spectacular and breathtaking performance. The *Volador*

is not performed very often nor in many places. (See
PAPANTLA.)

IMPORTANT FESTIVALS CELEBRATED BY THE ENTIRE NA-
TION: In some places they are more colorful than in others
but they are interesting everywhere.

The New Year. Midnight mass. Parties in homes and in
cabarets. In native villages newly elected officials often take
office on the New Year and this is sometimes the occasion for
a festival.

January 6. Day of Los Reyes Magos (Epiphany), when
at nightfall city children set out their shoes on the balconies
to receive presents. Indian children, who have neither shoes
nor balconies, find some compensation for the Epiphany in
special clay toys sold cheaply at their markets.

Totonac Performance at Papantla

294

February 2 (Candlemas). Blessing of seeds, candles, and animals in the churches.

February 5. A national holiday commemorating the Constitutions of 1857 and 1917, now governing Mexico.

Carnivals: Three days preceding Ash Wednesday: a movable date. In some villages still, as in Yautepec, Morelos, the carnival is celebrated on the weekend after Ash Wednesday. Traditional carnivals in cities like Mérida and Mazatlan. At *fiestas* in some villages, men dressed as women dance in the streets. Other villages stage elaborate representations of battles. (See HUEJOTZINGO.)

Lenten Fairs occur in many states; each centered around the Friday of each week and lasting several days. Third Friday celebrations of particular interest are held in Huachinango, Hidalgo, and Tepalcingo, Morelos.

Holy Week (movable date), beginning with the blessing of palms and plants on Palm Sunday and ending on Easter Sunday. Most villages have outdoor processions during Holy Week and some put on partial or complete representations of the Passion. (See TZINTZUNTZAN, Michoacán.)

May 1. Labor Day in Mexico, with workers' parades.

May 3. Day of the Holy Cross. Workers of the building trades celebrate this day by setting up flower-decked crosses on their jobs. At noon they shoot off fireworks and take *copitas*, or ceremonial drinks.

May 5. Mexico's victory over the French at Puebla. A National holiday. Picturesque sham battle, at Peñón, Mexico City, and in Puebla a great military parade.

During June (movable date) Corpus Christi is celebrated with services in all churches and *fiestas* in many places. (See PAPANTLA, VERACRUZ.) Around Lake Pátzcuaro and in mountain villages of Michoacán, the Corpus *fiestas* take the form of mock markets, in which all the handicrafts and industries of the villages in which they take place are made in miniature form and business is carried on with make-believe money, and there is much fun.

June 24. St. John's Day. It is customary for young folks to bathe after midnight of June 23rd and eat *tamales* with *atole* afterwards. Girls chop the ends of their hair with *machetes* so that it may grow better.

September 16. Mexico's Independence Day. In Mexico City the President of the Republic repeats the *grito,* or Hidalgo's Independence Proclamation, from the central balcony of the National Palace, on the night of the 15th, at 11 o'clock. Immediately afterward the Old Independence Bell is rung, followed by a deafening clang of bells from the cathedral towers, shouts from the mobs in the Zócalo, and fireworks. The same ceremony is repeated in every other city and town in the Republic at the same hour, governors or municipal presidents officiating, as the case may be. On the 16th, military parades are held in the cities. In some villages a youth representing Hidalgo, and a queen and her attendants chosen for the day, parade the streets on a platform or in carriages.

November 1 and 2. All Saints and Souls Day, the Days of Children and Adult Dead. The 2nd is a holiday when everyone visits cemeteries and decorates graves. Performances of *Don Juan Tenorio,* by Zorilla. Everywhere imitation skulls, crossbones, and skeletons in candies, bread, and clay toys. Politicians and public servants are mocked in verse, called *calaveras,* printed on colored sheets with amusing illustrations and sold on the streets. Some believe that their dead return on that day to partake of their dishes in spirit, so they set up *ofrendas,* or offerings of the best dishes of food they can afford, which they themselves eat afterward. Some take candles, with food and flowers to the graves, and toys for the dead children. (See JANITZIO, LAKE PÁTZCUARO.)

November 20. A national holiday, celebrating the outbreak of the 1910-20 Revolution. In Mexico City a great athletic parade, in which all government employees and federal school students take part. Similar parades throughout the Republic.

December 12. Virgin of Guadalupe Day, Mexico's patron saint. (See SANCTUARY AND VIRGIN OF GUADALUPE.)

December 16-25, the *Posadas,* commemorating the journey of Mary and Joseph to Bethlehem, which is represented during the eight consecutive nights before Christmas with religious processions, followed by parties during which a *piñata* is hilariously broken by someone blindfolded. The

296

piñata is a pottery jar filled with candy and delicacies, covered with a fantastic *papier-maché* figure. The festivities end on Christmas Eve, when a doll, representing the Infant Jesus, is sung to sleep in the manger or *nacimiento,* arranged with lovely clay figures, many of religious personages. Sometimes *pastorelas* are given or medieval representations announcing the birth of Christ. Midnight mass is celebrated in the churches, followed by a supper at home, for which traditional dishes are prepared.

FESTIVALS TO PATRON SAINTS: As stated above, it is impossible to vouch for dates; therefore, only those that are practically certain are included in the following list, if you are interested in seeing *fiestas,* ask about them as you travel.

January 1-7. Jojutla, near Cuernavaca. Picturesque festival with an interesting market.

January 17. St. Anthony's Day, when animals are painted and adorned with flowers and taken to church to be blessed.

Festival Dance

January 28-29. Cuilapan *fiesta*. A short distance from city of Oaxaca. Splendid plume dance.

February 2. In the Huave village of San Mateo del Mar, the *fiesta* is interesting with primitive dances. This village is on the Isthmus of Tehuantepec and can be reached via Juchitán. (See SAN JUAN DE LOS LAGOS, GUADALAJARA–SAN LUIS POTOSÍ HIGHWAY.)

May 1-8. Gay festival at Acapulco.

May 3. Festivals in Zimapan, Hidalgo, and Saltillo. Also at Amatlán, near Córdoba Veracruz.

May 15. San Isidro, patron saint of the peasants. Many harvest *fiestas* in his honor. A picturesque one at Metepec, with a parade of adorned oxen.

July 8. Festival at Teotitlán del Valle, *serape* village near Oaxaca. Plume dance and fireworks. Festival and fair in Motul, near Mérida.

July 16. A harvest festival around the Fortín at Oaxaca City, reminiscent of the one to the goddess of the harvest, Centeotl.

July 19. A pagan harvest festival at the *tirada de fruta,* at Juchitán, Tehuantepec, Oaxaca.

August 2. Big festival and fair at Tulancingo, Hidalgo.

August 10. Festival of the Rosario of Amozoc, Puebla.

August 10-18. Festival and fair of La Comisaría de Atemajac, at Zapopan, Jalisco, near Guadalajara.

August 15. Day of the Asunción. Festivals in many places. See Milpa Alta and Santa María Tonantzintla. Also one at Huamantla, Tlaxcala.

August 30. *Feria* in Ixtepec, Oaxaca, Isthmus of Tehuantepec, which lasts until October 3, with celebrations on August 31; September 8, 9, 23, 27, 28, 29; October 1, 2, and 3. It is very gay with many social, religious, and folk dances, horse races, fireworks. The Tehuanas turn out in their best and gayest costumes.

September 8. (See LOS REMEDIOS and TEPOZTLÁN, Morelos.)

September 29. San Miguel, or Michael's Day. Festival at Chalma and many other places. As San Miguel is the saint of horsemen, many rodeos are held on this date.

In San Miguel Allende, Guanajuato, the *fiesta* begins

on nearest weekend to actual date, is losing spontaneity and color under city officials' guidance; but some Conchero dancers still attend.

October 3. Festival at Tlacolula, near Oaxaca.

October 4. Festival to the miraculous Virgin of Zapopan, Jalisco, and in many other places to San Francisco.

November 3-12. Festival and fair at San Martin Texmelucan, near Puebla.

December 2-6. Festivals in San Francisco Ecatepec and Santa María Tonantzintla, near Puebla.

December 8. *Fiesta* and fair at Juquila, Oaxaca, to the miraculous Virgin of same name.

MISCELLANEOUS INFORMATION

SPANISH PHRASES: Those given here are necessarily limited, but they will help. For conversations on every conceivable need, including flirting and slang, see *Easy Spanish for Mexico, Cuba and All Latin America,* by Frances Toor.

Pronunciation hints: Spanish vowels have one basic sound—A, as in father; E, a little longer than in met; I, like the double e in meet; O, as in ought; U, like the double o in food. Most of the consonants are similar to those in English, excepting the J and Ge and Gi, which are aspirated like the ch in Bach. R and RR are vibrated, as in throat; ll, like y in yet. H is always silent.

Do you understand English?	¿Entiende Ud. el inglés?
Very little.	Muy poco, muy poquito.
Yes, sir. No, Madam.	Sí, señor. No, señora.
I do not speak Spanish.	No hablo el español.
Please speak slowly.	Favor de hablar despacio.
Does anyone here speak English?	¿Hay alguien aquí que hable el inglés?
Where is the best hotel here?	¿Dónde está el mejor hotel aquí?
Please watch my car.	Favor de cuidar mi coche.
What is the price of this?	¿Cuál es el precio de ésto?

Enough. Too much.	Bastante. Demasiado.
Give me thirty liters of gasoline.	Déme treinta litros de gasolina.
Fill the gas tank.	Llene el tanque.
Please check oil, water and tires.	Revise el aceite, agua, las llantas.
Clean the windshield.	Limpie el parabrisa.
Where is the road to . . .?	¿Dónde está el camino a . . .?
Left, right.	Izquierda, dérecha.
Straight ahead.	Derecho, adelante.
How far is it to . . .?	¿Qué distancia hay a . . .?
Wash, grease my car.	Lave, engrase mi coche.
Change the oil.	Cambie el aceite.
There is something wrong with my motor.	El motor tiene algo.
What do I owe you?	¿Cuánto le debo?
What have you to eat?	¿Qué hay de comer?
Bring me the bill.	Tráigame la cuenta.
Thank you very much.	Muchísimas gracias.
You are welcome.	Por nada. De nada. No hay de qué.
I don't want any more.	No quiero nada más.
I am sorry.	Lo siento mucho.
Good morning. Good afternoon.	Buenos días. Buenas tardes.
Good evening, good night.	Buenas noches.
Good-bye. Until later.	Adiós. Hasta luego.
Hot water, cold water.	Agua caliente, fría.
Breakfast.	El desayuno. El almuerzo.
Dinner. Supper.	La comida. La cena.
Coffee, tea, milk.	Café, té, leche.
Eggs soft, hard, fried.	Huevos, tibios, duros, fritos.
Vegetables, fruit.	Legumbres, fruta.
Bread and butter.	Pan y mantequilla.
Meat, fish, chicken.	Carne, pescado, pollo.
I am hungry, thirsty, cold, warm.	Tengo hambre, sed, frío, calor.
I am in a hurry.	Tengo prisa.
Hurry, please.	Aprisa, por favor.

Money. Mexican dollar.		Dinero. Un peso.	
I have only checks.		Tengo solamente cheques.	
I have no change.		No tengo cambio.	
1	uno	17	diez y siete
2	dos	18	diez y ocho
3	tres	19	diez y nueve
4	cuatro	20	viente
5	cinco	21	vientiuno
6	seis	22	vientidós
7	siete	23	vientitrés
8	ocho	30	trienta
9	nueve	40	cuarenta
10	diez	50	cincuenta
11	once	60	sesenta
12	doce	70	setenta
13	trece	80	ochenta
14	catorce	90	noventa
15	quince	100	cien
16	diez y seis	1000	mil

PRONUNCIATION OF DIFFICULT PLACE NAMES

Actopan—Ahk-*toh*-pahn.
Ajusco—Ah-*hoos*-koh.
Chapultepec—Chah-pool-teh-*peck*.
Chiapas—Chee-*ah*-pahs.
Chichén Itzá—Chee-*chen*-Ee-*tsah*.
Chihuahua—Chee-*wah*-wah.
Coahuila—Koh-ah-*weel*-ah.
Coatlinchán—Kwaht-leen-*chahn*.
Cuautla—*Kwau*-tlah.
Guadalajara—Gwah-dah-lah-*hah*-rah.
Guanajuato—Gwah-nah-hoo-*ah*-toh.
Guaymas—*Gwah-ee*-mahs.
Ixtaccíhuatl—Ees-tah-*see*-wahtl.
Jacala—Hah-*kah*-lah.
Janitzio—Hah-*neets*-yoh.
Jarácuaro—Hah-rah-*kwah*-roh.

Juárez—*Hwah*-rehs.
México—*Meh*-hee-koh.
Oaxaca—Wah-*hah*-kah.
Pátzcuaro—*Pahts*-kwah-roh.
Popocatépetl—Poh-poh-kat-*teh*-pehtl.
Puebla—*Pweh*-blah.
Quetzalcoatl—Ket-sahl-*koh*-ahtl.
Tacubaya—Tah-koo-*bah*-yah.
Tamazunchale—Tah-mah-soon-*chah*-leh.
Taxco—*Tahs*-koh.
Tehuacán—Teh-wah-*kahn*.
Tenayucan—Tehn-ah-*yoo*-kahn.
Tenochtitlán—Teh-noch-tee-*tlahn*.
Tepotzotlán —Teh-poht-soht-*lahn*.
Tepoztlán—Teh-pohs-*tlan*.
Tlaquepaque—Tlah-keh-*pah*-keh.
Tuxpan—*Toos*-pahn.
Tzintzuntzán—Tseen-*tsoon*-tsahn.
Uruapan—Oo-roo-*ah*-pahn.
Uxmal—Oosh-*mahl*.
Valles—*Vah*-yehs.
Xochicalco—Soh-chee-*kahl*-koh.
Xochimilco—Soh-chee-*meel*-koh.

For Transportation in General but Especially Buses: Ask at any one of the tourist agencies for a copy of the guide entitled *Guía de Transportes Aereos y Autotransportes de Mexico*. This guide also contains a hotel directory.

Postage: For ordinary mail within Mexico 40 *centavos* for letters; 20 for postcards; airmail 80 *centavos* for 20 grams. To the U.S.A., Canada, Cuba 40 *centavos* ordinary and 80 *centavos* airmail for 10 grams. Special delivery (*Entrega immediata*) 50 *centavos;* registry of a letter or package 50 *centavos* extra.

Telephones are dialed, and the greeting is "bueno." Hotels and business houses usually charge for local calls.

Telegraph service is administered by the federal government, and all towns of any importance have offices. Telegrams in English can be sent to the U.S. over the Mexican lines.

STREETCARS (*tranvias* or *trenes*) and BUSES (*camiones*) are found in all cities. Fares are low but no transfers.

MILEAGE: Multiply kilometers by .62 to get miles. (Or multiply by 6 and drop the last figure, for an approximation.) Or more exactly:

    5 km. = 3.1 mi.
   10 km. = 6.2 mi.
   25 km. = 15.5 mi.
   40 km. = 25 mi.
   60 km. = 37 mi.
  100 km. = 62 mi.

GASOLINE: Sold by the liter, roughly equivalent to U.S. quart. Divide liters by 4 to get gallons. Or more exactly:

    5 liters = 1.3 gal.
   10 liters = 2.6 gal.
   50 liters = 13.2 gal.
   60 liters = 16 gal.

CURRENCY: 100 *centavos* equal 1 *peso*. 1 *peso* ($1.00) equals 8¢. Multiply *pesos* by .08 to get U.S. equivalent. (The dollar sign in Mexico indicates *pesos*.)

	Mexican	U.S.
$	1.00 =	$0.08
	10.00 =	.80
	12.50 =	1.00
	25.00 =	2.00
	50.00 =	4.00
	75.00 =	6.00
	100.00 =	8.00

TEMPERATURE:

Fahrenheit	32	41	50	68	86	100
Centigrade	0	5	10	20	30	38

WEIGHTS AND MEASURES: The metric system is official and used exclusively in Mexico.

EQUIVALENTS

1 centimeter *(centímetro)* ...... = 0.39 inch.
1 meter *(metro)* .... = 39.37 inches, or
                                            3.28 feet, or
                                            1.09 yards
1 kilometer (1,000 meters) ...... = 0.6214 mile
1 hectare *(hectárea)* .... = 2.4711 acres
1 kilogram *(kilo)* .... = 2.2046 pounds
1 liter *(litro)* .... = 0.264 gallon or 1.056 qts.
1 inch *(pulgada)* .... = 2.54 centímetros (cm.)
1 foot *(pie)* .... = 30.48 centímetros (cm.)
                                            0.305 (mm.)
1 yard *(yarda)* .... = 0.914 metros
1 mile *(milla)* .... = 1.6 kilómetros (km.)
1 ounce *(onza)* .... = 28.35 gramos
1 pound *(libra)* .... = 453.59 grams
                                            .45 kilograms

For rapid calculations to obtain sufficiently close equivalents, multiply kilos by 2.2 to obtain pounds.

MAGAZINES, NEWSPAPERS, AND BOOKLETS IN ENGLISH:

Mexican Life, an illustrated monthly magazine.

El Excelsior and *El Universal, leading* Spanish dailies, have good English pages.

Novedades publishes *The News,* an all-English daily.

Mexico City *Daily Bulletin* (gratis). Good coverage of Mexican and foreign news; fiestas and daily events.

This Week In Mexico (Esta Semana) (gratis). A well-established weekly. Good information.

The *Gazer* is distributed free.

MEXICAN BIBLIOGRAPHY

The following is a list of some of the best basic books on Mexico. Those out of print can be consulted in libraries. In Mexico City the American bookstore, the Librería Británica, and the Central de Publicaciones specialize in English books and most of the Spanish bookstores on Avenida Juárez carry English books of interest to tourists.

ANCIENT AND COLONIAL MEXICO (See also HISTORY below):
    Ancient Civilizations of Mexico, by H. J. Spinden
    Ancient Life in Mexico and Central America,
        by E. L. Hewett
    Ancient Mexico, by Frederick Peterson
    Ancient Past of Mexico, by Alma Reed
    Aztecs in Mexico, by George Vaillant
    Conquest of Mexico and Peru, by William H. Prescott
    Digging in Yucatán, by Ann Axtell Morris
    Discovery and Conquest of Mexico (translation),
        by Bernal Días del Castillo
    History of the Maya, by Gann and Thompson
    Letters of Hernán Cortés (translation)
    Many Mexicos, by Lesley Simpson
    Mexico, by Stuart Chase
    Mexican Archaeology, by Thomas A. Joyce
    Rise and Fall of Maya Civilization,
        by J. Eric S. Thompson

ART AND ARCHITECTURE:
    Diego Rivera, by Bertram D. Wolfe
    Idols Behind Altars, by Anita Brenner
    Mexican Architecture, by Atlie B. Ayers
    Modern Mexican Artists,
        by Carlos Merida and Frances Toor
    Modern Mexican Painters, by MacKinley Helm
    Orozco, by Alma Reed
    Story of Architecture in Mexico, by Trent E. Sanford
    The New Architecture in Mexico, by Esther Born

BULLFIGHTING:
    La Fiesta Brava, by Barnaby Conrad
    To the Bullfight, by John Marks

COOKING:
   Mexican Cook Book, by Natalie Scott
FICTION:
   Black River, by Carleton Beals
   Sunburst (translation), by Mauricio Magdaleno
   The Brave Bulls, by Tom Lea
   The Fair Gods, by Lew Wallace
   The Plumed Serpent, by D. H. Lawrence
   The Power and the Glory, by Graham Greene
   The Singer, Not the Song, by Audrey Erskine
   The Stones Awake, by Carleton Beals
   The Under Dogs (translation), by Azuela
HISTORY:
   History of Mexico, by Parkes
   In the Footsteps of Cortés (translation),
      by Fernando Benitez
   Mexico—A Land of Volcanoes, by J. H. Sharman
   The Mexican Nation, by Hubert Priestly
GENERAL:
   A Treasury of Mexican Folkways, by Frances Toor
   Burning Water, by Laurette Sejourné
   Firefly in the Night, by Irene Nicholson
   House in the Sun, by Dane Chandos
   Life in Mexico, by Mme. Calderon de la Barca
   Life in a Mexican Village (also paperback condensed
      version), *Five Families,* and *Children of Sanchez*—
      all by Oscar Lewis
   Little Mexico, by William P. Spratling
   Mexican Maize, by Carleton Beals
   Mornings in Mexico, by D. H. Lawrence
   Seven Shares in a Gold Mine, by Margaret Larkin
   Tepoztlan, by Robert Redfield
   Viva Mexico, by Charles Flandrau
   Yucatán, by Robert Redfield
   Zapotec, by Helen Augur
TRAVEL:
   Inter-American Tourist Service, Pan American Union
publications: *Visit Mexico, Mexico, Motoring in Mexico,*
and *Directory of Hotels in Mexico.*

306

INDEX

Major entries are indicated in bold-face type.

307

308